Programming

Prentice Hall International Series in Computer Science

C. A. R. Hoare, Series Editor

BACKHOUSE, R. C., *Program Construction and Verification*
BACKHOUSE, R. C., *Syntax of Programming Languages: Theory and practice*
DEBAKKER, J. W., *Mathematical Theory of Program Correctness*
BARR, M. and WELLS, C., *Category Theory for Computing Science*
BEN-ARI, M., *Principles of Concurrent and Distributed Programming*
BIRD, R. and WADLER, P., *Introduction to Functional Programming*
BJÖRNER, D. and JONES, C. B., *Formal Specification and Software Development*
BORNAT, R., *Programming from First Principles*
BUSTARD, D., ELDER, J. and WELSH, J., *Concurrent Program Structures*
CLARK, K. L., and McCABE, F. G., *micro-Prolog: Programming in logic*
CROOKES, D., *Introduction to Programming in Prolog*
DROMEY, R. G., *How to Solve it by Computer*
DUNCAN, F., *Microprocessor Programming and Software Development*
ELDER, J., *Construction of Data Processing Software*
ELLIOTT, R. J. and HOARE, C. A. R., (eds.), *Scientific Applications of Multiprocessors*
GOLDSCHLAGER, L. and LISTER, A., *Computer Science: A modern introduction (2nd edn)*
GORDON, M. J. C., *Programming Language Theory and its Implementation*
HAYES, I. (ed.), *Specification Case Studies*
HEHNER, E. C. R., *The Logic of Programming*
HENDERSON, P., *Functional Programming: Application and Implementation*
HOARE, C. A. R., *Communicating Sequential Processes*
HOARE, C. A. R., and JONES, C. B. (ed.), *Essays in Computing Science*
HOARE, C. A. R., and SHEPHERDSON, J. C. (eds.), *Mathematical Logic and Programming Languages*
HUGHES, J. G., *Database Technology: A software engineering approach*
INMOS LTD, *occam 2 Reference Manual*
JACKSON, M. A., *System Development*
JOHNSTON, H., *Learning to Program*
JONES, C. B., *Systematic Software Development using VDM (2nd edn)*
JONES, C. B. and SHAW, R. C. F. (eds.), *Case Studies in Systematic Software Development*
JONES, G., *Programming in occam*
JONES, G. and GOLDSMITH, M., *Programming in occam 2*
JOSEPH, M., PRASAD, V. R. and NATARAJAN, N., *A Multiprocessor Operating System*
KALDEWAIJ, A., *Programming: The Derivation of Algorithms*
LEW, A., *Computer Science: A mathematical introduction*
MARTIN, J. J., *Data Types and Data Structures*
MEYER, B., *Introduction to the Theory of Programming Languages*
MEYER, B., *Object-orientated Software Construction*
MILNER, R., *Communication and Concurrency*
MORGAN, C., *Programming from Specifications*
PEYTON JONES, S. L., *The Implementation of Functional Programming Languages*
POMBERGER, G., *Software Engineering and Modula-2*
POTTER, B., SINCLAIR, J., TILL, D., *An Introduction to Formal Specification and Z*
REYNOLDS, J. C., *The Craft of Programming*
RYDEHEARD, D. E. AND BURSTALL, R. M., *Computational Category Theory*
SLOMAN, M. and KRAMER, J., *Distributed Systems and Computer Networks*
SPIVEY, J. M., *The Z Notation: A reference manual*
TENNENT, R. D., *Principles of Programming Languages*
WATT, D. A., *Programming Languages Concepts and Paradigms*
WATT, D. A., WICHMANN, B. A. and FINDLAY, W., *ADA: Language and methodology*
WELSH, J. and ELDER, J., *Introduction to Modula-2*
WELSH, J. and ELDER, J., *Introduction to Pascal (3rd edn)*
WELSH, J., ELDER, J., and BUSTARD, D., *Sequential Program Structures*
WELSH, J. and HAY, A., *A Model Implementation of Standard Pascal*
WELSH, J. and McKEAG, M., *Structured System Programming*
WIKSTRÖM, Å., *Functional Programming using Standard ML*

Programming

The Derivation of Algorithms

A. Kaldewaij
Eindhoven University of Technology

Prentice Hall
New York   London   Toronto   Sydney   Tokyo   Singapore

First published 1990 by
Prentice Hall International (UK) Ltd
66 Wood Lane End, Hemel Hempstead
Hertfordshire HP2 4RG
A division of
Simon & Schuster International Group

© Prentice Hall International (UK) Ltd, 1990

All rights reserved. No part of this publication may be
reproduced, stored in a retrieval system, or transmitted,
in any form, or by any means, electronic, mechanical,
photocopying, recording or otherwise, without prior
permission, in writing, from the publisher.
For permission within the United States of America
contact Prentice Hall Inc., Englewood Cliffs, NJ 07632.

Printed and bound in Great Britain by
Dotesios Printers Limited, Trowbridge, Wiltshire

Library of Congress Cataloguing-in-Publication Data

Kaldewaij, A. (Anne)
  Programming: the derivation of algorithms/A. Kaldewaij.
    p. cm. — (Prentice-Hall international series in computer
science)
  Includes bibliographical references and index.
  ISBN 0-13-204108-1 : $32.95
  1. Electronic digital computers — Programming. 2. Algorithms.
I. Title. II. Series.
QA76.6. K3417   1990
005. 1 — dc 20   90-14158
                                                              CIP

British Library Cataloguing in Publication Data

Kaldewaij, A. (Anne)
  Programming : the derivation of algorithms. – (Prentice
  Hall International series in computer science).
  1. Computer systems. Programming. Algorithms. Design
  I. Title
  0045.12028

  ISBN 0-13-204108-1

1 2 3 4 5   94 93 92 91 90

Contents

	Preface	ix
0	Introduction	1
1	Predicate Calculus	4
2	The Guarded Command Language	13
	2.0 Introduction	13
	2.1 Skip	16
	2.2 Assignment	17
	2.3 Catenation	20
	2.4 Selection	23
	2.5 Repetition	28
	2.6 Constants, Inner Blocks, and Arrays	38
	2.7 Summary	42
3	Quantifications	44
4	General Programming Techniques	51
	4.0 Introduction	51
	4.1 Taking conjuncts as invariant	52
	4.2 Replacing constants by variables	57
	4.3 Strengthening invariants	63
	4.4 Tail invariants	72
	4.5 Summary	80

5 Deriving Efficient Programs — 83
- 5.0 Introduction — 83
- 5.1 Integer division — 83
- 5.2 Fibonacci — 88

6 Searching — 92
- 6.0 Introduction — 92
- 6.1 Linear Search — 92
- 6.2 Bounded Linear Search — 95
- 6.3 Binary Search — 98
- 6.4 Searching by Elimination — 104

7 Segment Problems — 110
- 7.0 Introduction — 110
- 7.1 Longest segments — 110
  - 7.1.0 All zeros — 111
  - 7.1.1 Left-minimal segments — 115
  - 7.1.2 At most ten zeros — 117
  - 7.1.3 All elements different — 119
- 7.2 Shortest segments — 122

8 Slope Search — 127
- 8.0 Introduction — 127
- 8.1 The basic principle — 127
  - 8.1.0 Searching — 130
  - 8.1.1 Decomposition in a sum of two squares — 133
  - 8.1.2 Minimal distance — 136
- 8.2 Longest and shortest segments — 140
  - 8.2.0 Longest segments — 141
  - 8.2.1 Shortest segments — 144
  - 8.2.2 At least two zeros revisited — 146

9 Mixed Problems — 148

10 Array Manipulations — 152

- 10.0 Introduction 152
- 10.1 Array assignments 152
- 10.2 Swaps 159
  - 10.2.0 The Dutch National Flag 161
  - 10.2.1 Rotation 164

11 Sorting — 170

- 11.0 Introduction 170
- 11.1 Quadratic sorting algorithms 172
  - 11.1.0 Insertion Sort 172
  - 11.1.1 Selection Sort 174
  - 11.1.2 Bubble Sort 176
- 11.2 Advanced sorting algorithms 178
  - 11.2.0 Quicksort 179
  - 11.2.1 Mergesort 183
  - 11.2.2 Heapsort 187

12 Auxiliary Arrays — 195

- 12.0 At most K zeros 195
- 12.1 Largest square under a histogram 198
- 12.2 The length of a longest common subsequence 201
- 12.3 A shortest segment problem 206

Index — 214

Preface

Programming is the art of designing efficient algorithms that meet their specifications. During the 1980s the *art* of programming became more and more a *discipline* of programming. Problems that were hard to solve ten years ago are now used as examples in an introductory programming course. What happened?

There are two factors by which algorithms may be judged: their correctness (do they solve the right problem?) and their performance (how fast do they run, and how much space do they use?). The classical way of judging the quality of an algorithm is by tracing execution patterns, by providing test inputs, or by supplying formal proofs. The process of proving the correctness of an algorithm after it has been designed is known as *verification*. Verification of algorithms is rather difficult, even for the designer of an algorithm. Many a programmer regards it as a waste of time and prefers to continue with another interesting programming problem. This is one of the reasons why formal methods were largely rejected or neglected by the software community.

As time went by it became obvious that neither tracing nor testing can guarantee the absence of errors. To be sure of the correctness of a program one *has* to prove that it meets its specification. This insight led to the development of specification languages and tools that might support program verification.

A quite different approach was advocated and developed by Edsger W. Dijkstra and others during the 1970s. In their approach a program and its correctness proof are constructed hand in hand, thereby making a posteriori program verification superfluous. The proof rules (semantics) of the program notation provide the guidelines for the construction of algorithms from specifications. The correctness of a program obtained in this way is implicit: following the rules of the game it is impossible to construct an incorrect algorithm. With the introduction of this method of programming it also became possible to reason about programs in a non-operational way.

During the 1980s W.H.J. Feijen and others refined this method to what is known as the *calculational style* of programming: to a large extent, programs are derived from their specification by means of formula manipulation. The calculations that lead to the algorithm are carried out in small steps, so that each individual step is easily verified. In this way the design decisions become manifest. Such decisions are based on several considerations, such as efficiency, simplicity and symmetry. This method does not only help us in finding a solution, but it can also yield new solutions that are often quite surprising. Program derivation is not mechanical: it is a challenging activity and it requires creativity. This way of programming shows where creativity comes in. It is this method that is explained and exemplified in this textbook.

As a vehicle for the description of algorithms we use the guarded command language. It has the simplicity needed for educational reasons and it has the expressiveness needed for the description of algorithms. Procedures and recursion are not included: the modest constructs of the guarded command language provide more than enough latitude for an introduction to programming.

How to use this book

The material of this textbook can be presented in a one-year course. Such a course may be organized as follows: each week a two-hour lecture in which the theory is explained and exemplified and a three-hour training session in which exercises are solved in small groups. This is the way in which I present the material to first-year computing science students at the Eindhoven University of Technology. Each week one exercise is marked as a home-work assignment. That exercise has to be worked out with great precision. The same material has been used in a third-year course.

The only prerequisite is an introductory course in Pascal, just enough to give students some idea about programs and about program execution.

The pace of lecturing should be leisurely. It takes time to get used to the notation and to get used to the mathematical rigor that is needed. The exercises play a fundamental role: you can only understand and appreciate the strength and beauty of the method by using it.

A Teacher's Manual (including answers to exercises) is available from the publishers for adopters of this book.

Overview

In the first chapters, we introduce the predicate calculus and the guarded command language. Since this book is about programming and not about semantics, the presentation of the theory of predicates is kept as simple as possible. Each construct of the guarded command language is introduced together with its accompanying proof rule. These chapters form the basis for the development of programs. Many exercises have been included to help the reader gain familiarity with the notations and the proof rules.

Chapter 3 introduces quantifications, which are used in specifications and for which the manipulation rules are presented that are needed in program derivations.

In Chapter 4, we present the general programming techniques that underlie the more specific techniques presented in the chapters that follow. Chapter 5 discusses efficiency and presents two examples of efficient algorithms. This chapter gives the teacher the opportunity to show how one can reason about such programs without operational arguments.

In Chapters 6, 7, and 8 the general programming techniques of Chapter 4 are applied to more specific classes of problems. Chapter 6 addresses searching paradigms: the Linear Search, the Bounded Linear Search, the Binary Search, and Searching by Elimination are presented. In Chapter 7 segment problems are discussed, which provide an excellent training in the calculus needed for program derivation. Chapter 8 deals with two-dimensional searches and applies the Slope Search technique to segment problems. These chapters are followed by a set of mixed programming problems.

The final chapters deal with array operations. The proof rule for the array assignment is introduced and applied to various problems. In Chapter 12 the introduction of auxiliary arrays is discussed and exemplified by some more complicated programming problems.

Bibliography

The proof format used in this book was invented by W.H.J. Feijen. Much of the notation, such as the square brackets for universal quantification over a state space, is due to E.W. Dijkstra. Many of the examples and many exercises occur also in *A Method of Programming* by Edsger W. Dijkstra and W.H.J. Feijen, Addison Wesley, 1988. Another source is *The Science of Programming* by David Gries, Springer-Verlag New York Inc., 1981. For instance, the exercise called 'Welfare Crook' is an example from this book. Both books are recommended.

Searching by Elimination was invented by Berry Schoenmakers. Some of the exercises have been composed by Jan L.A. van de Snepscheut.

Two other books have to be mentioned. My first contact with the science of programming was *A Discipline of Programming* by Edsger W. Dijkstra, Prentice-Hall, 1976. You will find it a pleasure to read it after you have studied this textbook. For those interested in the theory of predicate transformers, I recommend *Predicate Calculus and Program Semantics* by Edsger W. Dijkstra and Carel S. Scholten, Springer-Verlag New York Inc., 1990.

Acknowledgements

It is a pleasure to express my gratitude to Wim Feijen, who spent so much time teaching me all he knows about programming. This book would not have been written without him.

The Eindhoven Algorithm Club, in particular Lex Bijlsma, Victor Dielissen, Joop van den Eijnde, Wim Nuij and Berry Schoenmakers, is gratefully acknowledged for pointing out errors and obscurities in earlier versions.

My thanks go to all those colleagues and students who made comments on parts of this book. I want to mention W.H.J. Feijen, Ria van Ouwerkerk, Martin Rem, Rob Nederpelt, Asia van de Mortel, and Tom Verhoeff.

The ATAC (Austin Tuesday Afternoon Club), in particular Edsger W. Dijkstra, is acknowledged for comments on the first part of this book.

Finally, my special thanks go to Rob Hoogerwoord who carefully studied the final draft of this text, and who suggested many methodological improvements.

Eindhoven, September 1990

Anne Kaldewaij

Chapter 0

Introduction

There are many different views on programming. A common view is that a program is just a kind of recipe that explains what steps have to be performed to achieve a certain goal. Such a program is often presented in an operational way: 'first do this, then apply that' and 'perform the following N times'. This approach can be found in many textbooks on programming. Often such textbooks treat a specific programming language, such as FORTRAN-77, COBOL or MODULA-2, and usually those books only differ in the language that is used.

In this book we present a completely different approach. A program together with its specification is viewed as a theorem. The theorem expresses that the program satisfies the specification. Hence, all programs require proofs (as theorems do). We shall derive programs according to their specifications in a constructive way, such that program development and correctness proof go hand in hand.

As an example, we consider the following Pascal program.

    program *maximum* (input,output);
    var x, y : integer;
    begin
        read(x);
        read(y);
        if $x < y$ **then** $x := y$;
        write(x)
    end.

Program variables define a so-called state space. Variables x and y introduced in the second line of this program define state space $\mathcal{Z} \times \mathcal{Z}$, where $\mathcal{Z}$ denotes the set of integers. The coordinates of this state space correspond to the variables, the first one to x and the second one to y. Elements of a state space are called states. Typical states are $\langle 1, 2 \rangle$ and $\langle 0, -5 \rangle$. Sets of states, i.e. subsets of the state space, are characterized by predicates (boolean functions), such as $x \geq y$ and $x \geq 0 \wedge y \geq 0$.

When values A and B are supplied as input to the program above, execution of read(x); read(y) establishes $x = A \wedge y = B$, or, phrased differently, leads to state $\langle A, B \rangle$. Execution of

$\quad$ **if** $x < y$ **then** $x := y$

establishes $x = A \max B$, the maximum of A and B. Finally, execution of write(x) will print the value of x, i.e. $A \max B$, at some output device.

The heart of the program is the selection statement:

$\quad$ **if** $x < y$ **then** $x := y$

The relation between

$\quad x = A \wedge y = B$,
$\quad$ **if** $x < y$ **then** $x := y$, and
$\quad x = A \max B$

is denoted as

$\quad \{ x = A \wedge y = B \}$ **if** $x < y$ **then** $x := y$ $\{ x = A \max B \}$

The operational interpretation of this triple is

$\quad$ Execution of '**if** $x < y$ **then** $x := y$' starting in a state satisfying $x = A \wedge y = B$ terminates in a state satisfying $x = A \max B$.

Predicate $x = A \wedge y = B$ is called the *pre-condition* and predicate $x = A \max B$ is called the *post-condition* of this statement. How the pre-condition (in particular, the initial state) has been established is not relevant. In this book we will not be concerned with input or output, but we focus our attention on the design of the algorithm that expresses the computation of the output in terms of the input.

We will use Edsger W. Dijkstra's guarded command language to denote our programs. This language is quite modest but sufficiently rich to represent sequential algorithms in a succinct and elegant way. The language is not a main subject of the course, it is only used to represent programs. In the guarded commands notation the program presented above is denoted as

$\lVert$ **var** x, y : int;
   $\{\, x = A \land y = B \,\}$
   if $x < y \rightarrow x := y \,[\!]\, x \geq y \rightarrow$ **skip fi**
   $\{\, x = A \max B \,\}$
$\rVert$.

Specifications have the same shape as programs, for instance, a possible specification for the program above is

$\lVert$ **var** x, y : int;
   $\{\, x = A \land y = B \,\}$
   $maximum$
   $\{\, x = A \max B \,\}$
$\rVert$,

in which *maximum* is the name of the program we are looking for.

In general, a specification consists of the definition of a state space (a set of program variables), a pre-condition and a post-condition. Program S satisfies a specification if all executions of S starting in a state satisfying the pre-condition terminate in a state satisfying the post-condition.

The fact that program S satisfies a specification with pre-condition P and post-condition Q is denoted as

$\{P\}\, S\, \{Q\}$

The guarded command language will be introduced in such a way that $\{P\}\, S\, \{Q\}$ can be inferred from the structure of S. For each construct S an inference rule is presented which is based on an operational interpretation of S. However, as soon as the rules have been defined, the operational interpretation will not be used any more.

Thus, before we can start with the main subject of this book, i.e. programming, we have to define the program notation and the rules of the game. The predicate calculus needed for this is the topic of the next chapter.

Any notation used in this book is introduced when it is needed. One convention is mentioned here: for function application we use a dot, so instead of $F(x)$ we write $F.x$. Function application is left-binding: $f.x.y$ should be interpreted as $(f.x).y$.

Chapter 1

Predicate Calculus

In programming, predicate logic is used as a calculus, as opposed to its use in other disciplines where logic plays a more static role. This chapter is not a short introduction to logic, but a presentation of a (rather modest) notation and set of rules that will be used in the subsequent chapters.

A predicate is a boolean function: for set X, function $P\colon X \to \{\text{false}, \text{true}\}$ is called a predicate on X. In our applications set X will be a *state space* defined by a set of program variables. Each program variable is of a certain type and X is the Cartesian product of these types. The coordinates of X are identified by the names of the program variables. For instance, x and y of type integer define state space $X = \mathcal{Z} \times \mathcal{Z}$. Let the first coordinate correspond to x and let the second coordinate correspond to y. Typical predicates on X are $x \geq y$ and $x = 2 \land y = 3$. The latter has value true in point $\langle 2, 3 \rangle$ and value false in all other points of the state space.

For each state space the (constant) predicate that is true in each point of that space is also denoted by true. Similarly, false denotes the predicate that is false in all points of the state space. The following operators are defined on the set of predicates on a state space.

$\land$ (conjunction)
$\lor$ (disjunction)
$\equiv$ (equivalence)
$\Rightarrow$ (implication)
$\neg$ (negation)

These operators are defined as follows:

$P \land Q$ is the predicate that is true in each point where P is true and Q is true; it is false in all other points.

$P \vee Q$ is the predicate that is false in each point where P is false and Q is false; it is true in all other points.

$P \equiv Q$ is the predicate that is true in each point where P and Q have the same value; it is false in all other points.

$P \Rightarrow Q$ is the predicate that is false in each point where P is true and Q is false; it is true in all other points.

$\neg P$ is the predicate that is true in each point where P is false; it is false in each point where P is true.

For $P \Rightarrow Q$ we may also write $Q \Leftarrow P$ ('Q follows from P'). To avoid parentheses in expressions we introduce the following priorities. Negation has the highest priority. From the binary operators, conjunction and disjunction have the highest priority followed by implication and then equivalence. For instance, $P \Rightarrow Q \equiv \neg P \vee Q$ should be read as $(P \Rightarrow Q) \equiv ((\neg P) \vee Q)$.

We are often interested in predicates that hold everywhere, i.e., predicates that are true at each point of the state space. Examples of such predicates are $Q \equiv Q$, $(x+1)^2 = x^2 + 2x + 1$, and true. The proposition 'P is true for all states' is denoted as

$$[P]$$

which is pronounced as 'for all states P' or 'P, for all states'.
For instance, $[x \geq 1 \Rightarrow x \geq 0]$ and [true] hold, whereas $[x \geq 0 \Rightarrow x \geq 1]$ does not hold, since

$$0 \geq 0 \wedge \neg(0 \geq 1)$$

Note that $[P \equiv Q]$ expresses that predicates P and Q denote the same function. In particular, Q may be substituted for P. This substitution rule (known as Leibniz's Rule) may be formulated as follows:

If $[P \equiv Q]$ then any occurrence of P in expression R may be replaced by Q without changing the value of R.

We assume that the reader is familiar with most of the properties of the operators introduced above. The following list shows some of these properties. This list is not exhaustive and not all of the listed properties will be used frequently. Their use will become apparent in the chapters that follow. In the following P, Q, and R are predicates on the same state space.

6   Predicate Calculus

idempotence: $[P \wedge P \equiv P]$
$[P \vee P \equiv P]$

commutativity: $[P \wedge Q \equiv Q \wedge P]$
$[P \vee Q \equiv Q \vee P]$
$[(P \equiv Q) \equiv (Q \equiv P)]$

associativity: $[(P \wedge Q) \wedge R \equiv P \wedge (Q \wedge R)]$
$[(P \vee Q) \vee R \equiv P \vee (Q \vee R)]$
$[((P \equiv Q) \equiv R) \equiv (P \equiv (Q \equiv R))]$

These associativity properties permit us to omit parentheses.

distributivity: $[P \wedge (Q \vee R) \equiv (P \wedge Q) \vee (P \wedge R)]$
$[P \vee (Q \wedge R) \equiv (P \vee Q) \wedge (P \vee R)]$
$[P \vee (Q \equiv R) \equiv P \vee Q \equiv P \vee R]$

absorption: $[P \wedge (P \vee R) \equiv P]$
$[P \vee (P \wedge R) \equiv P]$

false-true rules: $[P \wedge \text{true} \equiv P]$ $[P \wedge \text{false} \equiv \text{false}]$
$[P \vee \text{false} \equiv P]$ $[P \vee \text{true} \equiv \text{true}]$

De Morgan: $[\neg(P \wedge Q) \equiv \neg P \vee \neg Q]$ $[\neg(P \vee Q) \equiv \neg P \wedge \neg Q]$

negation: $[\neg\neg P \equiv P]$ $[P \vee \neg P \equiv \text{true}]$
$[\neg(P \equiv Q) \equiv \neg P \equiv Q]$ $[P \wedge \neg P \equiv \text{false}]$

implication: $[P \Rightarrow Q \equiv \neg P \vee Q]$ $[\text{false} \Rightarrow P]$
$[P \Rightarrow Q \equiv P \wedge Q \equiv P]$ $[P \Rightarrow \text{true}]$
$[P \Rightarrow Q \equiv P \vee Q \equiv Q]$ $[\text{true} \Rightarrow P \equiv P]$
$[P \Rightarrow P \vee Q]$ $[P \Rightarrow \text{false} \equiv \neg P]$
$[P \wedge Q \Rightarrow P]$

equivalence: $[P \equiv P]$
$[P \equiv P \equiv \text{true}]$
$[\neg P \equiv P \equiv \text{false}]$

A theorem of the form $[P \equiv Q]$ is often proved in a number of steps, for instance, by showing $[P \equiv A]$, $[A \equiv B]$, and $[B \equiv Q]$, for certain predicates A and B. To avoid writing down A and B twice, we use the following notation for such a proof:

$\quad P$
$\equiv \quad \{\text{hint why } [P \equiv A]\}$
$\quad A$
$\equiv \quad \{\text{hint why } [A \equiv B]\}$
$\quad B$
$\equiv \quad \{\text{hint why } [B \equiv Q]\}$
$\quad Q$

Similarly $[P \Rightarrow Q]$ may be proved by, for instance, $[P \equiv A]$, $[A \Rightarrow B]$, and $[B \Rightarrow Q]$. We will denote such a proof as follows:

$\quad P$
$\equiv \quad \{\text{hint why } [P \equiv A]\}$
$\quad A$
$\Rightarrow \quad \{\text{hint why } [A \Rightarrow B]\}$
$\quad B$
$\Rightarrow \quad \{\text{hint why } [B \Rightarrow Q]\}$
$\quad Q$

As an example we show $[P \wedge (\neg P \vee Q) \equiv P \wedge Q]$, a so-called 'complement rule':

$\quad P \wedge (\neg P \vee Q)$
$\equiv \quad \{\text{distributivity of } \wedge \text{ over } \vee\}$
$\quad (P \wedge \neg P) \vee (P \wedge Q)$
$\equiv \quad \{\text{negation rule}\}$
$\quad \text{false} \vee (P \wedge Q)$
$\equiv \quad \{\text{false-true rule}\}$
$\quad P \wedge Q$

When $[P \Rightarrow Q]$ holds then P is called *stronger* than Q and Q is called *weaker* than P. For example, $x \geq 2$ is stronger than $x \geq 1$ and $x^2 \geq 0$ is weaker than $x \geq 0$. The weakest predicate is predicate true, since $[P \Rightarrow \text{true}]$ for all P, and the strongest predicate is predicate false, since $[\text{false} \Rightarrow P]$ for all P.

Equation $Y : [Y \Rightarrow P]$ has P as weakest solution, since

8   Predicate Calculus

(i) $[P \Rightarrow P]$, i.e., P is a solution, and

(ii) for any solution Y, $[Y \Rightarrow P]$, i.e., P is weaker than Y.

Note that false is the strongest solution of this equation. Similarly, equation $Y: [P \Rightarrow Y]$ has P as its strongest solution, and true as its weakest solution.

We use predicates that are expressions in the program variables of the state space. An important operation on expressions is *substitution*. Substitution of expression E for variable x in expression Q is denoted as

$$Q(x := E)$$

to be pronounced as 'Q in which x is replaced by E'. Multiple substitution of x and y by E and F, respectively, is denoted as

$$Q(x, y := E, F)$$

Substitution has a higher priority than all other operators, for instance, $[P \equiv Q(x := E)]$ should be read as $[P \equiv (Q(x := E))]$. Substitution distributes over all other operators.

Examples

$$[(x^2 + 2 * x)(x := x+1) \;=\; (x+1)^2 + 2 * (x+1)]$$
$$[(x \geq y)(x := x+1) \;\equiv\; x+1 \geq y]$$
$$[(x + 2 * y = z)(x, y := y, x) \;\equiv\; y + 2 * x = z]$$
$$[(x = E)(x := E) \;\equiv\; E = E(x := E)] \qquad \text{(Note that } x \text{ may occur in E)}$$
$$[(P(x := y))(x := y) \;\equiv\; P(x := y)]$$
$$[(P(x := y))(y := x) \;\equiv\; P(y := x)]$$
$$[(P \wedge Q)(x := E) \;\equiv\; P(x := E) \wedge Q(x := E)]$$

We will use *existential quantification* and *universal quantification*. Existential quantification is a generalization of the disjunction. Let, for $i \geq 0$, $P.i$ be a predicate. For $n \geq 0$ the disjunction

$$P.0 \vee \cdots \vee P.(n-1)$$

is denoted as

$(\exists i : 0 \leq i < n : P.i)$

We have

$[(\exists i : 0 \leq i < 0 : P.i) \equiv \text{false}]$
$[(\exists i : 0 \leq i < n{+}1 : P.i) \equiv (\exists i : 0 \leq i < n : P.i) \vee P.n]$

In derivations this last line is accompanied by the hint 'split off $i = n$'. Due to the symmetry and associativity of $\vee$ any term may be split off. In general, existential quantification is of the form

$(\exists i : R : P)$

where i is a variable (or a list of variables), R is a predicate, called the *range* of the quantification, and P is called the *term*. The range need not be finite, for instance, 'x is an even natural number' is expressed by

$(\exists i : i \in \mathcal{Z} \wedge i \geq 0 : x = 2i)$

The term should be defined for all i that satisfy R. In general R and P depend on i. In some formulae we make this dependence more explicit and we write

$(\exists i : R.i : P.i)$

We have

$[(\exists i : \text{false} : P) \equiv \text{false}]$

When the range of a quantification is false we say that the range is empty. Similarly, a non-empty range means that the range is not false.

In $(\exists i : R : P)$ variable i is called a *bound variable* or a *dummy*. The expression $(\exists i : R : P)$ does *not* depend on i. We will always use fresh names for dummies. In particular, program variables will never occur as the name of a bound variable. Dummies may be renamed: for fresh variable j we have

$[(\exists i : R : P) \equiv (\exists j : R(i := j) : P(i := j))]$

Unless stated otherwise, dummies have type $\mathcal{Z}$ and we omit this type indication in the range. For instance, 'x is an even natural number' is denoted as

$(\exists i : i \geq 0 : x = 2i)$

10 Predicate Calculus

We mention some properties of existential quantification.

$[(\exists i : \text{false} : P) \equiv \text{false}]$
$[(\exists i : i = x : P) \equiv P(i := x)]$ (one-point rule)

$[(\exists i : R \wedge S : P) \equiv (\exists i : R : S \wedge P)]$ (trading)

$[Q \wedge (\exists i : R.i : P.i) \equiv (\exists i : R.i : Q \wedge P.i)]$
$[Q \vee (\exists i : R.i : P.i) \equiv (\exists i : R.i : Q \vee P.i)]$ for R non-empty

$[(\exists i : R : P) \vee (\exists i : R : Q) \equiv (\exists i : R : P \vee Q)]$
$[(\exists i : R : P) \vee (\exists i : S : P) \equiv (\exists i : R \vee S : P)]$

$[(\exists i : R.i : P.i) \wedge (\exists i : S.i : Q.i) \equiv (\exists i, j : R.i \wedge S.j : P.i \wedge Q.j)]$

Universal quantification is a generalization of the conjunction. It is denoted as

$(\forall i : R : P)$

We have similar (dual) rules for universal quantification:

$[(\forall i : \text{false} : P) \equiv \text{true}]$
$[(\forall i : i = x : P) \equiv P(i := x)]$ (one-point rule)

$[(\forall i : R \wedge S : P) \equiv (\forall i : R : S \Rightarrow P)]$ (trading)

$[Q \vee (\forall i : R.i : P.i) \equiv (\forall i : R.i : Q \vee P.i)]$
$[Q \wedge (\forall i : R.i : P.i) \equiv (\forall i : R.i : Q \wedge P.i)]$ for R non-empty

$[(\forall i : R : P) \wedge (\forall i : R : Q) \equiv (\forall i : R : P \wedge Q)]$
$[(\forall i : R : P) \wedge (\forall i : S : P) \equiv (\forall i : R \vee S : P)]$

$[(\forall i : R.i : P.i) \vee (\forall i : S.i : Q.i) \equiv (\forall i, j : R.i \wedge S.j : P.i \vee Q.j)]$

Universal and existential quantification are coupled by De Morgan's Law:

$[\neg(\exists i : R : P) \equiv (\forall i : R : \neg P)]$

Note that $[P]$ is also a form of universal quantification; it may also be written as $(\forall x : x \in X : P)$, where X is the state space. For universal quantification over a state space, however, we always use the square brackets.

Exercises

0. Prove the 'Golden Rule': $[P \land Q \equiv P \equiv Q \equiv P \lor Q]$

1. Prove

    (i) $[(P \Rightarrow Q) \lor \neg R \equiv P \land R \Rightarrow Q]$
    (ii) $[P \land B \Rightarrow R \equiv P \Rightarrow (B \Rightarrow R)]$
    (iii) $[(P \Rightarrow Q) \Rightarrow (P \land R \Rightarrow Q \land R)]$

2. Prove or disprove

    (i) $[(P \Rightarrow Q) \lor (Q \Rightarrow P)]$
    (ii) $[P \Rightarrow Q] \lor [Q \Rightarrow P]$

3. Prove

    (i) $[P \equiv Q \equiv P \Rightarrow Q \equiv Q \Rightarrow P]$
    (ii) $[P \equiv Q \equiv (P \Rightarrow Q) \land (Q \Rightarrow P)]$

4. Prove

    (i) $[(\forall i : i \geq 0 : P.i) \Rightarrow P.0]$
    (ii) $[P.0 \Rightarrow (\exists i : i \geq 0 : P.i)]$

5. Determine how the following pairs of predicates are related (which of the predicates is the weakest or strongest), if they are related at all:

    (i) $x \leq 0$ and $x \leq 1$
    (ii) $x \geq 0$ and $x^2 + y^2 = 9$
    (iii) $x \geq 1 \Rightarrow x \geq 0$ and $x \geq 1$
    (iv) $x \geq 1$ and $(\exists i : i \geq 0 : x = i)$
    (v) $(\forall i : P : Q)$ and $(\exists i : P : Q)$

6. Determine the strongest and the weakest solutions of the following equations in Y:

    (i) $Y : [Y \Rightarrow P \lor Q]$
    (ii) $Y : [Y \lor Q \Rightarrow P \lor Q]$
    (iii) $Y : [Y \Rightarrow P \land Q]$
    (iv) $Y : [Y \land Q \Rightarrow P \land Q]$

Predicate Calculus

7. Disprove

$$[(\exists i : R : P) \wedge (\exists i : R : Q) \equiv (\exists i : R : P \wedge Q)]$$

8. Perform the following substitutions:

   (i) $(x^2 + 2x + 1)(x := x+a)$

   (ii) $(x^2 \geq y)(x, y := y+1, x-1)$

   (iii) $x^2 \geq y(x, y := y+1, x-1)$

   (iv) $(x \geq y+1 \wedge y \geq z)(x, y := x + 3 * z, x - y + 1)$

   (v) $(a \equiv b)(a := a \equiv b)$

9. Simplify the following expressions

   (i) $(\exists i : i \geq 0 : x = 2 * i)$

   (ii) $(\forall i : i \geq a : x \leq i)$

   (iii) $(\exists i : i \geq 0 : (\exists j : 0 \leq j < i : x = 2 * j))$

Chapter 2

The Guarded Command Language

2.0 Introduction

A program is specified by its state space, a pre-condition and a post-condition. For example, consider the specification of a program for the computation of the greatest common divisor of two positive natural numbers X and Y:

$$\begin{array}{l} \|[\,\mathbf{var}\ x, y : \text{int};\\ \quad \{\,X > 0 \land Y > 0 \land x = X \land y = Y\,\}\\ \quad\quad S\\ \quad \{\,x = X\,\mathbf{gcd}\,Y\,\}\\ \,]\!|. \end{array}$$

The first line defines state space $\mathcal{Z} \times \mathcal{Z}$, in which the first coordinate corresponds to x and the second coordinate corresponds to y. In this chapter we restrict ourselves to types int and bool. The latter denotes the set of boolean values, {true, false}. The second line contains the pre-condition of the program. Variables X and Y are called *specification variables*. They are not program variables and thus may not occur in program statements. They may occur in predicates; specifications are universally quantified over all of the specification variables that occur in it. The third line contains the name of the program specified. Finally, the fourth line states the post-condition.

The operational interpretation of the specification is as follows: program S satisfies the specification if for all integers X and Y, execution of S starting in a state satisfying $X > 0 \land Y > 0 \land x = X \land y = Y$ terminates in a state satisfying $x = X\,\mathbf{gcd}\,Y$.

Programs, also called *statements*, are introduced in the next sections. For each statement S of the guarded command language a proof rule (inference rule) is presented that shows how to prove that S satisfies a given specification. These rules are inspired by the operational interpretation of S and by the operational interpretation of $\{P\}\,S\,\{Q\}$, which states

> each execution of S terminates in a state satifying Q when applied to a state satisfying P.

As soon as the rules have been given, we will not rely on this operational interpretation any more. As a preliminary, we discuss some general rules on programs. We shall then define the guarded command language in such a way that the general rules are not violated.

The first relation that we discuss is $\{P\}\,S\,\{\text{false}\}$ which states that execution of S starting in a state satisfying P terminates in a state satisfying false, i.e. in no state. To exclude miracles, we require that the following rule is valid for all our programs:

$$\{P\}\,S\,\{\text{false}\} \text{ is equivalent to } [P \equiv \text{false}]$$

Note that $\{P\}\,S\,\{\text{true}\}$ expresses the fact that execution of S terminates when applied to a state satisfying P.

Another rule is the fact that the pre-condition may be strengthened and the post-condition may be weakened. This is formulated as follows:

$$\{P\}\,S\,\{Q\} \text{ and } [P_0 \Rightarrow P] \text{ implies } \{P_0\}\,S\,\{Q\}$$
$$\{P\}\,S\,\{Q\} \text{ and } [Q \Rightarrow Q_0] \text{ implies } \{P\}\,S\,\{Q_0\}$$

Suppose that $\{P\}\,S\,\{Q\}$ and $\{P\}\,S\,\{R\}$ hold. Then, execution of S starting in a state satisfying P terminates in a state satisfying Q and also in a state satisfying R, hence, in a state satisfying $Q \wedge R$. This observation leads to the rule of conjunctivity:

$$\{P\}\,S\,\{Q\} \text{ and } \{P\}\,S\,\{R\} \text{ is equivalent to } \{P\}\,S\,\{Q \wedge R\}$$

The last rule of this kind is

$$\{P\}\,S\,\{Q\} \text{ and } \{R\}\,S\,\{Q\} \text{ is equivalent to } \{P \vee R\}\,S\,\{Q\}$$

A more precise way in which constructs may be introduced is as follows. For each construct S one defines a *predicate transformer*, denoted by $wp.S$, which is a function from predicates to predicates. For construct S and predicate Q, $wp.S.Q$ is interpreted as the weakest predicate P for which $\{P\} S \{Q\}$ holds. It is called the *weakest precondition* of S with respect to Q. The relation between the expressions $\{P\} S \{Q\}$ and $wp.S.Q$ is given by

$$\{P\} S \{Q\} \text{ is equivalent to } [P \Rightarrow wp.S.Q]$$

We shall use proof rules in terms of $\{P\} S \{Q\}$. For the interested reader, however, we provide proof rules in terms of weakest pre-conditions as well. The rules of this section follow from the following rules for $wp.S$:

$[wp.S.\text{false} \equiv \text{false}]$
$[wp.S.Q \wedge wp.S.R \equiv wp.S.(Q \wedge R)]$
$[wp.S.Q \vee wp.S.R \Rightarrow wp.S.(Q \vee R)]$

We do not have

$[wp.S.Q \vee wp.S.R \equiv wp.S.(Q \vee R)]$

since we allow so-called *non-determinism* in our programs. We will see examples of non-determinism in Section 2.4.

The examples used in this chapter may seem to be rather contrived. Their purpose is to show how the proof rules should be used and not how programs are derived. The derivation of programs is the subject of subsequent chapters: in this chapter programs are merely presented. Moreover, these programs are not supposed to be 'meaningful' nor is the reader expected to figure out 'what they do'.

Exercises

0. Give an operational description of $\{\text{true}\} S \{\text{true}\}$ and of $\{\text{false}\} S \{\text{true}\}$.

1. Deduce from the rules of this section that

    $\{P_0\} S \{Q_0\}$ and $\{P_1\} S \{Q_1\}$

    implies

    $\{P_0 \wedge P_1\} S \{Q_0 \wedge Q_1\}$ and $\{P_0 \vee P_1\} S \{Q_0 \vee Q_1\}$

2. Show $\{\text{false}\} S \{P\}$ for any P and S.

16 The Guarded Command Language

3. As explained in this section, we denote for construct S and predicate Q the weakest predicate X for which $\{X\} S \{Q\}$ holds as $wp.S.Q$. Then $\{P\} S \{Q\}$ is equivalent to

$$[P \Rightarrow wp.S.Q]$$

Show that the rules of this section follow from the following rules for $wp.S$:

$$[wp.S.\text{false} \equiv \text{false}]$$
$$[wp.S.Q \land wp.S.R \equiv wp.S.(Q \land R)]$$
$$[wp.S.Q \lor wp.S.R \Rightarrow wp.S.(Q \lor R)]$$

4. Statement **abort** is specified by

$$\{P\} \textbf{ abort } \{Q\} \text{ is equivalent to } [P \equiv \text{false}]$$

(i) Give an operational interpretation of **abort**.
(ii) Determine $wp.\textbf{abort}$.
(iii) Show that **abort** satisfies the rules of this section.

2.1 Skip

The first statement that we consider is skip. Execution of skip does not have any effect on the current state. As we will see later, it is important to be able to denote such an action by a word like skip. From the operational interpretation of $\{P\} S \{Q\}$ we conclude that skip may be characterized by $\{Q\} \text{skip} \{Q\}$ for all predicates Q. Since the pre-condition may be strengthened, we prefer to characterize it by

$$\boxed{\{P\} \text{skip} \{Q\} \text{ is equivalent to } [P \Rightarrow Q]}$$

For example,

$$[\![\textbf{var } x, y : \text{int}; \ \{x \geq 1\} \text{skip} \{x \geq 0\}]\!]$$

follows from

$$[x \geq 1 \Rightarrow x \geq 0]$$

The weakest solution of X: $\{X\} \text{skip} \{Q\}$ is Q, hence, in terms of weakest pre-conditions skip is defined by

$$[wp.\text{skip}.Q \equiv Q]$$

Exercises

0. Prove:

    (i) $[\![\,\textbf{var}\ x, y : \text{int};\ \{x > 0 \land y > 0\}\ \textbf{skip}\ \{x > 0\}\,]\!]$.
    (ii) $[\![\,\textbf{var}\ x, y : \text{int};\ \{x > 0 \land y > 0\}\ \textbf{skip}\ \{y \geq 0\}\,]\!]$.
    (iii) $[\![\,\textbf{var}\ x, y : \text{bool};\ \{x \equiv y\}\ \textbf{skip}\ \{x \Rightarrow y\}\,]\!]$.

1. Disprove:

    (i) $[\![\,\textbf{var}\ x, y : \text{int};\ \{x > 0 \land y > 0\}\ \textbf{skip}\ \{x = 1\}\,]\!]$.
    (ii) $[\![\,\textbf{var}\ x, y : \text{int};\ \{x > 0 \land y > 0\}\ \textbf{skip}\ \{y \geq x\}\,]\!]$.
    (iii) $[\![\,\textbf{var}\ x, y : \text{bool};\ \{x \equiv y\}\ \textbf{skip}\ \{x \lor y\}\,]\!]$.

2. Show that the general rules of Section 2.0 hold for skip.

2.2 Assignment

Any change of state that occurs during execution of a program is due to the execution of an assignment statement. The assignment statement is of the form $x := E$, where x is a program variable and E is an expression of x's type. Its operational interpretation is: execution of $x := E$ replaces the value of x by the value of E. In predicates this replacement corresponds to substitution. For predicate Q, we have that Q holds after execution of $x := E$ if $Q(x := E)$ held before execution. This observation yields the following rule for the assignment statement.

$$\{P\}\ x := E\ \{Q\} \text{ is equivalent to } [P \Rightarrow Q(x := E)]$$

For example,

$$\{x \geq 3\}\ x := x+1\ \{x \geq 0\}$$

follows from

$\quad (x \geq 0)(x := x+1)$
$\equiv \quad \{\,\text{substitution}\,\}$
$\quad x+1 \geq 0$
$\equiv \quad \{\,\text{arithmetic}\,\}$
$\quad x \geq -1$
$\Leftarrow \quad \{\,\text{arithmetic}\,\}$
$\quad x \geq 3$

18   The Guarded Command Language

The weakest solution of X: $\{X\}\, x := E\, \{Q\}$ is $Q(x := E)$, hence, in terms of weakest pre-conditions the assignment statement is defined by

$$[wp.(x := E).Q \equiv Q(x := E)]$$

For instance, the weakest P for which $\{P\}\, x := x+1\, \{x \geq 0\}$ holds is $x \geq -1$.

It is not difficult to show that the general rules of Section 1.0 are valid for the assignment. We will also use *multiple assignments*. For example,

$$\{x = A \wedge y = B\}\, x, y := y, x\, \{x = B \wedge y = A\}$$

follows from

$$[(x = B \wedge y = A)(x, y := y, x) \equiv x = A \wedge y = B]$$

Integer expressions consist of integer constants (represented in the usual way), variables of type int, and combinations of these, formed by operators. We will use the unary operator $-$ and the binary operators

+	addition
−	subtraction
*	multiplication
max	maximum
min	minimum
div	quotient of integer division
mod	remainder of integer division

Binary operators $+$ and $-$ have a lower priority than the other operators. Expressions $a\,\mathbf{div}\,b$ and $a\,\mathbf{mod}\,b$ are defined for $b \neq 0$ by

$$a\,\mathbf{div}\,b = q \wedge a\,\mathbf{mod}\,b = r \equiv a = b*q + r \wedge 0 \leq r < |b|$$

Note that equation $\langle q, r \rangle : a = b*q + r \wedge 0 \leq r < |b|$ has for $b \neq 0$ precisely one solution.

As an example, we show $(a+b)\,\mathbf{mod}\,b = a\,\mathbf{mod}\,b$ for $b \neq 0$. We derive

$$\begin{aligned}
&\quad a \,\mathbf{div}\, b = q \;\wedge\; a \,\mathbf{mod}\, b = r \\
&\equiv \quad \{\text{definition of } \mathbf{div} \text{ and } \mathbf{mod}\,\} \\
&\quad a = b*q + r \;\wedge\; 0 \leq r < |b| \\
&\equiv \quad \{\text{arithmetic}\,\} \\
&\quad a + b = b*(q+1) + r \;\wedge\; 0 \leq r < |b| \\
&\equiv \quad \{\text{definition of } \mathbf{div} \text{ and } \mathbf{mod}\,\} \\
&\quad (a+b) \,\mathbf{div}\, b = q+1 \;\wedge\; (a+b) \,\mathbf{mod}\, b = r
\end{aligned}$$

Hence, $(a+b) \,\mathbf{div}\, b = a \,\mathbf{div}\, b + 1$ and $(a+b) \,\mathbf{mod}\, b = a \,\mathbf{mod}\, b$.

In boolean expressions we use the unary operator $\neg$ and the binary operators $\wedge$, $\vee$, $\Rightarrow$, $\Leftarrow$, and $\equiv$. Furthermore, one may form boolean expressions by applying the relational operators $<, \leq, >, \geq, =,$ and $\neq$ to integer expressions. These operators have a higher priority than the boolean operators and a lower priority than the arithmetic operators. Examples of boolean expressions are, for $a, b :$ int, $p :$ bool,

$a*b \leq a \;\wedge\; a \,\mathbf{mod}\, 3 = 0$
$a \geq b{-}1 \;\vee\; p$

Expressions such as $a \,\mathbf{div}\, b$ are not defined for all values of a and b. The predicate that defines for which values of its variables expression E is defined, is denoted by def.E. For instance,

$[\text{def.}(a \,\mathbf{mod}\, b) \equiv b \neq 0]$
$[\text{def.}(a + b) \equiv \text{true}]$
$[\text{def.}(x \,\mathbf{div}\, (a - b)) \equiv a \neq b]$
$[\text{def.}(x \,\mathbf{div}\, y + y \,\mathbf{div}\, x) \equiv x \neq 0 \wedge y \neq 0]$

Since assignment $x := E$ is only defined when def.E holds, we extend the definition of the assignment to

$$\boxed{\{P\}\, x := E\, \{Q\} \text{ is equivalent to } [P \Rightarrow \text{def.}E \wedge Q(x := E)]}$$

Since for most expressions E [def.E] holds, we usually omit def.E and calculate $Q(x := E)$ only. In terms of weakest pre-conditions we have

$$[wp.(x := E).Q \equiv \text{def}.E \wedge Q(x := E)]$$

Exercises

0. Determine the weakest predicate P that satisfies

   (i) $\{P\}\, x := x+1\, \{x > 0\}$
   (ii) $\{P\}\, x := x*x\, \{x > 0\}$
   (iii) $\{P\}\, x := x*x*x - 2*x + 4\, \{x > 0\}$
   (iv) $\{P\}\, x := x+1\, \{x^3 - 5x^2 + 2x > 0\}$
   (v) $\{P\}\, x := x*x*x - 2*x + 4\, \{x^3 - 5x^2 + 2x > 0\}$
   (vi) $\{P\}\, x := x+1\, \{x = x+1\}$
   (vii) $\{P\}\, x := E\, \{x = E\}$
   (viii) $\{P\}\, x := x \bmod 2\, \{x = x \bmod 2\}$
   (ix) $\{P\}\, x,y := x+1, y-1\, \{x+y > 0\}$
   (x) $\{P\}\, x,y := y+1, x-1\, \{x > 0\}$
   (xi) $\{P\}\, x,y := y*x, x*y\, \{x+y > 0\}$
   (xii) $\{P\}\, a := a \equiv b\, \{a\}$
   (xiii) $\{P\}\, a := a \Rightarrow b\, \{a \vee b\}$

1. Show that execution of $x := x+1$ terminates.

2. Prove for $b \neq 0$:

   (i) $(a \bmod b) \bmod b = a \bmod b$
   (ii) $a \bmod b = a \bmod (-b)$
   (iii) $(a \bmod b + c \bmod b) \bmod b = (a + c) \bmod b$

2.3 Catenation

Catenation allows us to describe sequences of actions. The catenation of S and T is denoted as $S\,;T$. Its operational interpretation is: first S is executed after which T is executed. To prove $\{P\}\, S;T\, \{Q\}$, we have to invent predicate R such that $\{P\}\, S\, \{R\}$ and $\{R\}\, T\, \{Q\}$ hold. Then execution of S starting in a state satisfying P terminates in a state satisfying R, and execution of T starting in that state terminates in a state satisfying Q. This leads to the following rule:

> $\{P\}\, S;T\, \{Q\}$ is equivalent to
>
> a predicate R exists such that $\{P\}\, S\, \{R\}$ and $\{R\}\, T\, \{Q\}$

Note that the semi-colon is not used as a separator or a terminator: it is the composition operator for combining two statements. The weakest P that satisfies $\{P\}\, S;T\, \{Q\}$ is obtained by taking the weakest R in $\{R\}\, T\, \{Q\}$ and for that weakest R the weakest P for which $\{P\}\, S\, \{R\}$ holds. In terms of weakest preconditions this is captured by the following definition:

$$[wp.(S;T).Q \;\equiv\; wp.S.(wp.T.Q)]$$

i.e., the semi-colon corresponds to function composition. In particular, catenation is associative. As an example, we prove

$\|[\,$ **var** $a, b : \text{bool};$
$\quad \{(a \equiv A) \land (b \equiv B)\}$
$\quad a := a \equiv b$
$\quad ; b := a \equiv b$
$\quad ; a := a \equiv b$
$\quad \{(a \equiv B) \land (b \equiv A)\}$
$\,]\|.$

We calculate the weakest predicates that are allowed as intermediate predicates, proceeding from the bottom to the top, starting with the post-condition:

$\quad ((a \equiv B) \land (b \equiv A))(a := a \equiv b)$
$\equiv \quad \{\,\text{substitution}\,\}$
$\quad (a \equiv b \equiv B) \land (b \equiv A)$

and

$\quad ((a \equiv b \equiv B) \land (b \equiv A))(b := a \equiv b)$
$\equiv \quad \{\,\text{substitution}\,\}$
$\quad (a \equiv a \equiv b \equiv B) \land (a \equiv b \equiv A)$
$\equiv \quad \{\,\text{predicate calculus}\,\}$
$\quad (b \equiv B) \land (a \equiv b \equiv A)$

and, finally,

$$((b \equiv B) \land (a \equiv b \equiv A))(a := a \equiv b)$$
$\equiv$ { substitution }
$$(b \equiv B) \land (a \equiv b \equiv b \equiv A)$$
$\equiv$ { predicate calculus }
$$(b \equiv B) \land (a \equiv A)$$
$\equiv$ { predicate calculus }
$$(a \equiv A) \land (b \equiv B)$$

From these results we conclude

$$\{(a \equiv A) \land (b \equiv B)\}\ a := a \equiv b\ \{(b \equiv B) \land (a \equiv b \equiv A)\}$$
$$\{(b \equiv B) \land (a \equiv b \equiv A)\}\ b := a \equiv b\ \{(a \equiv b \equiv B) \land (b \equiv A)\}$$
$$\{(a \equiv b \equiv B) \land (b \equiv A)\}\ a := a \equiv b\ \{(a \equiv B) \land (b \equiv A)\}$$

which had to be proved. To avoid this duplication of predicates, these three arguments may be given in a so-called *annotated* program:

$\|[$ **var** $a, b :$ bool;
$\quad \{(a \equiv A) \land (b \equiv B)\}$
$\quad a := a \equiv b$
$\quad \{(b \equiv B) \land (a \equiv b \equiv A),\ \text{Proof 0}\ \}$
$\quad ; b := a \equiv b$
$\quad \{(a \equiv b \equiv B) \land (b \equiv A),\ \text{Proof 1}\ \}$
$\quad ; a := a \equiv b$
$\quad \{(a \equiv B) \land (b \equiv A),\ \text{Proof 2}\ \}$
$]|,$

and Proofs 0, 1, and 2 are the derivations above (in the order 2, 1, and 0).

Exercises

0. Determine the weakest predicate P that satisfies

   (i) $\{P\}\ x := x+1\ ; x := x+1\ \{x > 0\}$
   (ii) $\{P\}\ x := x * x\ ; x := x+1\ \{x > 0\}$
   (iii) $\{P\}\ x := x+y\ ; y := x-y\ ; x := x-y\ \{x = A \land y = B\}$
   (iv) $\{P\}\ x := y\ ; y := x\ \{x = A \land y = B\}$

(v) $\{P\}\, x := x+1\, ;\mathbf{skip}\, \{x^3 > 0\}$

(vi) $\{P\}\, x := E\, ;x := E\, \{x = E\}$

1. Show that $\mathbf{skip}\, ;\mathbf{skip}$ is equivalent to $\mathbf{skip}$.

2. Calculate expressions E such that

    (i) $\{A = q*B + r\}\, q := E\, ;r := r{-}B\, \{A = q*B + r\}$

    (ii) $\{true\}\, y := E\, ;x := x\, \mathbf{div}\, 2\, \{2*x = y\}$

    (iii) $\{x*y + p*q = N\}\, x := x{-}p\, ;q := E\, \{x*y + p*q = N\}$

3. Prove

$\|\![\, \mathbf{var}\, x, y : \text{int};$
$\quad \{x = A \wedge y = B\}$
$\quad x := x{-}y\, ;y := x{+}y\, ;x := y{-}x$
$\quad \{x = B \wedge y = A\}$
$\,]\!\|.$

2.4 Selection

Selection takes the form

$\quad \mathbf{if}\, B.0 \rightarrow S.0\, [\!]\, \cdots\, [\!]\, B.n \rightarrow S.n\, \mathbf{fi}$

in which for $0 \le i \le n$, $B.i$ is a boolean expression (a guard) and $S.i$ is a statement. The construct $B.i \rightarrow S.i$ is called a *guarded command*. An operational interpretation of selection is as follows:

> Upon execution of a selection all guards are evaluated. If none of the guards evaluates to true then execution of the selection aborts, otherwise one of the guards that has the value true is chosen *non-deterministically* and the corresponding statement is executed.

Abortion may be interpreted as 'fails to terminate'. A possible implementation of the selection is as follows: the guards are evaluated until one of these evaluates to true after which the corresponding statement is executed.

As an example we derive a statement S that satisfies

$\quad \|\![\, \mathbf{var}\, x, y, z : \text{int};\, \{true\}\, S\, \{z = x\, \mathbf{max}\, y\}\,]\!\|$

From

$$z = x \max y \equiv (z = x \vee z = y) \wedge z \geq x \wedge z \geq y$$

we conclude that $z := x$ is a candidate for S. As a pre-condition we then have

$$((z = x \vee z = y) \wedge z \geq x \wedge z \geq y)(z := x)$$
$$\equiv \quad \{ \text{substitution} \}$$
$$(x = x \vee x = y) \wedge x \geq x \wedge x \geq y$$
$$\equiv \quad \{ \text{calculus} \}$$
$$x \geq y$$

which leads to the guarded command $x \geq y \rightarrow z := x$. On account of symmetry we also have $y \geq x \rightarrow z := y$. Combining these two leads to S:

if $x \geq y \rightarrow z := x \;[\!]\; y \geq x \rightarrow z := y$ **fi**

From $[x \geq y \vee y \geq x]$ we infer that the selection will not abort. Since guards need not exclude each other, we were able to exploit the symmetry of **max**.

We are now ready to present the definition of selection. It is formulated for a selection statement that has two guarded commands.

$\{P\}$ **if** $B_0 \rightarrow S_0 \;[\!]\; B_1 \rightarrow S_1$ **fi** $\{Q\}$ is equivalent to

(i) $[P \Rightarrow B_0 \vee B_1]$ and

(ii) $\{P \wedge B_0\} S_0 \{Q\}$ and $\{P \wedge B_1\} S_1 \{Q\}$

In Section 2.2, we added def.E to the definition of $x := E$. For selection, we have a similar situation:

if $B_0 \rightarrow S_0 \;[\!]\; B_1 \rightarrow S_1$ **fi**

may only be executed in states where def.$B_0 \wedge$ def.B_1 holds. Hence, instead of (i) the formal proof obligation is

(i') $[P \Rightarrow \text{def}.B_0 \wedge \text{def}.B_1 \wedge (B_0 \vee B_1)]$

Since for most expressions B [def.B] holds, we usually omit def.$B_0 \wedge$ def.B_1 and consider $B_0 \vee B_1$ only.

The fact that only one of the guards is chosen, is demonstrated in the following example in which both guards are true. Its post-condition, $x = 1$, may not be replaced by $x = 2$. We prove

$\{x = 0\}$ **if** true $\to x := x+1$ [] true $\to x := x+1$ **fi** $\{x = 1\}$

Proof:

(i)   true ∨ true
         ≡   { predicate calculus }
         true
         ⇐   { predicate calculus }
         $x = 0$

(ii) $(x = 1)(x := x+1)$
         ≡   { substitution }
         $x+1 = 1$
         ≡   { arithmetic }
         $x = 0$

Hence, $\{x = 0 \wedge \text{true}\}\, x := x+1\, \{x = 1\}$

In programs we will use the following annotation and corresponding proofs for the selection:

$\{P\}$
if $B_0 \to \{P \wedge B_0\}\, S_0\, \{Q, \text{Proof 0}\}$
[] $B_1 \to \{P \wedge B_1\}\, S_1\, \{Q, \text{Proof 1}\}$
fi
$\{Q, \text{Proof 2}\}$

with

Proof 0: a proof of $\{P \wedge B_0\}\, S_0\, \{Q\}$;
Proof 1: a proof of $\{P \wedge B_1\}\, S_1\, \{Q\}$;
Proof 2: a proof of $[P \Rightarrow B_0 \vee B_1]$ and, if relevant,
           a proof of $[P \Rightarrow \text{def}.B_0 \wedge \text{def}.B_1]$.

The next example exhibits the non-determinism of selection. Its post-condition may be replaced neither by $x = 1$ nor by $x = -1$. We annotate the following program and we supply a proof for its correctness.

$\{x = 0\}$ **if** true $\to x := 1$ [] true $\to x := -1$ **fi** $\{x = 1 \vee x = -1\}$

The annotated version is

$\{x = 0\}$
if true $\to$ $\{x = 0\}$ $x := 1$ $\{x = 1 \lor x = -1,\ \text{Proof 0}\}$
$[\!]$ true $\to$ $\{x = 0\}$ $x := -1$ $\{x = 1 \lor x = -1,\ \text{Proof 1}\}$
fi
$\{x = 1 \lor x = -1,\ \text{Proof 2}\}$

Proof 0:

$\quad (x = 1 \lor x = -1)(x := 1)$
$\equiv \quad \{\text{substitution}\}$
$\quad 1 = 1 \lor 1 = -1$
$\equiv \quad \{\text{calculus}\}$
$\quad \text{true}$
$\Leftarrow \quad \{\text{predicate calculus}\}$
$\quad x = 0$

Proof 1: Similarly.

Proof 2:

$\quad \text{true} \lor \text{true}$
$\equiv \quad \{\text{predicate calculus}\}$
$\quad \text{true}$
$\Leftarrow \quad \{\text{predicate calculus}\}$
$\quad x = 0$

Hence, execution of this selection is guaranteed to terminate in a state satisfying $x = 1 \lor x = -1$, but neither termination in a state satisfying $x = 1$ nor termination in a state satisfying $x = -1$ can be guaranteed.

In terms of weakest pre-conditions selection is characterized by

$[wp.(\textbf{if}\ B_0 \to S_0\ [\!]\ B_1 \to S_1\ \textbf{fi}).Q$
$\equiv \text{def}.B_0 \land \text{def}.B_1 \land (B_0 \lor B_1) \land (B_0 \Rightarrow wp.S_0.Q) \land (B_1 \Rightarrow wp.S_1.Q)]$

Since for most expressions B $[\text{def}.B]$ holds, we usually omit $\text{def}.B_0 \land \text{def}.B_1$ in calculations with this weakest pre-condition.

Exercises

0. Prove:

   (i) $\{\text{true}\}\ \textbf{if}\ x \geq 1 \to x := x+1\ [\!]\ x \leq 1 \to x := x-1\ \textbf{fi}\ \{x \neq 1\}$.

   (ii) $\{\text{true}\}\ \textbf{if}\ x \geq y \to \text{skip}\ [\!]\ x \leq y \to x, y := y, x\ \textbf{fi}\ \{x \geq y\}$.

   (iii) $[\![\ \textbf{var}\ x, y : \text{int};$
   $\qquad \{\text{true}\}$
   $\qquad x, y := y*y, x*x$
   $\qquad ;\textbf{if}\ x \geq y \to x := x-y\ [\!]\ y \geq x \to y := y-x\ \textbf{fi}$
   $\qquad \{x \geq 0 \land y \geq 0\}$
   $]\!]$.

   (iv) $[\![\ \textbf{var}\ a, b : \text{bool};$
   $\qquad \{\text{true}\}$
   $\qquad \textbf{if}\ \neg a \lor b \to a := \neg a$
   $\qquad [\!]\ a \lor \neg b \to b := \neg b$
   $\qquad \textbf{fi}$
   $\qquad \{a \lor b\}$
   $]\!]$.

1. Prove: $\{P\}\ \textbf{if}\ B_0 \to S_0\ ; S\ [\!]\ B_1 \to S_1\ ; S\ \textbf{fi}\ \{Q\}$ is equivalent to
   $\{P\}\ \textbf{if}\ B_0 \to S_0\ [\!]\ B_1 \to S_1\ \textbf{fi}\ ; S\ \{Q\}$.

2. Prove: $\{P\}\ \textbf{if}\ B_0 \to S_0\ [\!]\ B_1 \to S_1\ \textbf{fi}\ \{Q\}$ implies
   $\{P\}\ \textbf{if}\ B_0 \to S_0\ [\!]\ B_1 \land \neg B_0 \to S_1\ \textbf{fi}\ \{Q\}$.

3. Determine the weakest P such that

   $[\![\ \textbf{var}\ x : \text{int};$
   $\quad \{P\}$
   $\quad x := x+1$
   $\quad ;\textbf{if}\ x > 0 \to x := x-1$
   $\quad\ \ [\!]\ x < 0 \to x := x+2$
   $\quad\ \ [\!]\ x = 1 \to \text{skip}$
   $\quad \textbf{fi}$
   $\quad \{x \geq 1\}$
   $]\!]$.

2.5 Repetition

The next construct of the language is repetition. Programs composed from the previous constructs have execution times proportional to their length. It is possible to specify, using repetition, a statement that is to be executed more than once. It has the form

$$\textbf{do } B.0 \rightarrow S.0 \, [\!] \, \cdots \, [\!] \, B.n \rightarrow S.n \textbf{ od}$$

in which for $0 \leq i \leq n$, $B.i$ is a boolean expression (a guard) and $S.i$ is a statement. An operational interpretation of repetition is the following.

> Upon execution of a repetition all guards are evaluated. If all guards evaluate to false then skip is executed. Otherwise one of the guards that has value true is chosen *non-deterministically* and the corresponding statement is executed after which the repetition is executed again.

At the end of this section, we present a (rather complicated) expression for the weakest pre-condition of a repetition. In the design of programs we do not use this weakest pre-condition. Instead, we use a rule known as the Invariance Theorem. In order to explain this rule we consider repetitions with one guarded command, i.e. repetitions of the form **do** $B \rightarrow S$ **od**. From the operational description above we conclude

$$\{P\} \textbf{ do } B \rightarrow S \textbf{ od } \{Q\}$$

is equivalent to

$$\{P\} \textbf{ if } \neg B \rightarrow \textbf{skip} \, [\!] \, B \rightarrow S \, ; \textbf{do } B \rightarrow S \textbf{ od } \textbf{ fi } \{Q\}$$

Annotation of the selection yields

$$\{P\}$$
$$\textbf{if } \neg B \rightarrow \{P \wedge \neg B\} \textbf{ skip } \{Q\}$$
$$[\!] \quad B \rightarrow \{P \wedge B\} \, S \, ; \textbf{do } B \rightarrow S \textbf{ od } \{Q\}$$
$$\textbf{fi}$$
$$\{Q\}$$

Since $\{P\}$ **do** $B \rightarrow S$ **od** $\{Q\}$ should hold, we choose P as intermediate predicate in the catenation S ; **do** $B \rightarrow S$ **od**. Thus, we have

$$\{P\}$$
$$\textbf{if } \neg B \rightarrow \{P \wedge \neg B\} \textbf{ skip } \{Q\}$$
$$[\!] \quad B \rightarrow \{P \wedge B\} \, S \, \{P\} \, ; \textbf{do } B \rightarrow S \textbf{ od } \{Q\}$$
$$\textbf{fi}$$
$$\{Q\}$$

with proof obligations

(i) $[P \wedge \neg B \Rightarrow Q]$
(ii) $\{P \wedge B\} S \{P\}$
(iii) $\{P\} \mathbf{do}\, B \to S \,\mathbf{od}\, \{Q\}$

in which (iii) gives rise to (i), (ii), and (iii) again. If we can ensure that the repetition terminates, (i) and (ii) suffice. This is formulated for a repetition with two guarded commands as follows.

(i) $[P \wedge \neg B_0 \wedge \neg B_1 \Rightarrow Q]$ and
(ii) $\{P \wedge B_0\} S_0 \{P\}$ and $\{P \wedge B_1\} S_1 \{P\}$

implies

$\{P\} \mathbf{do}\, B_0 \to S_0 \,[\!]\, B_1 \to S_1 \,\mathbf{od}\, \{Q\}$

provided that this repetition terminates.

A predicate P that satisfies (ii), i.e. $\{P \wedge B_0\} S_0 \{P\}$ and $\{P \wedge B_1\} S_1 \{P\}$, is called an *invariant* of $\mathbf{do}\, B_0 \to S_0 \,[\!]\, B_1 \to S_1 \,\mathbf{od}$.

Before discussing termination, we consider Edsger W. Dijkstra's example of the computation of the greatest common divisor of positive integers X and Y. Its specification is

$$[\![\mathbf{var}\, x, y : \mathrm{int}; \{x = X \wedge y = Y \wedge x > 0 \wedge y > 0\} S \{x = X \,\mathbf{gcd}\, Y\}]\!]$$

where $X \,\mathbf{gcd}\, Y$ denotes the greatest common divisor of X and Y; for $x \,\mathbf{gcd}\, y$ with $x > 0 \wedge y > 0$, we have

(0) $x \,\mathbf{gcd}\, x = x$
(1) $x \,\mathbf{gcd}\, y = y \,\mathbf{gcd}\, x$
(2) $x > y \Rightarrow x \,\mathbf{gcd}\, y = (x - y) \,\mathbf{gcd}\, y$ and, applying (1):
$y > x \Rightarrow x \,\mathbf{gcd}\, y = x \,\mathbf{gcd}\, (y - x)$

A *derivation* of a program based on these properties is presented in Chapter 4. Here we supply an invariant without further justification and we focus our attention on the proof obligations. Predicate P is defined as

$P:\ x > 0 \wedge y > 0 \wedge x \,\mathbf{gcd}\, y = X \,\mathbf{gcd}\, Y$

The pre-condition of the specification implies P. Furthermore,

$$
\begin{aligned}
&\quad P \wedge x > y \\
&\equiv \quad \{\text{definition of } P\} \\
&\quad x > 0 \wedge y > 0 \wedge x \gcd y = X \gcd Y \wedge x > y \\
&\Rightarrow \quad \{(2)\} \\
&\quad x > 0 \wedge y > 0 \wedge (x-y) \gcd y = X \gcd Y \wedge x > y \\
&\equiv \quad \{\text{arithmetic}\} \\
&\quad x - y > 0 \wedge y > 0 \wedge (x-y) \gcd y = X \gcd Y \\
&\equiv \quad \{\text{definition of } P\} \\
&\quad P(x := x - y)
\end{aligned}
$$

Hence, $\{P \wedge x > y\}\, x := x - y\, \{P\}$ and by symmetry $\{P \wedge y > x\}\, y := y - x\, \{P\}$. Finally, we derive

$$
\begin{aligned}
&\quad P \wedge \neg(x > y) \wedge \neg(y > x) \\
&\equiv \quad \{\text{arithmetic}\} \\
&\quad P \wedge x = y \\
&\Rightarrow \quad \{\text{definition of } P\} \\
&\quad x \gcd x = X \gcd Y \\
&\equiv \quad \{(0)\} \\
&\quad x = X \gcd Y
\end{aligned}
$$

Application of the rule for repetition yields

$$\{P\}$$
$$\textbf{do } x > y \rightarrow x := x - y \ [\!]\ y > x \rightarrow y := y - x \ \textbf{od}$$
$$\{x = X \gcd Y\}$$

provided that this repetition terminates.

Since $x = X \wedge y = Y \wedge x > 0 \wedge y > 0$ is stronger than P, we also have

$$\{x = X \wedge y = Y \wedge x > 0 \wedge y > 0\}$$
$$\textbf{do } x > y \rightarrow x := x - y \ [\!]\ y > x \rightarrow y := y - x \ \textbf{od}$$
$$\{x = X \gcd Y\}$$

provided that this repetition terminates.

Termination of a repetition is proved by means of an integer function on the state space that is bounded from below and that decreases in each step of the repetition. Such a function is called a *bound function*. For the repetition above, a suitable bound function is $x + y$. From invariant P we infer $x + y > 0$, and both $x := x - y$ and $y := y - x$ decrease $x + y$, i.e., for any constant C we have

$$\{P \wedge x > y \wedge x + y = C\} \; x := x - y \; \{x + y < C\} \quad \text{and}$$
$$\{P \wedge y > x \wedge x + y = C\} \; y := y - x \; \{x + y < C\}$$

Combining the previous rule with the termination requirement, we obtain

---

(i) $[P \wedge \neg B_0 \wedge \neg B_1 \Rightarrow Q]$
(ii) $\{P \wedge B_0\} \, S_0 \, \{P\}$ and $\{P \wedge B_1\} \, S_1 \, \{P\}$
(iii) an integer function t on the state space exists such that
$\quad [P \wedge (B_0 \vee B_1) \Rightarrow t \geq 0]$,
$\quad \{P \wedge B_0 \wedge t = C\} \, S_0 \, \{t < C\}$, and
$\quad \{P \wedge B_1 \wedge t = C\} \, S_1 \, \{t < C\}$

implies

$\{P\} \; \textbf{do} \; B_0 \rightarrow S_0 \; [\!] \; B_1 \rightarrow S_1 \; \textbf{od} \; \{Q\}$

This rule is known as the Invariance Theorem. Such a repetition is annotated as follows.

$\{\,\text{invariant } P : \cdots, \text{ bound } t : \cdots\}$
$\textbf{do} \; B_0 \rightarrow \{P \wedge B_0\} \, S_0 \, \{P, \text{Proof 1}\}$
$[\!] \quad B_1 \rightarrow \{P \wedge B_1\} \, S_1 \, \{P, \text{Proof 2}\}$
$\textbf{od}$
$\{Q, \text{Proof 3, termination: Proof 4}\,\}$

with

Proof 1: proof of $\{P \wedge B_0\} \, S_0 \, \{P\}$;

Proof 2: proof of $\{P \wedge B_1\} \, S_1 \, \{P\}$;

Proof 3: proof of $[P \wedge \neg B_0 \wedge \neg B_1 \Rightarrow Q]$;

Proof 4: proof of (i) $[P \wedge (B_0 \vee B_1) \Rightarrow t \geq 0]$,
$\qquad\qquad\qquad$ (ii) $\{P \wedge B_0 \wedge t = C\} \, S_0 \, \{t < C\}$, and
$\qquad\qquad\qquad$ (iii) $\{P \wedge B_1 \wedge t = C\} \, S_1 \, \{t < C\}$.

Often, the invariant is the post-condition of a statement that precedes the repetition. That statement is sometimes called 'the initialization of P' or 'the statement establishing P'. If S is such a statement and H is its pre-condition, the annotation is

$\{H\}$
S
$\{$ invariant: P, Proof 0, bound: $\cdots\}$
; **do** $B_0 \to \{P \land B_0\}\, S_0\, \{P,\, \text{Proof 1}\}$
 $[\!]\ B_1 \to \{P \land B_1\}\, S_1\, \{P,\, \text{Proof 2}\}$
od
$\{Q,\, \text{Proof 3, termination: Proof 4}\,\}$

with Proof 0 containing a proof of $\{H\}\, S\, \{P\}$.

As with selection,

do $B_0 \to S_0\ [\!]\ B_1 \to S_1$ **od**

is only defined when $\text{def}.B_0 \land \text{def}.B_1$ holds. Hence, another proof obligation is

$[P \Rightarrow \text{def}.B_0 \land \text{def}.B_1]$

When relevant, a proof thereof is added to Proof 3.

It is clear that repetition is the most complex construct of the guarded command language. Indeed, repetition is the essence of sequential programming. Programming is mainly the use of suitable techniques to derive invariants. These techniques are the subject of subsequent chapters. For instance, it is shown in Chapter 4 how this repetition for the computation of the greatest common divisor can be derived.

The derivation of a program is based on an invariant. However, in this chapter, for educational reasons, we give proofs of programs rather than deriving the program with its proof from scratch. Moreover, the examples and exercises are rather artificial: their only purpose is to show how the rules should be applied. An illustration thereof is given below. We prove

$[\![$ **var** $x, y, N :$ int; $\{N \geq 0\}$
  $x, y := 0, 0$
  ; **do** $x \neq 0\ \to x := x-1$
   $[\!]\ y \neq N\ \to x, y := x+1, y+1$
  od
  $\{x = 0 \land y = N\}$
$]\!]$.

It can be observed that the conjunction of the negations of the guards forms the postcondition. It remains to demonstrate termination. In the first guarded command x decreases and in the second guarded command $-y$ decreases. However, a decrease of $-y$ is accompanied by an increase of x. Weighting the decrease of $-y$ twice as much as the increase of x yields $x - 2y$ as a function that decreases in each step of this repetition. Since this function has $-2N$ as final value, we add $2N$ to it. This results in the bound function $x + 2(N-y)$. Clearly, the upper bound for y must be N and the lower bound for x must be 0, thus, we propose as invariant

$P: \; 0 \leq x \land y \leq N$

The annotated program is

$\quad$ [| **var** x, y, N : int; $\{N \geq 0\}$
$\quad\quad x, y := 0, 0$
$\quad\quad$ {invariant P: $0 \leq x \land y \leq N$, Proof 0, bound: $x + 2(N-y)$ }
$\quad\quad$; **do** $x \neq 0 \rightarrow \{P \land x \neq 0\}\; x := x-1\; \{P,\text{ Proof 1}\}$
$\quad\quad\quad$ [] $y \neq N \rightarrow \{P \land y \neq N\}\; x, y := x+1, y+1\; \{P,\text{ Proof 2}\}$
$\quad\quad$ **od**
$\quad\quad$ $\{x = 0 \land y = N,\text{ Proof 3, termination: Proof 4}\}$
$\quad$ |],

and the proofs are presented below.

Proof 0:

$\quad\quad P(x, y := 0, 0)$
$\quad \equiv \quad$ { substitution }
$\quad\quad 0 \leq 0 \land 0 \leq N$
$\quad \equiv \quad$ { calculus }
$\quad\quad 0 \leq N$

Proof 1:

$\quad\quad P(x := x-1)$
$\quad \equiv \quad$ { substitution }
$\quad\quad 0 \leq x-1 \land y \leq N$
$\quad \equiv \quad$ { arithmetic }
$\quad\quad 0 \leq x \land y \leq N \land x \neq 0$
$\quad \equiv \quad$ { definition of P }
$\quad\quad P \land x \neq 0$

The Guarded Command Language

Proof 2:

$$P(x, y := x+1, y+1)$$
$\equiv$ { substitution }
$$0 \leq x+1 \land y+1 \leq N$$
$\Leftarrow$ { arithmetic }
$$0 \leq x \land y \leq N \land y \neq N$$
$\equiv$ { definition of P }
$$P \land y \neq N$$

Proof 3:

$$P \land \neg(x \neq 0) \land \neg(y \neq N)$$
$\Rightarrow$ { calculus }
$$x = 0 \land y = N$$

Proof 4:

(i) $\quad P \land (x \neq 0 \lor y \neq N)$
$\quad\quad \Rightarrow$ { definition of P }
$\quad\quad 0 \leq x \land y \leq N$
$\quad\quad \Rightarrow$ { arithmetic }
$\quad\quad x + 2(N-y) \geq 0$

(ii) $\quad (x + 2(N-y))(x := x - 1)$
$\quad\quad =$ { substitution }
$\quad\quad x - 1 + 2(N-y)$
$\quad\quad <$ { arithmetic }
$\quad\quad x + 2(N-y)$

(iii) $\quad (x + 2(N-y))(x, y := x+1, y+1)$
$\quad\quad =$ { substitution }
$\quad\quad x + 1 + 2(N - (y+1))$
$\quad\quad =$ { arithmetic }
$\quad\quad x + 2(N-y) - 1$
$\quad\quad <$ { arithmetic }
$\quad\quad x + 2(N-y)$

For the interested reader we discuss the weakest pre-condition of **do** $B \to S$ **od**. As mentioned before, we define **do** $B \to S$ **od** as being equivalent to

if $\neg B \to$ skip $[\!]$ $B \to S$; **do** $B \to S$ **od fi**

We abbreviate **do** $B \to S$ **od** to DO, and we derive

$\quad wp.DO.Q$
$\equiv \quad \{\text{see above}\}$
$\quad wp.(\textbf{if } \neg B \to \text{skip } [\!] \ B \to S \ ; DO \ \textbf{fi}).Q$
$\equiv \quad \{\text{definition of selection}\}$
$\quad (\neg B \vee B) \wedge (\neg B \Rightarrow wp.\text{skip}.Q) \wedge (B \Rightarrow wp.(S\ ;DO).Q)$
$\equiv \quad \{[\neg B \vee B \equiv \text{true}], \text{definitions of skip and catenation}\}$
$\quad (\neg B \Rightarrow Q) \wedge (B \Rightarrow wp.S.(wp.DO.Q))$
$\equiv \quad \{\text{predicate calculus}\}$
$\quad (B \vee Q) \wedge (\neg B \vee wp.S.(wp.DO.Q))$

Hence,

$[\, wp.DO.Q \equiv (B \vee Q) \wedge (\neg B \vee wp.S.(wp.DO.Q))\,]$

i.e., $wp.DO.Q$ is a solution of the following equation in predicate X:

$X : [X \equiv (B \vee Q) \wedge (\neg B \vee wp.S.X)]$

This is a so-called *recursive* equation. We define $wp.(\textbf{do } B \to S \textbf{ od}).Q$ as the *strongest* solution of this equation (it can be shown that a strongest solution exists). With this definition the Invariance Theorem can be proved. Such a proof, however, is beyond the scope of this book.

As an example, we compute $wp.(\textbf{do } n \neq 0 \to n := n-2 \textbf{ od}).(n = 0)$. For this specific choice the equation is

$X : [X \equiv (n \neq 0 \vee n = 0) \wedge (n = 0 \vee wp.(n := n-2).X)]$

which may be simplified to

$X : [X \equiv n = 0 \vee X(n := n-2)]$

The strongest solution of this equation can be obtained by successive approximation, starting with false (the strongest predicate of all). Define for $k \geq 0$ predicate X_k by

$[X_0 \equiv \text{false}]$
$[X_{k+1} \equiv n = 0 \lor X_k(n := n-2)]$

then the strongest solution is

$(\exists k : 0 \leq k : X_k)$

Starting with $[X_0 \equiv \text{false}]$ we have

$\quad X_1$
$\equiv \quad \{\text{definition of } X_k, [X_0 \equiv \text{false}]\}$
$\quad n = 0 \lor \text{false}$
$\equiv \quad \{\text{predicate calculus}\}$
$\quad n = 0$

and

$\quad X_2$
$\equiv \quad \{\text{definition of } X_k, [X_1 \equiv n = 0]\}$
$\quad n = 0 \lor (n = 0)(n := n-2)$
$\equiv \quad \{\text{substitution}\}$
$\quad n = 0 \lor n = 2$

Similarly, we have $[X_3 \equiv n = 0 \lor n = 2 \lor n = 4]$ and with induction one can prove $[X_k \equiv 0 \leq n < 2k \land n \bmod 2 = 0]$. This result yields

$\quad wp.(\textbf{do } n \neq 0 \to n := n-2 \textbf{ od}).(n = 0)$
$\equiv \quad \{\text{strongest solution of the equation}\}$
$\quad (\exists k : 0 \leq k : X_k)$
$\equiv \quad \{\text{substitute } X_k\}$
$\quad (\exists k : 0 \leq k : 0 \leq n < 2k \land n \bmod 2 = 0)$
$\equiv \quad \{\text{calculus}\}$
$\quad 0 \leq n \land n \bmod 2 = 0$

Hence, $[wp.(\textbf{do } n \neq 0 \to n := n-2 \textbf{ od}).(n = 0) \equiv 0 \leq n \land n \bmod 2 = 0]$. It is easy to verify that $0 \leq n \land n \bmod 2 = 0$ is indeed a solution of

$X: [X \equiv n = 0 \lor X(n := n-2)]$.

Exercises

Prove the correctness of the following programs

0. $[\![$ **var** $x, N :$ int; $\{N \geq 0\}$
   $x := 0$
   ; **do** $x \neq N \to x := x+1$ **od**
   $\{x = N\}$
   $]\!]$.

1. $[\![$ **var** $x, y, N :$ int; $\{N \geq 0\}$
   $x, y := 0, 1$
   ; **do** $x \neq N \to x, y := x+1, y+y$ **od**
   $\{y = 2^N\}$
   $]\!]$.

2. $[\![$ **var** $y, N :$ int; $\{N \geq 0\}$
   $y := 1$
   ; **do** $y < N \to y := y+y$ **od**
   $\{y \geq N \land (\exists k : k \geq 0 : y = 2^k)\}$
   $]\!]$.

3. $[\![$ **var** $x, y, N :$ int; $\{N \geq 0\}$
   $x, y := 0, 0$
   ; **do** $x \neq 0 \to x := x-1$
   $[\!]\ y \neq N \to x, y := N, y+1$
   od
   $\{x = 0 \land y = N\}$
   $]\!]$.

4. $[\![$ **var** $x, y, z :$ int; $\{$true$\}$
   do $x < y \to x := x+1$
   $[\!]\ y < z \to y := y+1$
   $[\!]\ z < x \to z := z+1$
   od
   $\{x = y = z\}$
   $]\!]$.

5. The following program may be used to compute (non-deterministically) natural numbers x and y such that $x*y = N$. Prove:

$$
\begin{aligned}
&\|[\ \mathbf{var}\ p, x, y, N : \text{int};\ \{N \geq 1\} \\
&\ \ p, x, y := N{-}1, 1, 1 \\
&\ \ \{N = x*y + p\} \\
&\ ; \mathbf{do}\ p \neq 0 \\
&\ \ \ \ \to \mathbf{if}\ p \bmod x = 0\ \to\ y, p := y{+}1, p{-}x \\
&\ \ \ \ \ \ []\ p \bmod y = 0\ \to\ x, p := x{+}1, p{-}y \\
&\ \ \ \ \mathbf{fi} \\
&\ \ \mathbf{od} \\
&\ \ \{x*y = N\} \\
&\ ]\!|.
\end{aligned}
$$

6. For natural a and b, $a\,\mathbf{gcd}\,b$ denotes the greatest common divisor of a and b. By definition $0\,\mathbf{gcd}\,a = a\ \wedge\ a\,\mathbf{gcd}\,0 = a$. Prove

   (i) $a\,\mathbf{gcd}\,b = b\,\mathbf{gcd}\,(a \bmod b)$ for $a \geq b > 0$.

   (ii) $\|[\ \mathbf{var}\ x, y, A, B : \text{int};\ \{A \geq B > 0\}$
   $\ \ \ x, y := A, B$
   $\ ; \mathbf{do}\ y \neq 0 \to x, y := y, x \bmod y\ \mathbf{od}$
   $\ \ \{x = A\,\mathbf{gcd}\,B\}$
   $\ ]\!|.$

2.6 Constants, Inner Blocks, and Arrays

A possible specification for a program for the computation of the greatest common divisor of two positive integers is

$\|[\ \mathbf{var}\ A, B, x : \text{int};$
$\ \ \{A > 0\ \wedge\ B > 0\}$
$\ \ \ \ gcd$
$\ \ \{x = A\,\mathbf{gcd}\,B\}$
$\ ]\!|.$

This specification, however, has $A, B, x := 1, 1, 1$ as possible solution. Of course, this solution is not what we have in mind. To exclude such solutions, we might change the specification to

$\|[\,\textbf{var}\ A, B, x : \text{int};$
$\quad \{A = A_0 \land B = B_0 \land A > 0 \land B > 0\}$
$\quad \ gcd$
$\quad \{x = A\,\textbf{gcd}\,B \land A = A_0 \land B = B_0\}$
$\,]\!|,$

expressing that the final values of A and B equal their initial values. This specification still allows assignments to A and B. We use in the declaration **con** instead of **var** to express the fact that no value should be assigned to the listed names. Hence, a specification that avoids the problems mentioned above is

$\|[\,\textbf{con}\ A, B : \text{int}\ \{A > 0 \land B > 0\};$
$\quad \textbf{var}\ x : \text{int};$
$\quad \ gcd$
$\quad \{x = A\,\textbf{gcd}\,B\}$
$\,]\!|.$

Variables defined as **con** may not occur on the left-hand side of an assignment. Assertions about constants, such as $A > 0 \land B > 0$, should not be repeated in annotations and should not be part of an invariant. They are 'universally invariant' since the values of constants do not change. Assertions about constants provide a context of the program and may be used in proofs whenever appropriate. Constants are not part of the state space.

Another addition to the guarded command language are so-called *inner blocks*. These are used to extend the state space (locally) by means of new variables. An inner block has the form $\|[\,\textbf{var}\ \cdots\ ; S\,]\!|$. For variables introduced in an inner block, we use fresh names. As an example, we present a solution to *gcd*:

$\|[\,\textbf{con}\ A, B : \text{int};\ \{A > 0 \land B > 0\}$
$\quad \textbf{var}\ x : \text{int};$
$\quad \|[\,\textbf{var}\ y : \text{int};$
$\qquad x, y := A, B$
$\qquad ;\textbf{do}\ x > y \to x := x{-}y$
$\qquad \ [\!]\ y > x \to y := y{-}x$
$\qquad \textbf{od}$
$\qquad \{x = A\,\textbf{gcd}\,B \land y = A\,\textbf{gcd}\,B\}$
$\quad \,]\!|$
$\quad \{x = A\,\textbf{gcd}\,B\}$
$\,]\!|.$

In the inner block variable y of type int occurs. Between the inner scope symbols $[\![$ and $]\!]$ the state space has two coordinates, x and y. Outside the inner block the state space has one coordinate, x.

We formulate a rule for inner blocks for the case that the state space is extended with (fresh) variable y:

> For predicates P and Q in which y does not occur
>
> $\{P\} [\![\mathbf{var}\ y : \text{int}\ ; S]\!] \{Q\}$
>
> is equivalent to
>
> $\{P\}\ S\ \{Q\}$

Note that $\{P\} [\![\mathbf{var}\ y : \text{int}\ ; S]\!] \{Q\}$ is an assertion involving the states of the original state space, whereas $\{P\}\ S\ \{Q\}$ is an assertion over the state space extended with y. In terms of weakest pre-conditions, it is defined by

$$[wp.[\![\mathbf{var}\ y : \text{int}\ ; S]\!].Q \equiv (\forall y : y \in \mathcal{Z} : wp.S.Q)]$$

The universal quantification over y guarantees that $(\forall y : y \in \mathcal{Z} : wp.S.Q)$ depends on the variables of the original state space only. It says that, no matter what initial value y has, S should lead to a state satisfying Q.

Arrays are the final subject that we discuss in this chapter. Often arrays are considered as an abbreviation for a set of variables. We view arrays as functions on a finite consecutive subset of the integers. Such a subset is also called a *segment*. For $p \leq q$ the segment consisting of all i satisfying $p \leq i < q$ is denoted by $[p..q)$. It has length $q - p$. The statement

$$f : \mathbf{array}\ [p..q)\ \mathbf{of}\ \text{int}$$

defines a program variable f which has as value a function: $[p..q) \to \mathcal{Z}$. For the time being we use arrays defined as **con** only, and we restrict the operations on arrays to function application. For integer expression E, $f.E$ denotes f applied to E. Of course, $f.E$ is only defined when $p \leq E < q$, i.e.,

$$[\text{def}.(f.E) \equiv \text{def}.E \land p \leq E < q]$$

We also use notation such as $[p..q]$, $(p..q]$, and $(p..q)$. The sentence 'integer array $f[0..N)$' is short for 'f of type $\mathbf{array}\ [0..N)\ \mathbf{of}\ \text{int}$'. Instead of

$$f : \mathbf{array}\ [0..N)\ \mathbf{of}\ \mathbf{array}\ [0..M)\ \mathbf{of}\ \text{int}$$

we may also write

$$f : \mathbf{array}\ [0..N) \times [0..M)\ \mathbf{of}\ \text{int}.$$

Exercises

0. Prove

    $[\![\ \mathbf{var}\ x, y : \text{int}\ \{x = A \land y = B\};$
    $\quad [\![\ \mathbf{var}\ h : \text{int};$
    $\quad\quad h := x\ ; x := y\ ; y := h$
    $\quad]\!]$
    $\quad \{x = B \land y = A\}$
    $]\!].$

1. Determine $wp.[\![\ \mathbf{var}\ h : \text{int}\ ; h := x\ ; x := y\ ; y := h\ ]\!].(x = B \land y = A)$

2. Show that for P not depending on y

    $\{P\}\ S\ \{Q\}$

    implies

    $\{P\}[\![\ \mathbf{var}\ y : \text{int}\ ; S\ ]\!]\{(\exists y : y \in \mathcal{Z} : Q)\}$

3. Prove

    (i) $[\![\ \mathbf{con}\ N : \text{int}\ \{N \geq 0\};\ f\!:\ \mathbf{array}\ [0..N)\ \mathbf{of}\ \text{int};$
    $\quad\quad \mathbf{var}\ b : \text{bool};$
    $\quad\quad [\![\ \mathbf{var}\ n : \text{int};$
    $\quad\quad\quad b, n := \text{false}, 0$
    $\quad\quad\quad ; \mathbf{do}\ n \neq N \to b := b \lor f.n = 0\ ; n := n + 1\ \mathbf{od}$
    $\quad\quad]\!]$
    $\quad\quad \{b \equiv (\exists i : 0 \leq i < N : f.i = 0)\}$
    $\quad]\!].$

    (ii) $[\![\ \mathbf{con}\ N : \text{int}\ \{N \geq 0\};\ f\!:\ \mathbf{array}\ [0..N)\ \mathbf{of}\ \text{int};$
    $\quad\quad \mathbf{var}\ b : \text{bool};$
    $\quad\quad [\![\ \mathbf{var}\ n : \text{int};$
    $\quad\quad\quad b, n := \text{false}, 0$
    $\quad\quad\quad ; \mathbf{do}\ n \neq N \land \neg b \to b := f.n = 0\ ; n := n + 1\ \mathbf{od}$
    $\quad\quad]\!]$
    $\quad\quad \{b \equiv (\exists i : 0 \leq i < N : f.i = 0)\}$
    $\quad]\!].$

2.7 Summary

We have the following proof rules for constructs of the guarded command language.

skip:
$$\{P\}\operatorname{skip}\{Q\} \text{ is equivalent to } [P \Rightarrow Q]$$

assignment:
$$\{P\}\, x := E\, \{Q\} \text{ is equivalent to } [P \Rightarrow \operatorname{def}.E \wedge Q(x := E)]$$

catenation:
$$\{P\}\, S;T\, \{Q\} \text{ is equivalent to}$$
a predicate R exists such that $\{P\}\, S\, \{R\}$ and $\{R\}\, T\, \{Q\}$

selection:
$$\{P\} \text{ if } B_0 \to S_0 \,[\!]\, B_1 \to S_1 \text{ fi } \{Q\} \text{ is equivalent to}$$
(i) $[P \Rightarrow B_0 \vee B_1]$ and
(ii) $\{P \wedge B_0\}\, S_0\, \{Q\}$ and $\{P \wedge B_1\}\, S_1\, \{Q\}$

repetition:
(i) $[P \wedge \neg B_0 \wedge \neg B_1 \Rightarrow Q]$
(ii) $\{P \wedge B_0\}\, S_0\, \{P\}$ and $\{P \wedge B_1\}\, S_1\, \{P\}$
(iii) an integer function t on the state space exists such that
$[P \wedge (B_0 \vee B_1) \Rightarrow t \geq 0]$,
$\{P \wedge B_0 \wedge t = C\}\, S_0\, \{t < C\}$, and
$\{P \wedge B_1 \wedge t = C\}\, S_1\, \{t < C\}$

implies
$$\{P\} \text{ do } B_0 \to S_0 \,[\!]\, B_1 \to S_1 \text{ od } \{Q\}$$

inner blocks:

For predicates P and Q in which y does not occur
$$\{P\} \,[\![\, \textbf{var } y : \text{int}\, ; S \,]\!]\, \{Q\} \text{ is equivalent to } \{P\}\, S\, \{Q\}$$

The operational interpretation of $\{P\}\,S\{Q\}$ is

> All executions of S starting in a state satisfying P terminate in a state satisfying Q.

Statements of the guarded command language satisfy the following rules:

$\{P\}\,S\,\{\text{false}\}$ is equivalent to $[P \equiv \text{false}]$

$\{P\}\,S\,\{Q\}$ and $[P_0 \Rightarrow P]$ implies $\{P_0\}\,S\,\{Q\}$

$\{P\}\,S\,\{Q\}$ and $[Q \Rightarrow Q_0]$ implies $\{P\}\,S\,\{Q_0\}$

$\{P\}\,S\,\{Q\}$ and $\{P\}\,S\,\{R\}$ is equivalent to $\{P\}\,S\,\{Q \wedge R\}$

$\{P\}\,S\,\{Q\}$ and $\{R\}\,S\,\{Q\}$ is equivalent to $\{P \vee R\}\,S\,\{Q\}$

Chapter 3

Quantifications

Many practical programming problems involve the computation of a function over a sequence, such as the maximum element of a sequence of integers, the conjunction of a sequence of booleans, the sum of a sequence of integers, etc.. In order to specify such computations, we introduce a uniform notation, which is similar to that used for universal and existential quantification.

Let X be a set and let $\oplus$ be a binary operator on X such that $\oplus$ is commutative, associative and has e as identity, i.e.,

$$x \oplus y = y \oplus x$$
$$x \oplus (y \oplus z) = (x \oplus y) \oplus z$$
$$e \oplus x = x \oplus e = x$$

for all x, y, and z in X. For sequence $x.i$, $0 \leq i$, and natural number n, we write

$$x.0 \oplus \cdots \oplus x.(n{-}1)$$

as

$$(\oplus i : 0 \leq i < n : x.i)$$

for which we have

$$(\oplus i : 0 \leq i < 0 : x.i) = e$$
$$(\oplus i : 0 \leq i < n{+}1 : x.i) = (\oplus i : 0 \leq i < n : x.i) \oplus x.n$$

This last line may be accompanied by the note 'split off $i{=}n$'. Due to the commutativity and associativity of $\oplus$ any term may be split off. In general such a *quantification* is of the form

44

$(\oplus x : R : F)$

where x is a list of variables, R is a predicate, called the *range* of the quantification, and F is called the *term*. The term should be defined for all x that satisfy R. In general R and F depend on x. In some formulas we make this dependence more explicit and we write

$(\oplus x : R.x : F.x)$

We have

$(\oplus x : \text{false} : F) = e$, the identity of $\oplus$.

Addition and multiplication are well-known operators on $\mathcal{Z}$. For these we have, for instance,

$(+ i : 3 \leq i < 5 : i^2) = 3^2 + 4^2 = 25$
$(+ x, y : 0 \leq x < 3 \wedge 0 \leq y < 3 : x * y) = 9$
$(* k : 1 \leq k < 4 : k) = 1 * 2 * 3 = 6$
$(+ x : \text{false} : F.x) = 0$
$(* x : \text{false} : F.x) = 1$

As a more detailed example, we consider the binary operators **max** and **min** defined on $\mathcal{Z}$ by

$a \, \mathbf{max} \, b = c \equiv (a = c \vee b = c) \wedge a \leq c \wedge b \leq c$
$a \, \mathbf{min} \, b = c \equiv (a = c \vee b = c) \wedge a \geq c \wedge b \geq c$

An identity e for **max** should satisfy

$e \, \mathbf{max} \, a = a$ for all a in $\mathcal{Z}$, i.e.,
$e \leq a$ for all a in $\mathcal{Z}$

Since no such integer exists, we extend $\mathcal{Z}$ with the value $-\infty$ for which, by definition, $-\infty \leq a$ for all a in $\mathcal{Z}$. Similarly, we add ∞ as identity for **min**. Thus, we have

$(\mathbf{max} \, i : \text{false} : F.i) = -\infty$
$x \, \mathbf{max} \, -\infty = x$
$x \, \mathbf{min} \, -\infty = -\infty$
$(\mathbf{min} \, i : \text{false} : F.i) = \infty$
$x \, \mathbf{min} \, \infty = x$
$x \, \mathbf{max} \, \infty = \infty$

46   Quantifications

Addition and multiplication are not defined for ∞ and $-\infty$, hence, expressions like $\infty + a$ and $3 * -\infty$ are not allowed. Operators **min** and **max** distribute over each other:

$$x \text{ min } (\max i : R : F.i) = (\max i : R : x \text{ min } F.i)$$
$$x \text{ max } (\min i : R : F.i) = (\min i : R : x \text{ max } F.i)$$

Furthermore, we have for a *non-empty* range R

$$x + (\max i : R : F.i) = (\max i : R : x + F.i)$$
$$x + (\min i : R : F.i) = (\min i : R : x + F.i)$$

These rules are phrased as '+ distributes over **max** and **min** when the range is non-empty'. The fact that **max** is idempotent, i.e., $a \text{ max } a = a$ for all a, may be expressed by

$$(\max i : R \vee S : F) = (\max i : R : F) \text{ max } (\max i : S : F)$$

A similar equality holds for **min**.

This concludes our treatment of **min** and **max**. Other binary operators with other rules, and other lists of properties could be given. However, instead of doing so, we shall consider the general binary operator $\oplus$ again, for which we have

$$(\oplus i : \text{false} : F) = e$$
$$(\oplus i : i = x : F) = F(i := x)$$
$$(\oplus i : R : F) \oplus (\oplus i : S : F) = (\oplus i : R \vee S : F) \oplus (\oplus i : R \wedge S : F)$$
$$(\oplus i : R : F) \oplus (\oplus i : R : G) = (\oplus i : R : F \oplus G)$$
$$(\oplus i : R.i : (\oplus j : S.j : F.i.j)) = (\oplus j : S.j : (\oplus i : R.i : F.i.j))$$

When $\oplus$ is idempotent as well, i.e., $x \oplus x = x$ for all x, then

$$(\oplus i : R \vee S : F) = (\oplus i : R : F) \oplus (\oplus i : S : F)$$
$$x \oplus (\oplus i : R : F) = (\oplus i : R : x \oplus F) \quad \text{for } R \text{ non-empty}$$

Let $\otimes$ be a binary operator on X that distributes over $\oplus$, and has e as zero, i.e., $x \otimes e = e \otimes x = e$ for all x in X. Then

$$x \otimes (\oplus i : R : F) = (\oplus i : R : x \otimes F)$$
$$(\oplus i : R.i : F.i) \otimes (\oplus i : S.i : G.i) = (\oplus i, j : R.i \wedge S.j : F.i \otimes G.j)$$

The following associative and commutative operators will be used frequently:

+   identity 0,
    distributes over **max** and **min** when the range is non-empty;

*   identity 1,
    zero 0,
    distributes over +;

max   identity $-\infty$,
    zero ∞
    idempotent,
    distributes over **min**;

min   identity ∞,
    zero $-\infty$
    idempotent,
    distributes over **max**;

$\wedge$ identity true,
    zero false
    idempotent,
    distributes over $\vee$;

$\vee$ identity false,
    zero true
    idempotent,
    distributes over $\wedge$.

We mention some more rules for **max** and **min**.

For $x \geq 0$ and R non-empty:

$$x * (\mathbf{max}\, i : R.i : F.i) = (\mathbf{max}\, i : R.i : x * F.i)$$
$$x * (\mathbf{min}\, i : R.i : F.i) = (\mathbf{min}\, i : R.i : x * F.i)$$

and

$$-(\mathbf{max}\, i : R.i : F.i) = (\mathbf{min}\, i : R.i : -F.i)$$

Instead of $(\wedge i : R : F)$ we write the more common $(\forall i : R : F)$ and instead of $(\vee i : R : F)$ we use $(\exists i : R : F)$.

In derivations of programs, we often use the following relations (R is non-empty):

$$F.x = (\mathbf{max}\, i : R.i : F.i) \equiv R.x \wedge (\forall i : R.i : F.i \leq F.x)$$
$$F.x = (\mathbf{min}\, i : R.i : F.i) \equiv R.x \wedge (\forall i : R.i : F.i \geq F.x)$$

For summation, a common notation is $(\Sigma\, i : R : F)$ instead of $(+i : R : F)$, and for multiplication we use $(\Pi\, i : R : F)$ instead of $(*i : R : F)$.

A quite different quantifier is 'the number of'. We introduce it as follows. Function $\#\ :\ \{\text{false}, \text{true}\} \to \{0, 1\}$ is defined by $\#.\text{false} = 0$ and $\#.\text{true} = 1$. Expression

$$(\#\, i : R.i : F.i)$$

is defined as

$$(\Sigma\, i : R.i : \#.(F.i))$$

For this quantifier we have

$$(\#\, i : \text{false} : F.i) = 0$$

and, for $n \geq 0$,

$$(\#\, i : 0 \leq i < n{+}1 : F.i) = (\#\, i : 0 \leq i < n : F.i) + \#.(F.n)$$
$$= \begin{cases} (\#\, i : 0 \leq i < n : F.i) + 1 & \text{if } F.n \\ (\#\, i : 0 \leq i < n : F.i) & \text{if } \neg F.n \end{cases}$$

Notice that

$$(\exists\, i : R : F) \equiv (\#\, i : R : F) \geq 1$$
$$(\forall\, i : R : F) \equiv (\#\, i : R : F) = (\#\, i : R : \text{true})$$

We will use the following definitions for increasing, decreasing, ascending, and descending. Let $N \geq 0$ and let $X[0..N)$ be an array of integers. Then

$$\begin{aligned} X \text{ is increasing} &\equiv (\forall\, i, j : 0 \leq i < j < N : X.i < X.j) \\ X \text{ is decreasing} &\equiv (\forall\, i, j : 0 \leq i < j < N : X.i > X.j) \\ X \text{ is ascending} &\equiv (\forall\, i, j : 0 \leq i < j < N : X.i \leq X.j) \\ X \text{ is descending} &\equiv (\forall\, i, j : 0 \leq i < j < N : X.i \geq X.j) \end{aligned}$$

For example, a formal expression for 'r is the length of a longest ascending segment of X' is

$$r = (\mathbf{max}\, p, q : 0 \leq p \leq q \leq N \wedge (\forall\, i, j : p \leq i < j < q : X.i \leq X.j) : q - p)$$

Exercises

0. An integer array $X[0..N)$ is given, where $N \geq 1$. Express the following sentences in a formal way:

   (a) r is the sum of the elements of X.
   (b) m is the maximum of the array.
   (c) X is increasing.
   (d) all values of X are distinct.
   (e) all values of X are equal.
   (f) if X contains a 1 then X contains a 0 as well.
   (g) no two neighbors in X are equal.
   (h) the maximum of X occurs only once in X.
   (i) r is the length of a longest constant segment of X.
   (j) X is a permutation of $[0..N)$.
   (k) all elements of X are prime numbers.
   (l) the number of odd elements equals the number of even elements.
   (m) r is the product of the positive elements of X.
   (n) r is the maximum of the sums of the segments of X.
   (o) X contains a square.

1. An integer array $X[0..N)$ is given, where $N \geq 1$. Express the following expressions in a natural language.

   (a) $b \equiv (\forall i : 0 \leq i < N : X.i \geq 0)$
   (b) $r = (\max p, q : 0 \leq p \leq q \leq N \wedge (\forall i : p \leq i < q : X.i \geq 0) : q - p)$
   (c) $r = (\# k : 0 \leq k < N : (\forall i : 0 \leq i < k : X.i < X.k))$
   (d) $b \equiv (\exists i : 0 < i < N : X.(i{-}1) < X.i)$
   (e) $r = (\# p, q : 0 \leq p < q < N : X.p = 0 \wedge X.q = 1)$
   (f) $s = (\max p, q : 0 \leq p < q < N : X.p + X.q)$
   (g) $b \equiv (\forall p, q : 0 \leq p \wedge 0 \leq q \wedge p{+}q = N{-}1 : X.p = X.q)$
   (h) $b \equiv (\exists i : 0 \leq i < N : X.i = 0)$

2. Prove $a \max (b \min c) = (a \max b) \min (a \max c)$.

3. The greatest common divisor of natural numbers x and y is denoted by $x\,\mathbf{gcd}\,y$. By definition $0\,\mathbf{gcd}\,0 = 0$.

   (i) Give a formal definition of **gcd**.

   (ii) Show that **gcd** is commutative and associative.

   (iii) Prove that **gcd** has an identity.

   (iv) Investigate whether $*$ or $+$ distribute over **gcd**.

4. Prove

$$\begin{array}{l} \|[\,\mathbf{con}\ N : \mathrm{int}\ \{N \geq 1\};\ f\colon \mathbf{array}\ [0..N)\ \mathbf{of}\ \mathrm{int};\\ \quad\mathbf{var}\ x : \mathrm{int};\\ \quad\|[\ \mathbf{var}\ y : \mathrm{int};\\ \qquad x, y := 0, N{-}1\\ \qquad ; \mathbf{do}\ x \neq y\\ \qquad\quad \to \mathbf{if}\ f.x \leq f.y \to x := x{+}1\\ \qquad\qquad\ [\!]\ f.y \leq f.x \to y := y{-}1\\ \qquad\quad\ \mathbf{fi}\\ \qquad \mathbf{od}\\ \quad]\!|\\ \quad \{f.x = (\mathbf{max}\,i : 0 \leq i < N : f.i)\}\\ ]\!|. \end{array}$$

Chapter 4

General Programming Techniques

4.0 Introduction

The rest of this book is devoted to the derivation of programs. In the chapters that follow we shall discuss domain specific techniques. However, in this chapter some general underlying techniques are presented. The programming problems that we are studying typically have solutions in which repetitions occur. Thus, the design of suitable invariants is crucial in the derivation of solutions to these problems.

As will turn out in the next sections and chapters, there are many ways in which an invariant may be deduced from (the contents of) the pre- and post-condition of a specification. Program derivation is not mechanical: in general it is a challenging activity and it requires creativity. However, many programming problems may, to a large extent, be solved by pure calculation and by carefully applying the techniques discussed in this chapter. Moreover, the derivations show where the creativity comes in.

We do not always present completely annotated programs. Program derivations are carried out in such a way that the result is correct by design and that it is easy to deduce an annotated program with accompanying proofs.

The *efficiency* of a program is expressed as the upper bound of the number of steps that each repetition can take. This so-called time complexity is a function of (the values of) the constants in the specification. We use the $\mathcal{O}$-notation to express the time complexity. If, for instance, a program has natural N as constant then 'the time complexity is $\mathcal{O}(f.N)$' means that the number of steps is bounded by a constant times $f.N$. For instance, if the number of steps equals $\frac{1}{3}N^2 - 2N + 4$ then the time complexity is $\mathcal{O}(N^2)$.

Efficiency is of vital importance in computing science. Usually, programs are written only once and they are executed many times. To illustrate the role of efficiency, we consider a program consisting of a repetition of a statement which requires, in isolation, one second for each execution. The program contains integer N as constant. The execution time of the program is shown below for the cases that the repetition performs $^2\log N$, $\sqrt{N}$, N, and N^2 steps.

number of steps	$N = 1000$	$N = 1\,000\,000$
$^2\log N$	10 seconds	20 seconds
$\sqrt{N}$	30 seconds	15 minutes
N	15 minutes	300 hours
N^2	300 hours	30 000 years

If we succeed in speeding up the hardware such that execution of S takes a millisecond, i.e., we improve it by a factor 1000, then we obtain the following figures.

number of steps	$N = 1000$	$N = 1\,000\,000$
$^2\log N$	0.01 seconds	0.02 seconds
$\sqrt{N}$	0.03 seconds	1 second
N	1 second	15 minutes
N^2	15 minutes	30 years

A significant improvement of a program is not obtained by tricky adaptations that, for instance, save a variable or save an assignment within a repetition. Such changes often destroy the elegance and clarity of the original algorithm. Similarly, case analysis in which 'easy to compute' cases are treated separately does not really help.

A huge improvement is a reduction from, for instance, $\mathcal{O}(N)$ to $\mathcal{O}(\log N)$. Such an improvement is obtained by transforming the program into a more efficient one, or by deriving a completely different program. Examples of this are discussed in Chapter 5.

4.1 Taking conjuncts as invariant

When post-condition R is of the form $P \wedge Q$, one may try to take one of the conjuncts, say P, as an invariant, and the other one as negation of the guard of a repetition, leading to

$$\{P\}\ \mathbf{do}\ \neg Q \to S\ \mathbf{od}\ \{P \wedge Q\}$$

In its simplest form this method yields, taking true as invariant,

$$\{true\}\ \mathbf{do}\ \neg R \to S\ \mathbf{od}\ \{R\}$$

For instance, for integer variables x and y, $x \leq y$ can be established by

do $x > y \to x, y := y, x$ **od**

for which true is an invariant and $x - y$ is a bound function, as the reader may verify. A similar sorting program for four integers a, b, c, and d is obtained by taking true as invariant and the negations of the conjuncts of post-condition

$R: \quad a \leq b \wedge b \leq c \wedge c \leq d$

as guards, leading to

    $\{\text{true}\}$
    do $a > b \to a, b := b, a$
    $[\!]\ \ b > c \to b, c := c, b$
    $[\!]\ \ c > d \to c, d := d, c$
    od
    $\{a \leq b \leq c \leq d\}$

(Why does it terminate?)
A somewhat more interesting example is the computation of **div** and **mod** when only operators $+$ and $-$ may be used. Its specification reads

    $|[\ \textbf{con}\ A, B : \text{int}\ \{A \geq 0 \wedge B > 0\};$
      $\textbf{var}\ q, r : \text{int};$
      $divmod$
      $\{q = A\ \textbf{div}\ B \wedge r = A\ \textbf{mod}\ B\}$
    $]|.$

We rewrite post-condition R, using the definitions of **div** and **mod**, as

$R: \quad A = q * B + r \wedge 0 \leq r < B$

Conjunct $0 \leq r < B$ is an abbreviation of $0 \leq r \wedge r < B$; hence, we may write

$R: \quad A = q * B + r \wedge 0 \leq r \wedge r < B$

There are three conjuncts and possible solutions may, for instance, contain repetitions of the form

$\{P: 0 \leq r \wedge r < B\}$ do $A \neq q * B + r \rightarrow S$ od $\{R\}$,
$\{P: A = q * B + r \wedge r < B\}$ do $0 > r \rightarrow S$ od $\{R\}$, or
$\{P: A = q * B + r \wedge 0 \leq r\}$ do $r \geq B \rightarrow S$ od $\{R\}$

We choose as invariant

$P: \quad A = q * B + r \wedge 0 \leq r$

and as guard $r \geq B$, the negation of $r < B$, leading to a program of the form

$\{P\}$ do $r \geq B \rightarrow S$ od $\{R\}$

Invariant P is established by $q, r := 0, A$. Since P implies $0 \leq r$, we decide to take r as bound function. Then S has to decrease r. The guard is $r \geq B$, and, since $B > 0$, $r := r - B$ is a candidate for S. We derive

$\quad P(r := r - B)$
$\equiv \quad \{\text{substitution}\}$
$\quad A = q * B + r - B \wedge 0 \leq r - B$
$\equiv \quad \{\text{calculus}\}$
$\quad A = (q-1) * B + r \wedge r \geq B$

Hence,

$\quad P(q, r := q+1, r-B)$
$\equiv \quad \{\text{substitution, see above}\}$
$\quad A = q * B + r \wedge r \geq B$
$\Leftarrow \quad \{\text{definition of } P\}$
$\quad P \wedge r \geq B$

This yields the following solution to *divmod*:

$\quad q, r := 0, A$
$\quad \{\text{invariant } P: \ A = q * B + r \wedge 0 \leq r, \text{ bound: } r\}$
$\quad ; \text{do } r \geq B \ \rightarrow \ q, r := q+1, r-B \text{ od}$
$\quad \{R\}$

The initial value of q is 0, its final value is A div B, and in each step of the repetition q is increased by 1. We conclude that this program has time complexity $\mathcal{O}(A \text{ div } B)$.

In the next chapter we show that, if one allows **div** 2 and **mod** 2 as operators as well, a program can be derived that has time complexity $\mathcal{O}(\log(A \,\mathbf{div}\, B))$.

As another example, we derive a program for the computation of the square root, rounded down, of a natural number. It is specified by

$\|[\,\mathbf{con}\ N : \mathrm{int}\ \{N \geq 0\};$
  $\mathbf{var}\ x : \mathrm{int};$
   square root
  $\{x^2 \leq N \wedge (x+1)^2 > N\}$
$\,]\|.$

We try as invariant $P : x^2 \leq N$, which is established by $x := 0$. Negation of $(x+1)^2 > N$ yields $(x+1)^2 \leq N$ as guard, leading to

$$x := 0\ \{P\}\ ;\mathbf{do}\ (x+1) * (x+1) \leq N \rightarrow S\ \mathbf{od}\ \{x^2 \leq N \wedge (x+1)^2 > N\}$$

Since P implies $N - x^2 \geq 0$, $N - x^2$ seems appropriate as bound function. However, $N - x^2$ decreases for increasing x if and only if $0 \leq x$, which cannot be inferred from $P \wedge B$. This problem is solved by specifying a bound for x: strengthen P to

$P:\quad 0 \leq x \wedge x^2 \leq N$

We investigate an increase of x by 1:

$\quad P(x := x + 1)$
$\equiv\quad \{\,\text{substitution}\,\}$
$\quad 0 \leq x + 1 \wedge (x+1)^2 \leq N$
$\Leftarrow\quad \{\,\text{calculus}\,\}$
$\quad 0 \leq x \wedge (x+1)^2 \leq N$
$\Leftarrow\quad \{\,\text{definition of } P\,\}$
$\quad P \wedge (x+1)^2 \leq N$

leading to

$\quad \{N \geq 0\}$
$\quad x := 0$
$\quad \{\text{invariant } P : 0 \leq x \wedge x^2 \leq N,\ \text{bound}: N - x^2\}$
$\quad ;\mathbf{do}\ (x+1) * (x+1) \leq N \rightarrow x := x+1\ \mathbf{od}$
$\quad \{x^2 \leq N \wedge (x+1)^2 > N\}$

This program has time complexity $\mathcal{O}(\sqrt{N})$. In Chapter 6 we present a solution for *square root* that has time complexity $\mathcal{O}(\log N)$.

Instead of $x^2 \leq N$, we may also take $(x{+}1)^2 > N$ as invariant and $x * x > N$ as guard. This choice leads to

$\{N \geq 0\}$
$x := N$
$\{\text{invariant } P : 0 \leq x \land (x{+}1)^2 > N, \text{ bound: } x\}$
$;\textbf{do } x * x > N \to x := x{-}1 \textbf{ od}$
$\{x^2 \leq N \land (x{+}1)^2 > N\}$

Execution of this program, however, takes about $N - \sqrt{N}$ steps and has, therefore, time complexity $\mathcal{O}(N)$, which is worse than $\mathcal{O}(\sqrt{N})$.

As a final remark, we mention that it is quite common that invariants have to be strengthened with bounds for the variables involved. As a matter of fact, it is a good habit to include bounds for the variables right away.

Exercises

For each exercise that is specified in natural language, one has to supply a formal specification first.

0. Derive a program for the computation of $^3\log N$, rounded down, for positive integer N.

1. Derive, for given N, $N \geq 0$, a program for the computation of the smallest integer x that satisfies $x^3 - 6x^2 + 9x \geq N$.

2. Derive, for given N, $N \geq 0$, a program for the computation of the largest integer x that satisfies $x^3 - 6x^2 + 9x \leq N$.

3. Solve

  $[\![\textbf{con } A, B : \text{int } \{A > 0 \land B > 0\};$
  $\quad \textbf{var } x : \text{int};$
  $\quad \text{lcm}$
  $\quad \{x = A \operatorname{lcm} B\}$
  $]\!].$

  where **lcm** denotes the least common multiple, i.e., for $A > 0 \land B > 0$:

  $A \operatorname{lcm} B = (\textbf{min } i : 1 \leq i \land i \bmod A = 0 \land i \bmod B = 0 : i)$

4.2 Replacing constants by variables

We consider the computation of A to the power B for given naturals A and B. This problem is formally specified as

$\lVert$ **con** A, B : int $\{A \geq 0 \wedge B \geq 0\}$;
   var r : int;
      exponentiation
   $\{r = A^B\}$
$\rVert$,

where, by definition, $0^0 = 1$. There is no obvious way in which the post-condition can be weakened to a suitable invariant. In the state space defined by r predicate $r = A^B$ corresponds to a single point. When we extend the state space by introducing a fresh variable x, say, the state space defined by r and x contains the entire line satisfying $r = A^B$ and in this space this relation may be more easily established. A way in which fresh variables can be introduced is by replacing constants by variables. Such a replacement yields a possible invariant. For this specification possible choices are

$r = x^B$, $r = A^x$, and $r = x^y$

We use the invariant

P_0 : $r = A^x$

Then $P_0 \wedge x = B$ implies the post-condition, and P_0 is established by $r, x := 1, 0$. Furthermore, we specify an upper bound for x and add to the invariant

P_1 : $x \leq B$

This yields the program scheme

$r, x := 1, 0 \, \{P_0 \wedge P_1\}$; **do** $x \neq B \to S$ **od** $\{r = A^B\}$

We investigate the effect of increasing x by 1 in S:

$ P_0(x := x + 1)$
$\equiv \quad \{\,\text{substitution}\,\}$
$ r = A^{x+1}$

Hence, $\{r = A^{x+1}\} \, x := x+1 \, \{P_0\}$. Assuming $P_0 \wedge P_1 \wedge x \neq B$, we have

$$A^{x+1}$$
= { calculus }
$$A * A^x$$
= { P_0 }
$$A * r$$

from which we conclude

$$\{P_0 \wedge P_1 \wedge x \neq B\} \, r := A * r \, \{r = A^{x+1}\} \, ; x := x+1 \, \{P_0\}$$

The invariance of P_1, i.e.,

$$\{P_0 \wedge P_1 \wedge x \neq B\} \, r := A * r \, ; x := x+1 \, \{P_1\}$$

is easily proved and we obtain the following solution for *exponentiation*

$\|[$ **var** x : int;
   $r, x := 1, 0$
   {invariant: $P_0 \wedge P_1$, bound: $B - x$}
   ;**do** $x \neq B$
       $\rightarrow \{P_0 \wedge P_1 \wedge x \neq B\}$
         $r := r * A \, ; x := x+1$
         $\{P_0 \wedge P_1\}$
   od
   $\{P_0 \wedge P_1 \wedge x = B,$ hence, $r = A^B\}$
$]\|$
$\{r = A^B\}.$

This program has time complexity $\mathcal{O}(B)$. In Section 4.4 we derive a solution that has time complexity $\mathcal{O}(\log B)$.

Constants are usually denoted by capital letters, and we often use the same letter in lower-case for a variable that replaces a constant.

As a final example, we derive a solution to *summation*, which is specified below. To show how exercises should be worked out, we present a 'model solution' to the problem. Here is the specification:

$\|[$ **con** N : int $\{N \geq 0\}; f$: **array** $[0..N)$ **of** int;
   var x : int;
   summation
   $\{x = (\Sigma i : 0 \leq i < N : f.i)\}$
$]\|.$

Replacing constants by variables

The quantification that appears in the post-condition has two constants: 0 and N. Let us replace N by variable n and propose invariant

$P_0:$ $x = (\Sigma i : 0 \leq i < n : f.i)$

Then, by construction, $P_0 \wedge n = N$ implies the post-condition. Summation over an empty range equals 0, hence, P_0 is established by $n, x := 0, 0$. We investigate an increase of n by 1 and we derive, assuming $P_0 \wedge n \neq N$:

$\quad (\Sigma i : 0 \leq i < n+1 : f.i)$
$= \quad \{\text{split off } i = n, \, 0 \leq n < n+1 : \text{see below}\}$
$\quad (\Sigma i : 0 \leq i < n : f.i) + f.n$
$= \quad \{P_0\}$
$\quad x + f.n$

Evidently, $0 \leq n$ is needed in the derivation above, which must be added to P_0. From this derivation we conclude

$\{P_0 \wedge 0 \leq n\} \, x := x + f.n \, \{P_0(n := n+1)\}$

As a bound funtion $N - n$ seems appropriate; for the proof of termination we strengthen P_0 with $n \leq N$ as well. We now show how the solution is presented.

Solution:

Replacing constant N by variable n gives rise to the following invariants.

$P_0:$ $x = (\Sigma i : 0 \leq i < n : f.i)$
$P_1:$ $0 \leq n \leq N$

Proof 0:

$\quad (P_0 \wedge P_1)(n, x := 0, 0)$
$\equiv \quad \{\text{substitution}\}$
$\quad 0 = (\Sigma i : 0 \leq i < 0 : f.i) \wedge 0 \leq 0 \leq N$
$\equiv \quad \{0 \text{ is identity of } +\}$
$\quad 0 = 0 \wedge 0 \leq 0 \leq N$
$\equiv \quad \{\text{predicate calculus}\}$
$\quad 0 \leq N$

Proof 1: Assuming $P_0 \wedge P_1 \wedge n \neq N$,

$\ (\Sigma i : 0 \leq i < n+1 : f.i)$
$=\quad \{\text{split off } i = n,\ 0 \leq n < n+1\}$
$\ (\Sigma i : 0 \leq i < n : f.i) + f.n$
$=\quad \{P_0\}$
$\ x + f.n$

and

$\ 0 \leq n+1 \leq N$
$\Leftarrow\quad \{P_1\}$
$\ n \neq N$

Proof 2:

$\ P_0 \wedge P_1 \wedge n = N$
$\Rightarrow\quad \{\text{definition of } P_0\}$
$\ x = (\Sigma i : 0 \leq i < N : f.i)$

Proof 3:

$\ P_1$
$\Rightarrow\quad \{\text{definition of } P_1\}$
$\ N - n \geq 0$

and

$\ N - (n+1) < C$
$\Leftarrow\quad \{\text{calculus}\}$
$\ N - n = C$

Together with these proofs, the following annotated program solves *summation*.

$\lVert$ **var** n : int; $\{N \geq 0\}$
    $n, x := 0, 0$
    $\{$invariant: $P_0 \wedge P_1$, Proof 0, bound: $N - n\}$
    ; **do** $n \neq N$
        $\rightarrow \{P_0 \wedge P_1 \wedge n \neq N\}$
            $x := x + f.n$
            ; $n := n + 1$
            $\{P_0 \wedge P_1,$ Proof 1$\}$
    od
    $\{x = (\Sigma i : 0 \leq i < N : f.i),$ Proof 2, termination: Proof 3$\}$
$\rVert$
$\{x = (\Sigma i : 0 \leq i < N : f.i)\}.$

Some of the proofs presented above are really trivial (cf. Proof 2 and Proof 3) and they are omitted in other examples.

Verify that replacing constant 0 by variable n leads to invariants

P_0 : $x = (\Sigma i : n \leq i < N : f.i)$
P_1 : $0 \leq n \leq N$

to which the following program corresponds:

$\lVert$ **var** n : int;
    $n, x := N, 0$
    ; **do** $n \neq 0$
        $\rightarrow \quad x := x + f.(n-1)$
            ; $n := n - 1$
    od
$\rVert.$

Exercises

Derive solutions for the following programming problems.

0. $[\![\,\mathbf{con}\ N : \mathbf{int}\ \{N \geq 0\};\ f : \mathbf{array}\ [0..N)\ \mathbf{of}\ \mathrm{bool};$
   $\mathbf{var}\ r : \mathrm{bool};$
   S
   $\{r \equiv (\exists i : 0 \leq i < N : f.i)\}$
   $]\!]$.

1. $[\![\,\mathbf{con}\ N : \mathbf{int}\ \{N \geq 0\};\ f : \mathbf{array}\ [0..N)\ \mathbf{of}\ \mathrm{int};$
   $\mathbf{var}\ r : \mathrm{bool};$
   S
   $\{r \equiv (\forall i : 0 \leq i < N : f.i \geq 0)\}$
   $]\!]$.

2. $[\![\,\mathbf{con}\ N : \mathbf{int}\ \{N \geq 0\};\ f : \mathbf{array}\ [0..N)\ \mathbf{of}\ \mathrm{int};$
   $\mathbf{var}\ r : \mathrm{int};$
   S
   $\{r = (\mathbf{max}\, i : 0 \leq i < N : f.i)\}$
   $]\!]$.

3. $[\![\,\mathbf{con}\ N : \mathbf{int}\ \{N \geq 0\};\ f : \mathbf{array}\ [0..N)\ \mathbf{of}\ \mathrm{int};$
   $\mathbf{var}\ r : \mathrm{int};$
   S
   $\{r = (\#\, i : 0 \leq i < N : f.i\ \mathbf{mod}\ 2 = 0)\}$
   $]\!]$.

4. $[\![\,\mathbf{con}\ N, X : \mathbf{int}\ \{N \geq 0\};\ f : \mathbf{array}\ [0..N)\ \mathbf{of}\ \mathrm{int};$
   $\mathbf{var}\ r : \mathrm{int};$
   S
   $\{r = (\Sigma\, i : 0 \leq i < N : f.i * X^i)\}$
   $]\!]$.

5. $[\![\,\mathbf{con}\ N : \mathbf{int}\ \{N \geq 1\};\ f : \mathbf{array}\ [0..N)\ \mathbf{of}\ \mathrm{int};$
   $\mathbf{var}\ r : \mathrm{int};$
   S
   $\{r = (\mathbf{max}\, i : 0 \leq i \wedge i^2 < N : f.(i^2))\}$
   $]\!]$.

4.3 Strengthening invariants

When an invariant for a repetition has been chosen, the termination requirement guides the construction of the statement of the repetition. For such a candidate one applies the proof rules. This may lead to an expression E which cannot easily be expressed in terms of the program variables. A way to deal with this situation is to introduce a fresh program variable and an accompanying invariant stating that the variable equals E. Of course, the fact that this new invariant has to be established and kept invariant may pose other problems. We illustrate this point with some examples.

As a first example, we consider the Fibonacci function fib, defined by

fib.0 = 0, fib.1 = 1, and
fib.$(n+2)$ = fib.n + fib.$(n+1)$ for $n \geq 0$

We are asked to derive a program for the computation of fib.N, i.e., we have to solve

$[\![$ **con** N : int $\{N \geq 0\}$;
  var x : int;
  Fibonacci
  $\{x = \text{fib}.N\}$
$]\!]$,

and we propose as invariant $P_0 \wedge P_1$, where

$P_0:$ $x = \text{fib}.n$

$P_1:$ $0 \leq n \leq N$

which is established by $n, x := 0, 0$.

An increase of n by 1 leads to expression fib.$(n+1)$ which cannot be easily expressed in terms of x and n. Therefore, we introduce variable y of type int and invariant Q defined by

$Q:$ $y = \text{fib}.(n+1)$

The strengthened invariant $P_0 \wedge P_1 \wedge Q$ is established by $n, x, y := 0, 0, 1$.

The invariance of P_0 is now easily realized: from Q we infer that $x := y$ establishes $P_0(n := n+1)$.

For $Q(n := n+1)$ we derive, assuming $P_0 \wedge P_1 \wedge Q$:

$$\begin{aligned}&\text{fib.}(n{+}2)\\=\quad&\{\,\text{definition of fib},\ n\geq 0\,\}\\&\text{fib.}n+\text{fib.}(n{+}1)\\=\quad&\{\,P_0\text{ and }Q\,\}\\&x+y\end{aligned}$$

This leads to the following solution:

$$\begin{aligned}&\|[\,\mathbf{var}\ n,y:\text{int};\ \{N\geq 0\}\\&\quad n,x,y:=0,0,1\\&\quad\{\text{invariants: }P_0\wedge P_1\wedge Q,\ \text{bound: }N-n\}\\&\quad ;\mathbf{do}\ n\neq N\\&\qquad\to\ x,y:=y,x+y\\&\qquad\ ;n:=n+1\\&\quad\mathbf{od}\\&\quad\{x=\text{fib.}N\ \wedge\ y=\text{fib.}(N{+}1)\}\\&\,]\!|\\&\{x=\text{fib.}N\},\end{aligned}$$

a program that has time complexity $\mathcal{O}(N)$. In Chapter 5 we derive a program for *Fibonacci* that has time complexity $\mathcal{O}(\log N)$.

As a second example, we derive, given array $f[0..N)$, a program for the computation of the number of pairs (i,j) for which $0\leq i<j<N\ \wedge\ f.i\leq 0\ \wedge\ f.j\geq 0$. A formal specification is

$$\begin{aligned}&\|[\,\mathbf{con}\ N:\text{int}\ \{N\geq 0\};\ f:\mathbf{array}\ [0..N)\ \mathbf{of}\ \text{int};\\&\quad\mathbf{var}\ r:\text{int};\\&\quad S\\&\quad\{r=(\#\,i,j:0\leq i<j<N:f.i\leq 0\wedge f.j\geq 0)\}\\&\,]\!|.\end{aligned}$$

Replacing constant N by variable n gives rise to invariants

$P_0:\quad r=(\#\,i,j:0\leq i<j<n:f.i\leq 0\wedge f.j\geq 0)$

$P_1: \quad 0 \leq n \leq N$

which are initialized by $n, r := 0, 0$, since number-of quantification over an empty range is 0. Assuming $P_0 \wedge P_1 \wedge n \neq N$, we have

$\quad (\# i, j : 0 \leq i < j < n+1 : f.i \leq 0 \wedge f.j \geq 0)$
$= \quad \{ \text{split off } j = n \}$
$\quad (\# i, j : 0 \leq i < j < n : f.i \leq 0 \wedge f.j \geq 0) + (\# i : 0 \leq i < n : f.i \leq 0 \wedge f.n \geq 0)$
$= \quad \{ P_0 \}$
$\quad r + (\# i : 0 \leq i < n : f.i \leq 0 \wedge f.n \geq 0)$
$= \quad \{ \text{case analysis} \}$
$\quad \begin{cases} r & \text{if } f.n < 0 \\ r + (\# i : 0 \leq i < n : f.i \leq 0) & \text{if } f.n \geq 0 \end{cases}$
$= \quad \{ \text{introduction of } s \text{ with invariant } Q, \text{ see below} \}$
$\quad \begin{cases} r & \text{if } f.n < 0 \\ r + s & \text{if } f.n \geq 0 \end{cases}$

where s satisfies

$Q: \quad s = (\# i : 0 \leq i < n : f.i \leq 0)$

Substitution of $n = 0$ yields that Q is established by $n, s := 0, 0$. For the invariance of Q, we derive, assuming $P_1 \wedge Q \wedge n \neq N$,

$\quad (\# i : 0 \leq i < n+1 : f.i \leq 0)$
$= \quad \{ \text{split off } i = n,\ 0 \leq n < n+1 \leq N \}$
$\quad (\# i : 0 \leq i < n : f.i \leq 0) + \#.(f.n \leq 0)$
$= \quad \{ Q \}$
$\quad s + \#.(f.n \leq 0)$
$= \quad \{ \text{definition of } \# \}$
$\quad \begin{cases} s & \text{if } f.n > 0 \\ s + 1 & \text{if } f.n \leq 0 \end{cases}$

These derivations yield a program that solves the problem:

$\|[\textbf{var } n, s : \text{int}; \{N \geq 0\}$
    $n, r, s := 0, 0, 0$
    $\{\text{invariant: } P_0 \wedge P_1 \wedge Q, \text{ bound: } N - n\}$
    $;\textbf{do } n \neq N$
        $\to \{P_0 \wedge P_1 \wedge Q \wedge n \neq N\}$
            $\textbf{if } f.n < 0 \to \text{skip}$
            $[\!] \ f.n \geq 0 \to r := r+s$
            $\textbf{fi}$
            $\{P_0(n := n+1) \wedge P_1 \wedge Q \wedge n \neq N\}$
            $;\textbf{if } f.n > 0 \to \text{skip}$
            $[\!] \ f.n \leq 0 \to s := s+1$
            $\textbf{fi}$
            $\{(P_0 \wedge P_1 \wedge Q)(n := n+1)\}$
            $;n := n+1$
    $\textbf{od}$
$]\!|$
$\{r = (\#i, j : 0 \leq i < j < N : f.i \leq 0 \wedge f.j \geq 0)\}.$

The reader may verify that the two selections

$\textbf{if } f.n < 0 \to \text{skip}$
$[\!] \ f.n \geq 0 \to r := r+s$
$\textbf{fi}$
$;\textbf{if } f.n > 0 \to \text{skip}$
$[\!] \ f.n \leq 0 \to s := s+1$
$\textbf{fi}$

can be replaced by

$\textbf{if } f.n < 0 \ \to s := s+1$
$[\!] \ f.n = 0 \ \to r, s := r+s, s+1$
$[\!] \ f.n > 0 \ \to r := r+s$
$\textbf{fi}$

due to the fact that $P_0 \wedge P_1 \wedge Q \wedge n \neq N$ can be used as assumption for all the derivations.

In the calculations we derived that the value of $(\#i : 0 \leq i < n : f.i \leq 0)$ is needed for the invariance of P_0. We could have decided to introduce another repetition in which this value is computed, i.e., a repetition that establishes $s = (\# i : 0 \leq i < n : f.i \leq 0)$. This naive approach leads to an $\mathcal{O}(N^2)$ algorithm instead of the $\mathcal{O}(N)$ algorithm presented above.

Finally, we mention that the introduction of variables is always based upon some reasoning or derivation. They are not introduced by magic.

In the following example we consider the problem of the maximal sum of the elements of segments $A[p..q]$ of a given integer array A. A formal specification for this problem is

$\| [\mathbf{con}\ N : \text{int}\ \{N \geq 0\};\ A : \mathbf{array}\ [0..N)\ \mathbf{of}\ \text{int};$
$\quad \mathbf{var}\ r : \text{int};$
$\quad\quad maxsegsum$
$\quad \{r = (\mathbf{max}\, p, q : 0 \leq p \leq q \leq N : (\Sigma i : p \leq i < q : A.i))\}$
$\| .$

To make the expression in the post-condition more manageable, we define, for $0 \leq p \leq q \leq N$:

$S.p.q = (\Sigma i : p \leq i < q : A.i)$

Post-condition R becomes

$R: \quad r = (\mathbf{max}\, p, q : 0 \leq p \leq q \leq N : S.p.q)$

Replacing constant N by variable n yields invariants P_0 and P_1:

$P_0: \quad r = (\mathbf{max}\, p, q : 0 \leq p \leq q \leq n : S.p.q)$

$P_1: \quad 0 \leq n \leq N$

which are initialized by $n, r := 0, 0$, since $S.0.0 = 0$. Assuming $P_0 \wedge P_1 \wedge n \neq N$, we derive

$\quad (\mathbf{max}\, p, q : 0 \leq p \leq q \leq n+1 : S.p.q)$
$= \quad \{\text{split off } q = n+1\}$
$\quad (\mathbf{max}\, p, q : 0 \leq p \leq q \leq n : S.p.q)\ \mathbf{max}\ (\mathbf{max}\, p : 0 \leq p \leq n+1 : S.p.(n+1))$
$= \quad \{P_0\}$
$\quad r\ \mathbf{max}\ (\mathbf{max}\, p : 0 \leq p \leq n+1 : S.p.(n+1))$

At this point it seems appropriate to introduce the variable s and accompanying invariant

$$s = (\max p : 0 \leq p \leq n+1 : S.p.(n+1))$$

However, for n=N (which is not excluded by P_1) this predicate is not defined. Replacing all occurrences of n by $n-1$ yields an expression that is defined for all n, $0 \leq n \leq N$. Thus, if we define additional invariant Q by

$$Q: \quad s = (\max p : 0 \leq p \leq n : S.p.n)$$

then $Q(n := n+1)$ equals the relation that is needed, i.e.,

$$\begin{aligned}
& (\max p, q : 0 \leq p \leq q \leq n+1 : S.p.q) \\
=\ & \quad \{\text{ see previous derivation }\} \\
& r \max (\max p : 0 \leq p \leq n+1 : S.p.(n+1)) \\
=\ & \quad \{\text{ assume } Q(n := n+1) \} \\
& r \max s
\end{aligned}$$

This leads to a solution of the following form

$$\begin{aligned}
& \|[\ \mathbf{var}\ n, s : \text{int}; \\
& \quad \text{'establish } P_0 \land P_1 \land Q\text{'} \\
& \quad ; \mathbf{do}\ n \neq N \\
& \quad\quad \rightarrow\ \text{'establish } Q(n := n+1)\text{'} \\
& \quad\quad\quad ; r := r \max s \\
& \quad\quad\quad ; n := n+1 \\
& \quad\quad \mathbf{od} \\
& \ ]\|.
\end{aligned}$$

where 'establish $Q(n := n+1)$' is formally specified as

$$\begin{aligned}
& \|[\ \mathbf{con}\ N, n, r : \text{int};\ A : \mathbf{array}\ [0..N]\ \mathbf{of}\ \text{int}; \\
& \quad \{P_0 \land P_1 \land n \neq N\} \\
& \quad \mathbf{var}\ s : \text{int}; \\
& \quad \{Q\} \\
& \quad S \\
& \quad \{Q(n := n+1)\} \\
& \ ]\|.
\end{aligned}$$

For $Q(n := n+1)$, we derive, assuming $P_0 \land P_1 \land Q \land n \neq N$:

$$
\begin{aligned}
&\quad (\mathbf{max}\, p : 0 \leq p \leq n{+}1 : S.p.(n{+}1)) \\
&= \quad \{\text{split off } p = n{+}1,\, 0 \leq n{+}1 \leq N\,\} \\
&\quad (\mathbf{max}\, p : 0 \leq p \leq n : S.p.(n{+}1))\; \mathbf{max}\; S.(n{+}1).(n{+}1) \\
&= \quad \{\text{definition of } S,\text{ summation over an empty range is } 0\,\} \\
&\quad (\mathbf{max}\, p : 0 \leq p \leq n : S.p.(n{+}1))\; \mathbf{max}\; 0 \\
&= \quad \{\text{definition of } S\,\} \\
&\quad (\mathbf{max}\, p : 0 \leq p \leq n : S.p.n + A.n)\; \mathbf{max}\; 0 \\
&= \quad \{\;+\text{ distributes over } \mathbf{max}\text{ when the range is non-empty, } 0 \leq n\,\} \\
&\quad ((\mathbf{max}\, p : 0 \leq p \leq n : S.p.n) + A.n)\; \mathbf{max}\; 0 \\
&= \quad \{\,Q\,\} \\
&\quad (s + A.n)\, \mathbf{max}\, 0
\end{aligned}
$$

From this derivation it follows that $Q(n := n{+}1)$ is established by $s := (s + A.n)\,\mathbf{max}\, 0$. Thus, we arrive at the following non-annotated solution to *maxsegsum*:

$$
\begin{aligned}
&\|[\ \mathbf{var}\ n, s : \text{int}; \\
&\quad n, r, s := 0, 0, 0 \\
&\quad ;\mathbf{do}\ n \neq N \\
&\qquad \rightarrow\quad s := (s + A.n)\,\mathbf{max}\, 0 \\
&\qquad\quad\; ; r := r\,\mathbf{max}\, s \\
&\qquad\quad\; ; n := n{+}1 \\
&\quad\ \mathbf{od} \\
&\,]\!|.
\end{aligned}
$$

A nice solution to a not so simple problem. In order to get used to the calculations that are performed in such derivations, the reader should thoroughly analyse the derivation of this program. In these derivations we used the following properties of S:

$S.n.n = 0\quad \text{for } 0 \leq n \leq N$
$S.p.(n{+}1) = S.p.n + A.n\quad \text{for } 0 \leq p \leq n < N$

We summarize these examples by showing the general pattern of the derivations carried out. Post-condition R is of the form

$R:\quad r = F.N$

for some natural number N and function F defined on $[0..N]$. The choice of invariants

$P_0:\quad r = F.n$
$P_1:\quad 0 \leq n \leq N$

leads to a program of the form

$\lVert$ **var** n : int;
$\quad n, r := 0, F.0$
$\quad$;**do** $n \neq N$
$\quad\quad \rightarrow$ 'establish $r = F.(n+1)$'
$\quad\quad\quad ; n := n+1$
$\quad$ **od**
$\rVert$,

and a calculation of the form

$\quad F.(n+1)$
$=\quad$ { calculus }
$\quad F.n \oplus G.n$
$=\quad$ { P_0 }
$\quad r \oplus G.n$
$=\quad$ { introduction of variable s and invariant Q }
$\quad r \oplus s$

where s satisfies

$Q:\quad s = G.n$

Then $r := r \oplus s$ establishes $P_0(n := n+1)$. Computation of $G.(n+1)$ may similarly lead to a relation of the form $G.(n+1) = G.n \otimes H.n$ in which case another invariant is introduced. This process continues until (we hope) an expression comes up that is easily computed.

Sometimes, as in the derivation of *maxsegsum*, we obtain a relation of the form

$\quad F.(n+1) = F.n \oplus G.(n+1)$

in which case

$Q:\quad s = G.n$

is introduced and the statement establishing $Q(n := n+1)$ precedes the statement establishing $P_0(n := n+1)$.

Exercises

Derive solutions for the following programming problems.

0. $[\![$ **con** N : int $\{N \geq 1\}$; A : **array** $[0..N)$ **of** int;
   var r : int;
   S
   $\{r = (\max p, q : 0 \leq p < q < N : A.p - A.q)\}$
   $]\!]$.

1. $[\![$ **con** N : int $\{N \geq 1\}$; A : **array** $[0..N)$ **of** int;
   var r : int;
   S
   $\{r = (\# p, q : 0 \leq p < q < N : A.p * A.q \geq 0)\}$
   $]\!]$.

2. Derive for integer N, $N \geq 1$, and integer array $A[0..N)$ a program for the computation of the maximal sum of the *non-empty* segments of A.

3. $[\![$ **con** N : int $\{N \geq 1\}$; A : **array** $[0..N)$ **of** int;
   var r : int;
   S
   $\{r = (\max p, q : 0 \leq p < q < N : (A.p - A.q)^2)\}$
   $]\!]$.

4. $[\![$ **con** N : int $\{N \geq 0\}$; A : **array** $[0..N)$ **of** bool;
   var r : bool;
   S
   $\{r \equiv (\exists p : 0 \leq p \leq N : (\forall i : 0 \leq i < p : A.i) \land (\forall i : p \leq i < N : \neg A.i))\}$
   $]\!]$.

5. Let $N \geq 0$ and let $A[0..N)$ be an array of integers. For $0 \leq p \leq q \leq N$, the *credit* of $A[p..q)$ is defined by

   $\text{credit}.p.q = (\# i : p \leq i < q : A.i > 0) - (\# i : p \leq i < q : A.i < 0)$

   Derive a program for the computation of a segment of A with maximal credit.

6. $[\![\,\mathbf{con}\ N : \text{int}\ \{N \geq 0\};\ A : \mathbf{array}\,[0..N)\,\mathbf{of}\ \text{int};$
   $\mathbf{var}\ r : \text{int};$
   S
   $\{r = (\mathbf{max}\,p, q : 0 \leq p \leq q \leq N : (\Pi\,i : p \leq i < q : A.i))\}$
   $]\!]$.

4.4 Tail invariants

In this section we discuss tail recursion. We used a form of tail recursion when we discussed the greatest common divisor algorithm in Section 2.5. That algorithm is based on properties of the function F defined for positive integers x and y by $F.x.y = x\,\mathbf{gcd}\,y$. These properties are

$$F.x.x = x$$
$$F.x.y = \begin{cases} F.(x-y).y & \text{if } x > y \\ F.x.(y-x) & \text{if } y > x \end{cases}$$

which is an example of a so-called tail recursive definition. A repetition for the computation of $F.A.B$ is obtained by choosing as invariant

$$F.x.y = F.A.B$$

as we did for the algorithm in Section 2.5.

As another example, consider

$[\![\,\mathbf{con}\ N : \text{int}\ \{N \geq 0\};\ A : \mathbf{array}\,[0..N]\,\mathbf{of}\ \text{int};$
$\mathbf{var}\ r : \text{int};$
S
$\{r = (\mathbf{max}\,i : 0 \leq i \leq N : A.i)\}$
$]\!]$.

Define, for $0 \leq x \leq y \leq N$, the function F by

$$F.x.y = (\mathbf{max}\,i : x \leq i \leq y : A.i)$$

Then the post-condition of this specification can be written as

R: $r = F.0.N$

and F has the following properties:

(i) $x = y \Rightarrow F.x.y = A.x$

(ii) $x < y \Rightarrow \begin{cases} F.x.y = F.(x{+}1).y & \text{if } A.x \leq A.y \\ F.x.y = F.x.(y{-}1) & \text{if } A.y \leq A.x \end{cases}$

A repetition based on (i) and (ii) has invariant

P: $F.x.y = F.0.N \wedge 0 \leq x \leq y \leq N$

and its coding is straightforward:

$\begin{array}{l} \mathbf{[\![}\ \mathbf{var}\ x, y : \mathrm{int};\ \{N \geq 0\} \\ \quad x, y := 0, N \\ \quad \{\text{invariant } P\text{: } F.x.y = F.0.N \wedge 0 \leq x \leq y \leq N,\ \text{bound: } y - x\} \\ \quad ; \mathbf{do}\ x \neq y \\ \quad\quad \to \mathbf{if}\ A.x \leq A.y \to x := x{+}1 \\ \quad\quad\quad [\!]\ A.y \leq A.x \to y := y{-}1 \\ \quad\quad \mathbf{fi} \\ \quad \mathbf{od} \\ \quad \{P \wedge x = y,\ \text{hence},\ A.x = F.0.N\} \\ \quad ; r := A.x \\ \mathbf{]\!]} \\ \{r = (\mathbf{max}\, i : 0 \leq i \leq N : A.i)\}. \end{array}$

The general setting of tail recursion is as follows. A function F is given for which

(i) $F.x = h.x$ if $b.x$
(ii) $F.x = F.(g.x)$ if $\neg b.x$

and one is asked to derive a program that establishes $r = F.X$ for some X. Taking

$P: \quad F.x = F.X$

as a so-called *tail invariant*, yields

> $\|$ **var** x;
> $\quad x := X$
> $\quad \{\text{invariant: } F.x = F.X\}$
> $\quad ; \textbf{do } \neg b.x \rightarrow x := g.x \textbf{ od}$
> $\quad ; r := h.x$
> $\|$
> $\{r = F.X\}$
> provided that the repetition terminates.

Solving a problem by tail recursion amounts to finding a suitable function F. A special case of tail recursion is the following.

An associative operator $\oplus$ is given with identity e. A function G has the following properties:

(0) $G.x = a$ $\qquad\qquad$ if $b.x$
(1) $G.x = h.x \oplus G.(g.x)$ $\quad$ if $\neg b.x$

and one is asked to derive a program with post-condition $r = G.X$. This problem may be solved by a tail invariant of the form

$P: \quad G.X = r \oplus G.x$

which may be interpreted as

'the result' = 'what has been computed' $\oplus$ 'what still has to be computed'

Invariant P is stablished by $r, x := e, X$. Furthermore, if $b.x$ holds, then

$\qquad G.X = r \oplus G.x$
$\equiv \quad \{b.x, \text{ use } (0)\}$
$\qquad G.X = r \oplus a$

and, for $\neg b.x$

$$
\begin{aligned}
&\quad G.X = r \oplus G.x \\
&\equiv \quad \{\neg b.x,\ \text{use (1)}\,\} \\
&\quad G.X = r \oplus (h.x \oplus G.(g.x)) \\
&\equiv \quad \{\,\oplus \text{ is associative}\,\} \\
&\quad G.X = (r \oplus h.x) \oplus G.(g.x) \\
&\equiv \quad \{\,\text{definition of } P\,\} \\
&\quad P(r, x := r \oplus h.x, g.x)
\end{aligned}
$$

This yields the following program scheme

If $\oplus$ is associative and has identity e, and G is such that

(0) $G.x = a$ if $b.x$
(1) $G.x = h.x \oplus G.(g.x)$ if $\neg b.x$

then

{true}
|[**var** x;
    $x, r := X, e$ {invariant: $G.X = r \oplus G.x$}
   ; **do** $\neg b.x \rightarrow x, r := g.x, r \oplus h.x$ **od**
    $\{G.X = r \oplus a\}$
   ; $r := r \oplus a$
]|
$\{r = G.X\}$

provided that the repetition terminates.

Note that in almost each line of the derivation above '$G.X =$' occurs. When applying tail invariants, we only derive the relevant parts, leading to derivations of the following form:
If $b.x$ holds, then

$$
\begin{aligned}
&\quad r \oplus G.x \\
&= \quad \{\,b.x,\ \text{use (0)}\,\} \\
&\quad r \oplus a
\end{aligned}
$$

and, for $\neg b.x$

$$r \oplus G.x$$
$$= \quad \{\neg b.x, \text{ use } (1)\}$$
$$r \oplus (h.x \oplus G.(g.x))$$
$$= \quad \{\oplus \text{ is associative}\}$$
$$(r \oplus h.x) \oplus G.(g.x)$$

We illustrate tail recursion by two examples.

For natural number x, $G.x$ is the sum of the decimals of x, defined by

$$G.0 = 0$$
$$G.x = x \bmod 10 + G.(x \text{ div } 10) \quad \text{for } x > 0$$

We are asked for a program with post-condition $r = G.N$ for natural number N. The program scheme presented above yields as tail invariant

$P_0: \quad G.N = r + G.x$

and as a lower bound for x, we add

$P_1: \quad 0 \leq x$

For $x = 0$, we have $r + G.x = r$ and for $x > 0$:

$$r + G.x$$
$$= \quad \{\text{definition of } G,\ x > 0\}$$
$$r + (x \bmod 10 + G.(x \text{ div } 10))$$
$$= \quad \{+ \text{ is associative}\}$$
$$(r + x \bmod 10) + G.(x \text{ div } 10)$$

leading to

$\|[\text{ var } x : \text{int}; \{N \geq 0\}$
$\quad x, r := N, 0 \ \{\text{invariant: } P_0 \wedge P_1,\ \text{bound: } x\}$
$\quad ; \textbf{do } x \neq 0 \to x, r := x \text{ div } 10, r + x \bmod 10 \textbf{ od}$
$]\|$
$\{r = G.N\}.$

Note that a bound function is specified to satisfy the termination requirement. Termination follows from

$$x \operatorname{\bf div} 10 < x$$
$\equiv$ { heading for the definition of **div** }
$$10 * (x \operatorname{\bf div} 10) < 10 * x$$
$\equiv$ { calculus }
$$x \operatorname{\bf mod} 10 + 10 * (x \operatorname{\bf div} 10) < x \operatorname{\bf mod} 10 + 10 * x$$
$\equiv$ { definition of **div** and **mod** }
$$x < x \operatorname{\bf mod} 10 + 10 * x$$
$\Leftarrow$ { $x \operatorname{\bf mod} 10 \geq 0$ }
$$x < 10 * x$$
$\equiv$ { calculus }
$$0 < x$$

As a second example we reconsider *exponentiation* (cf. Section 4.2), specified by

$[\![$ **con** $A, B :$ int $\{A \geq 0 \land B \geq 0\}$;
  var r : int;
    exponentiation
  $\{r = A^B\}$
$]\!]$.

For exponentiation, i.e., for function G defined by $G.x.y = x^y$, we have, for $x \geq 0 \land y \geq 0$:

(0) $G.x.0 = 1$
(1) $G.x.y = 1 * G.(x*x).(y \operatorname{\bf div} 2)$ if $y \operatorname{\bf mod} 2 = 0$
     $G.x.y = x * G.x.(y-1)$ if $y \operatorname{\bf mod} 2 = 1$

A tail invariant corresponding to G is

P_0 : $r * x^y = A^B$

and a lower bound for y is given by

P_1 : $0 \leq y$

From the recurrence relations for G, we infer

$$P_0 \land y > 0 \land y \operatorname{\bf mod} 2 = 0 \Rightarrow P_0(x, y := x * x, y \operatorname{\bf div} 2)$$

and

$$P_0 \wedge y > 0 \wedge y \bmod 2 = 1 \Rightarrow P_0(r, y := r * x, y - 1)$$

resulting in

$\|[\,\mathbf{var}\ x, y : \text{int};\ \{A \geq 0 \wedge B \geq 0\}$
$\quad r, x, y := 1, A, B$
$\quad \{\text{invariant: } r * x^y = A^B \wedge 0 \leq y,\ \text{bound: } y\}$
$\quad ; \mathbf{do}\ y \neq 0$
$\quad\quad \to \mathbf{if}\ y \bmod 2 = 0 \to x, y := x * x, y\,\mathbf{div}\,2$
$\quad\quad\quad \|\ y \bmod 2 = 1 \to r, y := r * x, y - 1$
$\quad\quad \mathbf{fi}$
$\quad \mathbf{od}$
$\quad \{r * x^y = A^B \wedge y = 0,\ \text{hence},\ r = A^B\}$
$\,]\|$
$\{r = A^B\}.$

Since y halves at least every other step of the repetition, the time complexity of this program is $\mathcal{O}(\log B)$.

The purpose of this section is *not* to explain how a specific problem can be formulated in terms of F or G. In practice, we do not always define F or G explicitly. For instance, the exponentiation program would be introduced by
'We choose a tail invariant P, defined by

P: $r * x^y = A^B$

and we choose as guard $y \neq 0$'.
In later chapters we will see many applications of the tail invariant technique.

Exercises

0. Derive a program for the computation of $A * B$ where A and B are natural numbers. Apart from **div** 2, **mod** 2, and *2 only addition and subtraction are allowed.

1. Derive a program for the computation of the number of factors 3 of natural positive number N.

2. Solve

   $[\![$ **con** $N, X :$ int $\{N \geq 0\}; f :$ **array** $[0..N)$ **of** int;
      var $r :$ int;
      S
      $\{r = (\Sigma i : 0 \leq i < N : f.i * X^i)\}$
   $]\!]$,

   by defining for $0 \leq n \leq N$

   $G.n = (\Sigma i : n \leq i < N : f.i * X^{i-n})$

   and deriving a suitable recurrence relation for G.

3. The function fusc is defined on the natural numbers by

      fusc.$0 = 0$, fusc.$1 = 1$
      fusc.$(2*n) =$ fusc.n, and
      fusc.$(2*n+1) =$ fusc.$n +$ fusc.$(n+1)$ for $n \geq 0$

   Derive a program for the computation of fusc.N, $N \geq 0$. (Hint: compute fusc.78).

4. Solve

   $[\![$ **con** $N, X :$ int $\{N \geq 0\}; f :$ **array** $[0..N)$ **of** int;
      var $r :$ bool;
      S
      $\{r \equiv (\exists i : 0 \leq i < N : f.i = 0)\}$
   $]\!]$,

   by defining for $0 \leq n \leq N$

   $G.n \equiv (\exists i : n \leq i < N : f.i = 0)$

   and deriving a suitable recurrence relation for G.

5. An h-sequence is either a sequence consisting of the single element 0 or it is a 1, followed by two h-sequences. Syntactically, h-sequences may be defined by

$$\langle h \rangle \;=\; 0 \;\mid\; 1 \,\langle h \rangle \,\langle h \rangle$$

Solve

$$\begin{array}{l} [\![\,\mathbf{con}\; N : \mathbf{int}\; \{N \geq 0\};\; A :\; \mathbf{array}\,[0..2{*}N{+}1)\,\mathbf{of}\,[0..1]; \\ \quad \mathbf{var}\; r : \mathbf{bool}; \\ \qquad S \\ \quad \{r \equiv A \text{ is an } h\text{-sequence}\} \\ ]\!]. \end{array}$$

4.5 Summary

In this chapter we discussed some general techniques that show how a suitable invariant may be derived from a given pre- and post-condition. We summarize these ideas.

Taking conjuncts

When the post-condition is a conjunction of predicates, take some of the conjuncts as invariants and take the negations of the other conjuncts as guards for a repetition. As a special case, one can try true as invariant and the negation of the post-condition as guard.

Replacing constants by variables.

The replacement of one or more constants by variables yields a possible invariant for a repetition.

Strengthening invariants.

When a choice for an invariant has been made, calculations may lead to an expression E that is neither easily computed nor easily expressed in terms of the program variables. The extension of the state space with a variable and the addition of an invariant that expresses that this variable equals E may help obtain a solution to the problem.

Tail invariants

The general setting of tail recursion is as follows. A function F is given for which

$$F.x = h.x \quad \text{if } b.x$$
$$F.x = F.(g.x) \quad \text{if } \neg b.x$$

and one is asked to derive a program that establishes $r = F.X$ for some X. Then $F.x = F.X$ is a good candidate as invariant for a repetition that solves this problem.

A special case of tail recursion is applicable to the problem of computing $G.X$, where G is such that

(0) $\quad G.x = a \quad$ if $b.x$
(1) $\quad G.x = h.x \oplus G.(g.x) \quad$ if $\neg b.x$

in which $\oplus$ is an associative operator with identity e. Then $G.X = r \oplus G.x$ is good candidate for an invariant.

Exercises

Derive solutions to the following programming problems.

0. $[\![\, \textbf{con } N : \text{int } \{N \geq 1\}; \, A : \textbf{array } [0..N) \textbf{ of } \text{int};$
   $\textbf{var } b : \text{bool};$
   S
   $\{b \equiv (\exists p, q : 0 \leq p < q < N : A.p - A.q \leq 2)\}$
   $]\!].$

1. $[\![\, \textbf{con } N : \text{int } \{N \geq 1\}; \, A : \textbf{array } [0..N) \textbf{ of } \text{int};$
   $\textbf{var } r : \text{int};$
   S
   $\{r = (\# i : 0 \leq i < N : (\forall p : i \leq p < N : A.i \geq A.p))\}$
   $]\!].$

2. The function A is defined on the natural numbers by

   $A.0 = 1$
   $A.(2n) = 2 * A.n$, for $n \geq 1$
   $A.(2n+1) = n + A.(2n)$, for $n \geq 0$

Derive a program for the computation of $A.N$, $N \geq 0$.

3. $[\![\, \mathbf{con}\ N : \text{int}\ \{N \geq 2\};\ A : \mathbf{array}\ [0..N)\ \mathbf{of}\ \text{int};$
   $\mathbf{var}\ x, y : \text{int};$
   S
   $\{0 \leq x < y < N\ \wedge\ |A.x * A.y| = (\mathbf{max}\, p, q : 0 \leq p < q < N : |A.p * A.q|)\}$
   $]\!]$.

4. $[\![\, \mathbf{con}\ N : \text{int}\ \{N \geq 2\};\ A : \mathbf{array}\ [0..N)\ \mathbf{of}\ \text{int};$
   $\mathbf{var}\ r : \text{int};$
   S
   $\{r = (\Sigma\, p, q : 0 \leq p < q < N : (A.p - A.q)^2)\}$
   $]\!]$.

5. Derive an $\mathcal{O}(\log N)$ program for the computation of $(\Sigma\, i : 0 \leq i < N : A^i)$ where N and A are natural numbers.

6. $[\![\, \mathbf{con}\ N : \text{int}\ \{N \geq 0\};\ A : \mathbf{array}\ [0..N)\ \mathbf{of}\ \text{int};$
   $\mathbf{var}\ r : \text{int};$
   S
   $\{r = (\#\, k : 0 \leq k \leq N : (\forall\, i : k \leq i < N : A.i \geq 0))\}$
   $]\!]$.

7. $[\![\, \mathbf{con}\ N : \text{int}\ \{N \geq 1\};$
   $\mathbf{var}\ x : \text{int};$
   $\quad Fibolucci$
   $\{x = (\Sigma\, i : 0 \leq i \leq N : \text{fib}.i * \text{fib}.(N{-}i)\}$
   $]\!]$,
   where fib is defined by

   $\quad$ fib.0 = 0, fib.1 = 1, and
   $\quad$ fib.$(n{+}2)$ = fib.n + fib.$(n{+}1)$ for $n \geq 0$

   (Hint: replace both occurrences of N by n).

Chapter 5

Deriving Efficient Programs

5.0 Introduction

In this chapter we present two examples of efficient programs. The chapter may be skipped at first reading.

In Section 5.1 we present an efficient program for the computation of $A \operatorname{\mathbf{div}} B$ and $A \operatorname{\mathbf{mod}} B$. In Section 5.2 we show a technique that is applicable to a class of algorithms. In that section we assume that the reader is familiar with matrix multiplication.

Both examples are not simple and one of the purposes of this chapter is to show how one can reason about these programs in a non-operational way.

5.1 Integer division

Our first example is the derivation of an efficient solution to integer division, specified as

$\quad$ |[**con** A, B : int $\{A \geq 0 \land B > 0\}$;
$\quad\quad$ **var** q, r : int;
$\quad\quad\quad$ *divmod*
$\quad\quad\quad$ $\{q = A \operatorname{\mathbf{div}} B \land r = A \operatorname{\mathbf{mod}} B\}$
$\quad$]|.

in which apart from $\operatorname{\mathbf{div}} 2$, $\operatorname{\mathbf{mod}} 2$ and $*2$ (that are usually provided by machines) only addition and subtraction are allowed. As pointed out in Section 4.1, post-condition R may be written as

$R: \quad A = q * B + r \;\land\; 0 \leq r < B$

In Section 4.1 we chose as invariant $A = q*B + r \land 0 \leq r$ leading to

$q, r := 0, A$
$; \textbf{do } r \geq B \rightarrow q, r := q+1, r - B \textbf{ od}$

a program whose execution takes $A \textbf{ div } B$ steps.

It is quite easy to transform it into a program that is twice as efficient, by dividing by $2*B$ instead of B. Such a transformation leads to the following program.

$q, r := 0, A$
$\{A = q*2*B + r \land 0 \leq r\}$
$; \textbf{do } r \geq 2*B \rightarrow q, r := q+1, r - 2*B \textbf{ od}$
$\{A = q*2*B + r \land 0 \leq r < 2*B\}$
$; q := q*2$
$\{A = q*B + r \land 0 \leq r < 2*B\}$
$; \textbf{if } B \leq r \rightarrow q, r := q+1, r - B$
$[\!] \ r < B \rightarrow \textbf{skip}$
$\textbf{fi}$
$\{A = q*B + r \land 0 \leq r < B\}$

Execution of this program takes $\frac{1}{2} * (A \textbf{ div } B)$ steps. Of course, we can apply this idea again, leading to a program that is four times as efficient as the original program (at the price of two selections). In general we may start with a division by $2^k * B$ for some $k \geq 0$. This idea leads to an invariant that is obtained from the post-condition by replacing constant B by variable b:

$P_0: \quad A = q*b + r \land 0 \leq r < b$

To guarantee $b = 2^k * B$ for some natural k, we introduce variable k as well and define invariant P_1 by

$P_1: \quad b = 2^k * B \land 0 \leq k$

$P_0 \land P_1$ is established by a repetition for which

$Q: \quad A = q*b + r \land 0 \leq r \land b = 2^k * B \land 0 \leq k$

is an invariant and $r \geq b$ the guard. Its coding is straightforward:

$q, r, b, k := 0, A, B, 0$
$; \textbf{do } r \geq b \rightarrow b, k := b*2, k+1 \textbf{ od}$

Integer division 85

This part has time complexity $\mathcal{O}(\log(A \operatorname{\mathbf{div}} B))$, since k is 0 initially and has the minimum i for which $2^i > A \operatorname{\mathbf{div}} B$ as its final value.

As guard of the next repetition, we choose $b \neq B$. To obtain an efficient algorithm we investigate the effect of $b := b \operatorname{\mathbf{div}} 2$ and we derive

$$P_0 \wedge P_1 \wedge b \neq B$$
$$\equiv \quad \{\text{definitions of } P_0 \text{ and } P_1\}$$
$$A = q * b + r \wedge 0 \leq r < b \wedge b = 2^k * B \wedge 0 \leq k \wedge b \neq B$$
$$\equiv \quad \{\text{calculus}\}$$
$$A = q * b + r \wedge 0 \leq r < b \wedge b = 2^k * B \wedge 1 \leq k$$
$$\equiv \quad \{\text{heading for } b := b \operatorname{\mathbf{div}} 2\}$$
$$A = (q * 2) * (b \operatorname{\mathbf{div}} 2) + r \wedge 0 \leq r < 2 * (b \operatorname{\mathbf{div}} 2) \wedge b \operatorname{\mathbf{div}} 2 = 2^{k-1} * B$$
$$\wedge \; 0 \leq k{-}1$$

Hence,

$$\{P_0 \wedge P_1 \wedge b \neq B\}$$
$$q, b, k := q * 2, b \operatorname{\mathbf{div}} 2, k{-}1$$
$$\{A = q * b + r \wedge 0 \leq r < 2 * b \wedge b = 2^k * B \wedge 0 \leq k\}$$

Starting with the last line it is easy to establish $P_0 \wedge P_1$:

$$\{A = q * b + r \wedge 0 \leq r < 2 * b \wedge b = 2^k * B \wedge 0 \leq k\}$$
if $r < b \rightarrow$ skip $\{P_0 \wedge P_1\}$
[] $r \geq b \rightarrow q, r := q{+}1, r{-}b$ $\{P_0 \wedge P_1\}$
fi
$\{P_0 \wedge P_1\}$

Thus, we arrive at the following program:

|[**var** b, k : int;
　　$q, r, b, k := 0, A, B, 0$
　　; **do** $r \geq b \rightarrow b, k := b * 2, k{+}1$ **od**
　　; **do** $b \neq B$
　　　　$\rightarrow q, b, k := q * 2, b \operatorname{\mathbf{div}} 2, k{-}1$
　　　　; **if** $r < b \rightarrow$ skip [] $r \geq b \rightarrow q, r := q{+}1, r{-}b$ **fi**
　　od
]|.

In each step of the second repetition k is decreased by 1. Its final value is 0, hence execution of the second repetition takes $\log(A \operatorname{div} B)$ steps as well. We conclude that this program has time complexity $\mathcal{O}(\log(A \operatorname{div} B))$.

Variable k plays a specific role. No other variable depends on k and leaving out this variable does not affect the algorithm. But k does play a role, since the invariant (and, hence, the correctness of the algorithm) depends on k. When we remove k, what would be an invariant of the resulting program? The solution is not difficult: the above program shows the existence of integer k such that all relations are satisfied. Replacing invariants P_1 and Q by

$PP_1:\quad (\exists k: 0 \leq k: b = 2^k * B)$

$QQ:\quad A = q*b+r \wedge 0 \leq r \wedge (\exists k: 0 \leq k: b = 2^k * B)$

results in a program in which k does not occur any more:

$\{A \geq 0 \wedge B > 0\}$
$[\![\,\textbf{var}\ b: \text{int};$
$\quad q, r, b := 0, A, B$
$\quad ;\textbf{do}\ r \geq b \rightarrow b := b * 2\ \textbf{od}$
$\quad ;\textbf{do}\ b \neq B$
$\quad\quad \rightarrow q, b := q*2, b\ \textbf{div}\ 2$
$\quad\quad\quad ;\textbf{if}\ r < b \rightarrow \text{skip}\ [\!]\ r \geq b \rightarrow q, r := q+1, r-b\ \textbf{fi}$
$\quad \textbf{od}$
$]\!]$
$\{q = A \operatorname{div} B \wedge r = A \operatorname{mod} B\}.$

It is possible to derive this program in terms of P_0, PP_1, and QQ right from the beginning. As a disadvantage one has to perform all calculations with an existential quantification. Moreover, the efficiency considerations cannot be phrased in terms of k any more. The introduction of variable k makes it easier to reason about the program, and as k does not actually occur in the final program it is called a *ghost variable*.

Finally, we remark that the correctness of the program presented above is difficult to grasp without its derivation. Nevertheless, it is essentially the same division algorithm that is taught in primary school.

Exercises

0. Derive an $\mathcal{O}(\log N)$ algorithm for *square root*:

   $\lVert\mathbf{con}\ N : \text{int}\ \{N \geq 0\};$
   $\quad\mathbf{var}\ x : \text{int};$
   $\quad\quad\textit{square root}$
   $\quad\{x^2 \leq N \wedge (x+1)^2 > N\}$
   $\rVert,$

   by introducing variables y and k and invariants

   $P_0:\ x^2 \leq N \wedge (x+y)^2 > N$
   $P_1:\ y = 2^k \wedge 0 \leq k$

1. Derive a program that has time complexity $\mathcal{O}(\log N)$ for

   $\lVert\mathbf{con}\ N : \text{int}\ \{N \geq 1\};\ f : \mathbf{array}\ [0..N]\ \mathbf{of}\ \text{int}\ \{f.0 < f.N\};$
   $\quad\mathbf{var}\ x : \text{int};$
   $\quad\quad S$
   $\quad\{0 \leq x < N \wedge f.x < f.(x+1)\}$
   $\rVert.$

   by introducing variable y and invariants

   $P_0:\ f.x < f.y$
   $P_1:\ 0 \leq x < y \leq N$

2. Solve

   $\lVert\mathbf{con}\ A, B : \text{int}\ \{B > 0\};$
   $\quad\mathbf{var}\ q, r : \text{int};$
   $\quad\quad\textit{divmod}$
   $\quad\{q = A\ \mathbf{div}\ B \wedge r = A\ \mathbf{mod}\ B\}$
   $\rVert.$

5.2 Fibonacci

Our second example is the derivation of an $\mathcal{O}(\log N)$ program for *Fibonacci* (cf. Section 4.3), specified by

$\|[\,\mathbf{con}\ N : \text{int}\ \{N \geq 0\};$
$\quad\mathbf{var}\ x : \text{int};$
$\quad\quad Fibonacci$
$\quad\{x = \text{fib}.N\}$
$\,]\|,$

where fib is defined by

fib.0 = 0, fib.1 = 1, and
fib.$(n+2)$ = fib.n + fib.$(n+1)$ for $n \geq 0$

In Section 4.3, we chose as invariant $x = \text{fib}.n \wedge y = \text{fib}.(n+1)$, leading to

$\{N \geq 0\}$
$\|[\,\mathbf{var}\ y, n : \text{int};$
$\quad n, x, y := 0, 0, 1$
$\quad;\mathbf{do}\ n \neq N$
$\quad\quad \rightarrow\ x, y := y, x+y$
$\quad\quad;n := n + 1$
$\quad\quad\mathbf{od}$
$\,]\|$
$\{x = \text{fib}.N\},$

a program that has time complexity $\mathcal{O}(N)$. We derive from this program a more efficient one by a rather general technique exploiting the fact that the expressions assigned to x and y in the multiple assignment $x, y := y, x+y$ are *linear combinations* of x and y. In terms of matrices this assignment is denoted as

$$\begin{pmatrix} x \\ y \end{pmatrix} := \begin{pmatrix} 0 & 1 \\ 1 & 1 \end{pmatrix} \begin{pmatrix} x \\ y \end{pmatrix}$$

and the algorithm may be denoted as

|[**var** y, n : int;

$$n := 0 \,; \begin{pmatrix} x \\ y \end{pmatrix} := \begin{pmatrix} 0 \\ 1 \end{pmatrix}$$

;**do** $n \neq N$

$$\rightarrow \begin{pmatrix} x \\ y \end{pmatrix} := \begin{pmatrix} 0 & 1 \\ 1 & 1 \end{pmatrix} \begin{pmatrix} x \\ y \end{pmatrix}$$

$$; n := n + 1$$

od

$$\{ \begin{pmatrix} x \\ y \end{pmatrix} = \begin{pmatrix} 0 & 1 \\ 1 & 1 \end{pmatrix}^N \begin{pmatrix} 0 \\ 1 \end{pmatrix} = \begin{pmatrix} \text{fib.}N \\ \text{fib.}(N+1) \end{pmatrix} \}$$

]|
$\{x = \text{fib.}N\}$.

An invariant of the program for *Fibonacci* is

$$\begin{pmatrix} x \\ y \end{pmatrix} = \begin{pmatrix} 0 & 1 \\ 1 & 1 \end{pmatrix}^n \begin{pmatrix} 0 \\ 1 \end{pmatrix}$$

and its post-condition is

$$\begin{pmatrix} x \\ y \end{pmatrix} = \begin{pmatrix} 0 & 1 \\ 1 & 1 \end{pmatrix}^N \begin{pmatrix} 0 \\ 1 \end{pmatrix}$$

In Section 4.4 we developed an $\mathcal{O}(\log N)$ program for *exponentiation*, based on a tail invariant. A similar approach to the computation of $\begin{pmatrix} 0 & 1 \\ 1 & 1 \end{pmatrix}^N \begin{pmatrix} 0 \\ 1 \end{pmatrix}$ is appropriate, using invariants

$$P_0 : \begin{pmatrix} 0 & 1 \\ 1 & 1 \end{pmatrix}^N \begin{pmatrix} 0 \\ 1 \end{pmatrix} = A^n \begin{pmatrix} x \\ y \end{pmatrix}$$

$P_1 : \; 0 \leq n \leq N$

which are initialized by $n, x, y := N, 0, 1 \,; A := \begin{pmatrix} 0 & 1 \\ 1 & 1 \end{pmatrix}$ and for which we have

$$P_0 \wedge n = 0 \Rightarrow x = \text{fib.}N \wedge y = \text{fib.}(N+1)$$

Deriving Efficient Programs

This leads to the following program:

$$n, x, y := N, 0, 1 \; ; A := \begin{pmatrix} 0 & 1 \\ 1 & 1 \end{pmatrix}$$

$$; \mathbf{do}\ n \neq 0$$
$$\quad \rightarrow \mathbf{if}\ n \bmod 2 = 0 \rightarrow A := A * A \;; n := n\ \mathbf{div}\ 2$$
$$\quad [\!]\ n \bmod 2 = 1 \rightarrow \begin{pmatrix} x \\ y \end{pmatrix} := A \begin{pmatrix} x \\ y \end{pmatrix}\ ; n := n-1$$
$$\quad \mathbf{fi}$$
$$\mathbf{od}$$
$$\{x = \mathrm{fib}.N\}$$

A next step is the elimination of the matrix operations. We compute some powers of $\begin{pmatrix} 0 & 1 \\ 1 & 1 \end{pmatrix}$:

$$\begin{pmatrix} 0 & 1 \\ 1 & 1 \end{pmatrix}^2 = \begin{pmatrix} 0 & 1 \\ 1 & 1 \end{pmatrix}\begin{pmatrix} 0 & 1 \\ 1 & 1 \end{pmatrix} = \begin{pmatrix} 1 & 1 \\ 1 & 2 \end{pmatrix}$$

$$\begin{pmatrix} 0 & 1 \\ 1 & 1 \end{pmatrix}^4 = \begin{pmatrix} 1 & 1 \\ 1 & 2 \end{pmatrix}\begin{pmatrix} 1 & 1 \\ 1 & 2 \end{pmatrix} = \begin{pmatrix} 2 & 3 \\ 3 & 5 \end{pmatrix}$$

This leads to the conjecture that all these powers are of the form $\begin{pmatrix} a & b \\ b & a+b \end{pmatrix}$. Indeed,

$$\begin{pmatrix} a & b \\ b & a+b \end{pmatrix}\begin{pmatrix} a & b \\ b & a+b \end{pmatrix} = \begin{pmatrix} p & q \\ q & p+q \end{pmatrix}$$

where $p = a^2 + b^2$ and $q = ab + ba + b^2$. Hence, matrix A may be represented by two integers: pair $\langle a, b \rangle$ represents matrix $\begin{pmatrix} a & b \\ b & a+b \end{pmatrix}$. Then

$$A := A * A \quad \text{corresponds to} \quad a, b := a*a + b*b, a*b + b*a + b*b$$

and

$$\begin{pmatrix} x \\ y \end{pmatrix} := A \begin{pmatrix} x \\ y \end{pmatrix} \quad \text{corresponds to} \quad x, y := a*x + b*y, b*x + a*y + b*y$$

The final solution is presented below.

$\{N \geq 0\}$
$\|[$ **var** $a, b, n, y :$ int;
$\quad a, b, x, y, n := 0, 1, 0, 1, N$
$\quad ;$ **do** $n \neq 0$
$\quad\quad \rightarrow$ **if** $n \bmod 2 = 0 \rightarrow a, b := a * a + b * b, a * b + b * a + b * b \, ; n := n \, \textbf{div} \, 2$
$\quad\quad\quad [\!] \; n \bmod 2 = 1 \rightarrow x, y := a * x + b * y, b * x + a * y + b * y \, ; n := n{-}1$
$\quad\quad$ **fi**
$\quad$ **od**
$\quad \{x = \text{fib}.N\}$
$]\!|.$

Needless to say that this program cannot be easily understood without its derivation.

Exercises

Solve

0. $\|[$ **con** $A, B, N :$ int $\{N \geq 0\}$;
   $\quad$ **var** $x :$ int;
   $\quad S$
   $\quad \{x = (\Sigma i : 0 \leq i \leq N : A^{N-i} * B^i)\}$
   $]\!|.$

1. $\|[$ **con** $N :$ int $\{N \geq 1\}$;
   $\quad$ **var** $x :$ int;
   $\quad Fibolucci$
   $\quad \{x = (\Sigma i : 0 \leq i \leq N : \text{fib}.i * \text{fib}.(N{-}i)\}$
   $]\!|,$
   where fib is defined by

   fib.0 = 0, fib.1 = 1, and
   fib.$(n{+}2)$ = fib.n + fib.$(n{+}1)$ for $n \geq 0$.

Chapter 6

Searching

6.0 Introduction

Many programming problems can be viewed as a so-called searching problem. For instance, the square root problem of Section 4.1 may be formulated as 'search for the maximal natural number i for which $i^2 \leq N$', i.e., establish post-condition

$$x = (\mathbf{max}\, i : 0 \leq i \wedge i^2 \leq N : i)$$

It may also be formulated as

$$x = (\mathbf{min}\, i : 0 \leq i \wedge (i+1)^2 > N : i)$$

i.e., search for the minimal natural number i for which $(i+1)^2 > N$. In Section 6.1 we discuss a simple program called *Linear Search*. The *Bounded Linear Search* is presented in Section 6.2. In Section 6.3 we consider a more efficient scheme which is applicable to a large class of search problems. That program is known as the *Binary Search*. In Section 6.4 we discuss a less well-known program scheme called *Searching by Elimination*.

6.1 Linear Search

We consider the following problem. For integer variable x, $b.x$ is a boolean expression such that

$$(\exists i : 0 \leq i : b.i)$$

An example of such an expression is $(x+1) * (x+1) > N$. We are interested in the smallest natural i for which $b.i$ holds. A formal specification of this problem is

Linear Search

$\| \textbf{var } x : \text{int};$
$\{(\exists i : 0 \leq i : b.i)\}$
   Linear Search
$\{x = (\min i : 0 \leq i \wedge b.i : i)\}$
$\|.$

We rewrite the post-condition:

$R: \quad 0 \leq x \wedge b.x \wedge (\forall i : 0 \leq i < x : \neg b.i)$

A possible invariant is obtained by the technique of taking a conjunct: we define P by

$P: \quad 0 \leq x \wedge (\forall i : 0 \leq i < x : \neg b.i)$

which is initialized by $x := 0$. As guard we choose, of course, $\neg b.x$. Investigation of $x := x + 1$ leads to

$\quad P(x := x+1)$
$\equiv \quad \{\text{definition of } P\}$
$\quad 0 \leq x + 1 \wedge (\forall i : 0 \leq i < x + 1 : \neg b.i)$
$\Leftarrow \quad \{\text{heading for } P\}$
$\quad 0 \leq x \wedge (\forall i : 0 \leq i < x + 1 : \neg b.i)$
$\equiv \quad \{\text{split off } i = x, 0 \leq x < x + 1\}$
$\quad 0 \leq x \wedge (\forall i : 0 \leq i < x : \neg b.i) \wedge \neg b.x$
$\equiv \quad \{\text{definition of } P\}$
$\quad P \wedge \neg b.x$

This gives rise to the following program:

$\quad x := 0 \,; \textbf{do } \neg b.x \rightarrow x := x + 1 \textbf{ od}.$

For a proof of the correctness of this program we still have to provide a bound function. Note that we have not used the pre-condition yet. The pre-condition allows us to define constant X by

$\quad 0 \leq X \wedge b.X$

and we derive

Searching

$$P$$
$\Rightarrow$ { definition of P }
$$(\forall i : 0 \leq i \wedge i < x : \neg b.i)$$
$\equiv$ { predicate calculus: trading }
$$(\forall i : 0 \leq i \wedge b.i : i \geq x)$$
$\Rightarrow$ $\{ 0 \leq X \wedge b.X \}$
$$X \geq x$$

Hence, $X - x$ is a suitable bound function for the program presented above. We formulate our result as follows.

Linear Search

$\|[$ **var** x : int;
$\quad \{(\exists i : 0 \leq i : b.i)\}$
$\quad x := 0$
$\quad ;$ **do** $\neg b.x \rightarrow x := x + 1$ **od**
$\quad \{x = (\min i : 0 \leq i \wedge b.i : i)\}$
$]\|.$

Of course, the fact that 0 is a lower bound is not essential: the maximum i for which $b.i$ holds is obtained by initializing x with an upper bound and replacing $x := x + 1$ by $x := x - 1$.

As an example, we solve the following problem.

$\|[$ **con** N : int $\{N \geq 0\}$; A : **array** $[0..N]$ **of** int;
$\quad \{A.0 < A.N\}$
$\quad$ **var** r : int;
$\quad\quad S$
$\quad \{r = (\max i : 0 \leq i < N \wedge A.i < A.(i+1) : i)\}$
$]\|.$

This problem can be solved by replacing constant N by variable n, an approach that leads to a less elegant algorithm, as the reader may verify. Applying the Linear Search, we obtain as solution:

S: $\{(\exists i : 0 \leq i < N : A.i < A.(i+1)),$ see Proof, apply Linear Search$\}$
$r := N - 1$
$; \mathbf{do}\ A.r \geq A.(r+1) \rightarrow r := r - 1\ \mathbf{od}$
$\{r = (\mathbf{max}\, i : 0 \leq i < N \land A.i < A.(i+1) : i)\}$

Proof:

$\quad (\forall i : 0 \leq i < N : A.i \geq A.(i+1))$
$\Rightarrow \quad \{\text{transitivity of } \geq\}$
$\quad A.0 \geq A.N$

Hence,

$A.0 < A.N \Rightarrow (\exists i : 0 \leq i < N : A.i < A.(i+1))$

The program with its accompanying proof is all one has to provide as solution to the problem.

6.2 Bounded Linear Search

The Bounded Linear Search is a solution to the following problem. Given integer N, $N \geq 0$, and boolean array $b[0..N)$, one is asked to derive a program that assigns to variable x the least number i in $[0..N)$ for which $b.i$ holds. If no such number exists in this domain, N should be assigned to x. A solution with invariant

$0 \leq x \leq N \land (\forall i : 0 \leq i < x : \neg b.i)$

and program

$x := 0\, ; \mathbf{do}\ \neg b.x \land x \neq N \rightarrow x := x+1\ \mathbf{od}$

is *not* correct, since N does not belong to the domain of b and $x = N$ is not excluded by the invariant.

A formal specification of the problem is

$\lVert\ \mathbf{con}\ N : \text{int } \{N \geq 0\};\ b : \mathbf{array}\ [0..N)\ \mathbf{of}\ \text{bool};$
$\quad \mathbf{var}\ x : \text{int};$
$\quad\quad \textit{bounded linear search}$
$\quad \{x = (\mathbf{max}\, i : 0 \leq i \leq N \land (\forall j : 0 \leq j < i : \neg b.j) : i)\}$
$\rVert.$

Searching

When we define (without, of course, actually changing b) $b.N$ as true, the post-condition may be written as

$R: \quad 0 \leq x \leq N \land (\forall i : 0 \leq i < x : \neg b.i) \land b.x$

As explained above, a repetition with $\neg b.x$ as guard is not possible. When we take $b.x$ as part of the invariant, it should be established by $x := N$, since N is the only value for which it is known that b has the value true. On the other hand, the first two conjuncts of R require $x := 0$ as initialization. This 'conflict' is solved by the introduction of integer variable y: we choose as invariant

$P_0: \quad 0 \leq x \leq N \land (\forall i : 0 \leq i < x : \neg b.i) \land b.y$

Then P_0 is established by $x, y := 0, N$ and $P_0 \land x = y$ implies R. Hence, we choose $x \neq y$ as guard for the repetition and $y - x$ as bound function. As bounds for y we add

$P_1: \quad x \leq y \leq N$

to the invariant. Then $P_0 \land P_1 \land x \neq y \Rightarrow 0 \leq x < N$, and, hence, $b.x$ may occur in the statement of the repetition. It is now easy to derive

$$P_0 \land P_1 \land x \neq y \land \neg b.x \Rightarrow (P_0 \land P_1)(x := x+1)$$

and

$$P_0 \land P_1 \land x \neq y \land b.x \Rightarrow (P_0 \land P_1)(y := x)$$

This leads to the following solution:

Bounded Linear Search

$\|[$ **con** N : int $\{N \geq 0\}$; b: **array** $[0..N)$ **of** bool;
　var x : int;
　$\|[$ **var** y : int;
　　$x, y := 0, N$
　　; **do** $x \neq y$
　　　$\rightarrow$ **if** $\neg b.x \rightarrow x := x+1$
　　　　$[\!]$　$b.x \rightarrow y := x$
　　　fi
　　od
　$]\!|$
　$\{x = (\mathbf{max}\, i : 0 \leq i \leq N \land (\forall j : 0 \leq j < i : \neg b.j) : i)\}$
$]\!|.$

Exercises

Solve the following programming problems.

0. $[\![$ **con** N : int $\{\text{true}\}$;
    var x : int;
    S
    $\{x = (\min i : 0 \leq i \wedge 2^i \geq N : i)\}$
    $]\!]$.

1. $[\![$ **con** N : int $\{N > 0\}$;
    var x : int;
    S
    $\{x = (\max i : 0 \leq i \wedge 2^i \leq N : i)\}$
    $]\!]$.

2. $[\![$ **con** N : int $\{N \geq 2\}$; A : **array** $[0..N)$ **of** int;
    $\{(\exists i, j : 0 \leq i < j < N : A.i - A.j \leq 2)\}$
    var r : int;
    S
    $\{r = (\max i : 0 < i < N \wedge A.(i-1) - A.i \leq 2 : i)\}$
    $]\!]$.

3. Derive a linear program for the Bounded Linear Search problem, based on the invariant

    $$x = (\max i : n \leq i \leq N \wedge (\forall j : n \leq j < i : \neg b.j) : i)$$

    What is the disadvantage of this solution compared to the one presented in this section?

4. $[\![$ **var** x : int;
    $\{(\exists i : i \text{ int} : b.i)\}$
    S
    $\{b.x \wedge (\forall i : |i| < |x| : \neg b.i)\}$
    $]\!]$.

5. $\|[\,\mathbf{con}\ N : \mathrm{int}\ \{N \geq 0\};\ f : \mathbf{array}\ [0..N)\ \mathbf{of}\ \mathrm{int};$
    $\mathbf{var}\ r : \mathrm{int};$
    S
    $\{r = (\mathbf{max}\,i : 0 \leq i \leq N \wedge (\forall j : 0 \leq j < i : f.j \neq 0) : i)\}$
    $\,]\!|.$

6. $\|[\,\mathbf{con}\ N : \mathrm{int}\ \{N \geq 1\};\ A, B : \mathbf{array}\ [0..N]\ \mathbf{of}\ \mathrm{int};$
    $\{A.0 < B.0 \wedge A.N \geq B.N\}$
    $\mathbf{var}\ r : \mathrm{int};$
    S
    $\{r = (\mathbf{max}\,i : 0 \leq i < N \wedge A.i < B.i \wedge A.(i{+}1) \geq B.(i{+}1) : i)\}$
    $\,]\!|.$

6.3 Binary Search

For ascending and descending functions, searching may often be realized in a much more efficient way than by an application of the linear search. For instance, it is much easier to find one's telephone number in a phone book than to find a name, given a telephone number. We explain the so-called Binary Search by solving

$\|[\,\mathbf{con}\ N, A : \mathrm{int}\ \{N \geq 1\};\ f : \mathbf{array}\ [0..N]\ \mathbf{of}\ \mathrm{int}\ \{f.0 \leq A < f.N\};$
$\mathbf{var}\ x : \mathrm{int};$
  binary search
$\{f.x \leq A < f.(x{+}1)\}$
$\,]\!|.$

Note that, apart from $f.0 \leq A < f.N$, nothing is assumed about f.

The post-condition is a conjunction of two predicates: $f.x \leq A$, which is initialized by $x := 0$; and $A < f.(x{+}1)$, which is initialized by $x := N{-}1$. As we did for the Bounded Linear Search, we introduce a variable y and we define invariants P_0 and P_1 by

$P_0 :\ f.x \leq A < f.y$
$P_1 :\ 0 \leq x < y \leq N$

Then, on account of the pre-condition, $P_0 \wedge P_1$ is established by $x, y := 0, N$. As guard of the repetition we choose $x{+}1 \neq y$, and as bound function we choose $y{-}x$. For any h such that $x < h < y$, we have $y{-}h < y{-}x$ and $h{-}x < y{-}x$, hence, both $x := h$ and $y := h$ decrease $y{-}x$ and both maintain P_1. Furthermore,

$$P_0(x := h)$$
$\equiv$ { substitution }
$$f.h \leq A < f.y$$
$\Leftarrow$ { definition of P_0 }
$$P_0 \wedge f.h \leq A$$

and

$$P_0(y := h)$$
$\equiv$ { substitution }
$$f.x \leq A < f.h$$
$\Leftarrow$ { definition of P_0 }
$$P_0 \wedge A < f.h$$

This leads to

$\{f.0 \leq A < f.N\}$
$[\![$ **var** y : int;
$\quad x, y := 0, N$
$\quad$ {invariant: $P_0 \wedge P_1$, bound: $y - x$}
$\quad$; **do** $x+1 \neq y$
$\quad\quad \rightarrow [\![$ **var** h : int;
$\quad\quad\quad$ 'establish $x < h < y$'
$\quad\quad\quad$; **if** $f.h \leq A \rightarrow x := h$
$\quad\quad\quad\quad [\!]\ A < f.h \rightarrow y := h$
$\quad\quad\quad$ **fi**
$\quad\quad]\!]$
$\quad$ **od**
$]\!]$
$\{f.x \leq A < f.(x+1)\}$

Since $y - x$ is replaced either by $y - h$ or by $h - x$, the best choice for h is the middle of $[x..y]$, i.e., $(x+y)$ **div** 2. Indeed,

$$
\begin{array}{rl}
& x < (x+y) \,\mathbf{div}\, 2 < y \\
\equiv & \{\,\text{calculus}\,\} \\
& x+1 \leq (x+y) \,\mathbf{div}\, 2 \leq y-1 \\
\Leftarrow & \{\,\mathbf{div}\, 2 \text{ is ascending}\,\} \\
& 2x+2 \leq x+y \leq 2y-2 \\
\equiv & \{\,\text{calculus}\,\} \\
& x+2 \leq y \\
\equiv & \{\,\text{calculus}\,\} \\
& x < y \land x+1 \neq y \\
\Leftarrow & \{\,\text{definition of } P_1\,\} \\
& P_1 \land x+1 \neq y
\end{array}
$$

Hence, $h := (x+y)\,\mathbf{div}\,2$ is a valid choice. Substitution in the above algorithm yields the solution:

Binary Search

```
{0 < N ∧ f.0 ≤ A < f.N}
x, y := 0, N
; do x+1 ≠ y
    → ‖ var h : int;
         h := (x+y) div 2
         ; if f.h ≤ A   → x := h
           ‖  A < f.h  → y := h
           fi
       ‖
  od
{0 ≤ x < N ∧ f.x ≤ A < f.(x+1)}
```

Since $y - x$ has initial value N and halves in each step of the repetition, the time complexity of this program is $\mathcal{O}(\log N)$.

Variable h has been introduced to enable us to *name* a value between x and y. In the program above h is just short for $(x+y)$ **div** 2 and the only property of h that is relevant to the correctness of the program is $x < h < y$. This example shows another reason for the introduction of variables.

Note that $0 < h < N$, from which we infer that $f.0$ and $f.N$ are not inspected during the execution of the program. Pre-condition $f.0 \leq A < f.N$ is only used for the initialization of x and y. When this part of the pre-condition is replaced by true or, equivalently, by

$$f.0 \leq A < f.N \ \lor \ f.0 > A \ \lor \ f.N \geq A$$

the post-condition is

$$0 \leq x < N \ \land \ (f.x \leq A < f.(x+1) \ \lor \ f.0 > A \ \lor \ f.N \geq A)$$

We use this property in the following application of this algorithm. Let $N \geq 1$ and let $f[0..N)$ be an ascending array of integers. We are asked to derive a program for the computation of the boolean value 'integer A occurs in $f[0..N)$'. A formal specification is

$\|[$ **con** $N, A :$ int $\{N \geq 1\}; \ f :$ **array** $[0..N)$ **of** int ;
$\{(\forall i, j : 0 \leq i \leq j < N : f.i \leq f.j)\}$
var $r :$ bool;
$\quad S$
$\{r \equiv (\exists i : 0 \leq i < N : f.i = A)\}$
$]\|.$

In view of the remarks above, we define, since $f.N$ is not inspected, $f.N = \infty$ (without, of course, actually changing f). Then $A < f.N$ holds and the post-condition of the Binary Search is

$R: \quad 0 \leq x < N \ \land \ (f.x \leq A < f.(x+1) \ \lor \ A < f.0)$

At this point (and only here!) the ascendingness of f comes in. From R and the ascendingness of f we infer

Searching

$$(\exists i : 0 \leq i < N : f.i = A) \equiv f.x = A$$

Hence, we have

    $[\![$ **con** N, A : int $\{N \geq 1\}$; f : **array** $[0..N)$ **of** int $\{f$ is ascending$\}$;
      var b : bool;
        $[\![$ **var** x, y : int;
           $x, y := 0, N$
          ; **do** $x+1 \neq y$
                $\rightarrow [\![$ **var** h : int;
                      $h := (x+y)$ **div** 2
                    ; **if** $f.h \leq A \rightarrow x := h$
                       $[\!]$ $A < f.h \rightarrow y := h$
                    fi
                $]\!]$
        od
         ; $b := f.x = A$
      $]\!]$
      $\{b \equiv (\exists i : 0 \leq i < N : f.i = A)\}$
    $]\!]$.

This program is also known as 'the binary search'. It is an important algorithm and every programmer should know this program and its derivation by heart.

As a final example, we reconsider *square root* of Section 4.1, specified by

    $[\![$ **con** N : int $\{N \geq 0\}$;
      var x : int;
      square root
      $\{x^2 \leq N \land (x+1)^2 > N\}$
    $]\!]$.

For $N \geq 0$, we have $0^2 \leq N < (N+1)^2$. A straightforward application of the binary search yields the following $\mathcal{O}(\log N)$ program.

$\{N \geq 0\}$
$\|[\textbf{var } y : \text{int};$
    $x, y := 0, N+1 \ \{0 \leq x < y \land x^2 \leq N < y^2, \text{binary search}\}$
    $; \textbf{do } x+1 \neq y$
        $\rightarrow \|[\textbf{var } h : \text{int};$
            $h := (x+y) \textbf{ div } 2$
            $; \textbf{if } h * h \leq N \rightarrow x := h$
            $[\!]\ N < h * h \rightarrow y := h$
            $\textbf{fi}$
        $]\!|$
    $\textbf{od}$
$]\!|$
$\{x^2 \leq N < (x+1)^2\}$

Once again, we remark that the correctness of this program does *not* depend on the fact that x^2 is an ascending function of x on the natural numbers. However, when this program is used to establish $b \equiv (\exists p : 0 \leq p : N = p^2)$ for boolean variable b, then the ascendingness of x^2 is needed.

Exercises

Derive a program for the following specifications.

0. $\|[\textbf{con } N : \text{int } \{N \geq 0\};$
    $\textbf{var } r : \text{bool};$
    S
    $\{r \equiv (\exists p : p \geq 0 : N = p^3)\}$
   $]\!|.$

1. Derive for given N, $N \geq 0$, a program for the computation of the smallest integer x that satisfies $x^3 - 6x^2 + 9x \geq N$.

2. $\|[\textbf{con } N : \text{int } \{N \geq 1\}; A, B : \textbf{array } [0..N] \textbf{ of } \text{int};$
    $\{A.0 \leq B.0 \land A.N \geq B.N\}$
    $\textbf{var } r : \text{int};$
    S
    $\{0 \leq r < N \land A.r \leq B.r \land A.(r+1) \geq B.(r+1)\}$
   $]\!|.$

6.4 Searching by Elimination

Searching by elimination is the last technique discussed in this chapter. It may very well be studied at a later stage. Its derivation is a first example of so-called program refinement. The resulting program is obtained in a number of steps, and intermediate programs have, for instance, sets as variables.

We are given a finite set W and a boolean function S on W, such that $S.w$ holds for some $w \in W$. We are asked to derive a program with post-condition $S.x$. We identify boolean functions on W and subsets of W, i.e., S is identified with $\{x \in W \mid S.x\}$. Thus, the post-condition may also be written as $x \in S$ or as

$R: \quad S \cap \{x\} \neq \emptyset$

Note that in terms of sets the pre-condition '$S.w$ holds for some w in W' may be written as $S \cap W \neq \emptyset$. We replace $\{x\}$ by variable V and we define P, as a generalization of the pre- and post-condition, by

$P: \quad S \cap V \neq \emptyset \land V \subseteq W$

From $P \land |V| = 1$ we infer that the unique element of V satisfies R. This leads to

$\{S \cap W \neq \emptyset\}$
$V := W$
$\{\text{invariant } P : S \cap V \neq \emptyset \land V \subseteq W, \text{ bound: } |V|\}$
$;\mathbf{do}\ |V| \neq 1 \rightarrow \text{'decrease } |V| \text{ under invariance of } P\text{'}\ \mathbf{od}$
$; x := \text{'the unique element of } V\text{'}$

From $P \land |V| \neq 1$ we conclude that $|V| \geq 2$. Searching by elimination is based on the fact that of any two elements of V at least one may be removed without violating P. This yields the following approximation:

$V := W$
$;\mathbf{do}\ |V| \neq 1$
$\quad \rightarrow \text{'choose } a \text{ and } b \text{ in } V, \text{ such that } a \neq b\text{'}$
$\quad\quad \{a \in V \land b \in V \land a \neq b \land S \cap V \neq \emptyset\}$
$\quad\quad ;\mathbf{if}\ B_0 \rightarrow V := V \setminus \{a\}$
$\quad\quad \quad [\!]\ B_1 \rightarrow V := V \setminus \{b\}$
$\quad\quad \mathbf{fi}$
$\ \mathbf{od}$
$; x := \text{'the unique element of } V\text{'}$

From $S \cap V \neq \emptyset$ we infer $\neg S.a \Rightarrow S \cap V \setminus \{a\} \neq \emptyset$ and, since $b \in V \wedge a \neq b$, we also have $S.b \Rightarrow S \cap V \setminus \{a\} \neq \emptyset$. Hence, $\neg S.a \vee S.b$ is a good choice for B_0. More formally, this is derived as follows:

$\quad S \cap V \neq \emptyset \Rightarrow S \cap (V \setminus \{a\}) \neq \emptyset$
$\equiv \quad \{a \in V\}$
$\quad S.a \vee S \cap (V \setminus \{a\}) \neq \emptyset \Rightarrow S \cap (V \setminus \{a\}) \neq \emptyset$
$\equiv \quad \{\text{predicate calculus}\}$
$\quad S.a \Rightarrow S \cap (V \setminus \{a\}) \neq \emptyset$
$\Leftarrow \quad \{b \in V \setminus \{a\}\}$
$\quad S.a \Rightarrow S.b$
$\equiv \quad \{\text{predicate calculus}\}$
$\quad \neg S.a \vee S.b$

On account of the symmetry, $\neg S.b \vee S.a$ is a good choice for B_1. Note that this choice yields two guards whose disjunction is true. Substitution of these guards into our previous program yields the first version of searching by elimination.

Searching by Elimination (0)

```
{(∃w : w ∈ W : S.w)}
V := W
; do |V| ≠ 1
    → 'choose a and b in V, such that a ≠ b'
    ; if ¬S.a ∨ S.b → V := V \ {a}
      [] ¬S.b ∨ S.a → V := V \ {b}
      fi
  od
; x := 'the unique element of V'
{S.x}
```

We often encounter situations in which set W is $[0..N]$. In that case V may be represented by two integers a and b, $0 \leq a \leq b \leq N$, such that

106   Searching

$V = [a..b]$
$|V| \neq 1$ corresponds to $a \neq b$
$V := V \setminus \{a\}$ corresponds to $a := a + 1$
$V := V \setminus \{b\}$ corresponds to $b := b - 1$

and the program may be encoded as

Searching by Elimination (1)

$$\{(\exists i : 0 \leq i \leq N : S.i)\}$$
$$a, b := 0, N$$
$$; \mathbf{do}\ a \neq b$$
$$\quad \to \mathbf{if}\ \neg S.a \lor S.b \to a := a + 1$$
$$\quad \quad [\!]\ \neg S.b \lor S.a \to b := b - 1$$
$$\quad \mathbf{fi}$$
$$\mathbf{od}$$
$$; x := a$$
$$\{S.x\}$$

Our first application of searching by elimination is the derivation of a program that satisfies

$$[\![\ \mathbf{con}\ N : \mathrm{int}\ \{N \geq 0\};\ f : \mathbf{array}\ [0..N]\ \mathbf{of}\ \mathrm{int};$$
$$\mathbf{var}\ x : \mathrm{int};$$
$$maxlocation$$
$$\{0 \leq x \leq N \land f.x = (\mathbf{max}\ i : 0 \leq i \leq N : f.i)\}$$
$$]\!].$$

The post-condition may be rewritten as

$$0 \leq x \leq N \land (\forall i : 0 \leq i \leq N : f.i \leq f.x)$$

In order to use Searching by Elimination we define S by

$$S.x \equiv (\forall i : 0 \leq i \leq N : f.i \leq f.x)$$

Then

$\quad\quad \neg S.a \vee S.b$
$\equiv \quad \{\text{predicate calculus}\}$
$\quad\quad S.a \Rightarrow S.b$
$\equiv \quad \{\text{definition of } S\}$
$\quad\quad (\forall i : 0 \leq i \leq N : f.i \leq f.a) \Rightarrow (\forall i : 0 \leq i \leq N : f.i \leq f.b)$
$\Leftarrow \quad \{\text{transitivity of } \leq\}$
$\quad\quad f.a \leq f.b$

Hence, $f.a \leq f.b \Rightarrow \neg S.a \vee S.b$ and, by symmetry, $f.b \leq f.a \Rightarrow \neg S.b \vee S.a$ as well. This leads to the following solution to *maxlocation*

$\quad$|[**var** a, b : int;
$\quad\quad a, b := 0, N$
$\quad\quad$; **do** $a \neq b$
$\quad\quad\quad \rightarrow$ **if** $f.a \leq f.b \rightarrow a := a + 1$
$\quad\quad\quad\quad$ [] $f.b \leq f.a \rightarrow b := b - 1$
$\quad\quad\quad$ **fi**
$\quad\quad$ **od**
$\quad\quad$; $x := a$
$\quad$]|
$\quad \{0 \leq x \leq N \wedge f.x = (\mathbf{max}\, i : 0 \leq i \leq N : f.i)\}$

Our second example is known as the *celebrity problem*. It is described as follows. Among $N+1$ persons, a celebrity is someone who is known by everyone, but does not know anyone. This relation between persons is represented by a boolean matrix k:

$\quad k.i.j \equiv$ person i knows person j

Knowing that a celebrity exists among these persons, one is asked to determine such a celebrity. A formal specification is

$\quad$|[**con** N : int $\{N \geq 0\}$; k : **array** $[0..N] \times [0..N]$ **of** bool;
$\quad \{(\exists i : 0 \leq i \leq N : (\forall j : j \neq i : k.j.i \wedge \neg k.i.j))\}$
$\quad$ **var** x : int;
$\quad\quad$ *celebrity*
$\quad \{0 \leq x \leq N \wedge (\forall j : j \neq x : k.j.x \wedge \neg k.x.j))\}$
$\quad$]|.

We choose $S.x \equiv (\forall j : j \neq x : k.j.x \land \neg k.x.j)$ and we derive

$\quad \neg S.a \lor S.b$
$\Leftarrow \quad \{\text{predicate calculus}\}$
$\quad \neg S.a$
$\equiv \quad \{\text{definition of } S\}$
$\quad \neg(\forall j : j \neq a : k.j.a \land \neg k.a.j)$
$\equiv \quad \{\text{De Morgan}\}$
$\quad (\exists j : j \neq a : \neg k.j.a \lor k.a.j)$
$\Leftarrow \quad \{b \neq a\}$
$\quad \neg k.b.a \lor k.a.b$

By symmetry, $\neg S.b \Leftarrow \neg k.a.b \lor k.b.a$. Since $k.a.b \lor \neg k.a.b \equiv$ true, we strengthen the guards slightly, thereby destroying the symmetry, and we obtain as solution

$\|[\textbf{var } a, b : \text{int};$
$\quad a, b := 0, N$
$\quad ; \textbf{do } a \neq b$
$\qquad \rightarrow \textbf{if } k.a.b \rightarrow a := a+1$
$\qquad \quad [\!] \ \neg k.a.b \rightarrow b := b-1$
$\qquad \textbf{fi}$
$\quad \textbf{od}$
$\quad ; x := a$
$]\!|.$

Exercises

0. Derive a program that non-deterministically computes a number in the range $[0..N]$, $N \geq 0$.

1. Derive from general program scheme (0) a scheme for which $W = [0..N]$ and V is represented by integers a and b such that $0 \leq a < b \leq N+1$ and $V = \{a\} \cup [b..N]$.

2. What changes have to be made to the program schemes such that they satisfy

    pre-condition $\quad W \neq \emptyset$
    post-condition $\quad S \neq \emptyset \Rightarrow S.x$

3. Solve the bounded linear search problem of Section 6.2 by application of Searching by Elimination.

4. The *starting pit location* problem is stated as follows. There are $N+1$ pits located along a circular race-track. The pits are numbered clockwise from 0 up to and including N. At pit i, there are $p.i$ gallons of petrol available. To race from pit i to its clockwise neighbour one needs $q.i$ gallons of petrol. One is asked to determine a pit from which it is possible to race a complete lap, starting with an empty fuel tank. To guarantee the existence of such a starting pit it is given that

$$(\Sigma i : 0 \leq i \leq N : p.i) = (\Sigma i : 0 \leq i \leq N : q.i)$$

A formal specification of the problem is

$\lVert\,$ **con** $N :$ int $\{N \geq 0\}$; $p, q :$ **array** $[0..N]$ **of** int;
$\{(\Sigma i : 0 \leq i \leq N : p.i) = (\Sigma i : 0 \leq i \leq N : q.i)\}$
var $x :$ int;
   starting pit location
$\{0 \leq x \leq N \land (\forall i : 0 \leq i \leq N : D.x.i \geq 0)\}$
$\rVert,$

where $D.i.j$ is the difference of the number of gallons provided and the number of gallons needed, when racing from pit i to pit j in clockwise direction:

$D.i.j = (\Sigma k : k$ from i up to and not including j in clockwise direction $: p.k - q.k)$

Chapter 7

Segment Problems

7.0 Introduction

In this chapter we illustrate programming by so-called segment problems. Such problems involve the computation of a longest or shortest segment that satisfies a certain predicate, usually defined in terms of a given array. Many attempts have been made (and are still made) to classify these problems with respect to the predicates that define the segments one is interested in. In this chapter we do not classify these problems nor do we provide general program schemes that can be applied to all kinds of segment problems. Of course, some general aspects of this type of problem will emerge during our treatment.

The purpose of this chapter is to show *how* problems may be solved, what decisions are made in the derivations and which properties play a specific role. The techniques used in this chapter are applicable to other classes of programming problems as well.

In Chapter 8 we apply a technique called Slope Search to segment problems. That technique yields another way in which these problems may be solved.

7.1 Longest segments

Let $N \geq 0$ and let $X[0..N)$ be an integer array. We are interested in the length of a longest subsegment $[p..q)$ of $[0..N)$ that satisfies a certain predicate defined in terms of X. Examples of such predicates are

$(\forall i : p \leq i < q : X.i = 0)$	all elements are zero,
$(\forall i : p \leq i < q : X.p \leq X.i)$	the segment is left-minimal,
$(\# i : p \leq i < q : X.i = 0) \leq 10$	the segment contains at most 10 zeros,

$(\forall i, j : p \leq i < j < q : X.i \neq X.j)$ all values are different.

In the following sections we solve these problems. Each of them has its own characteristics.

7.1.0 All zeros

As our first example we solve the problem of determining the length of a longest segment of $X[0..N)$ that contains zeros only. It is about the simplest longest segment problem one can imagine and, hence, it is very well suited to illustrating the calculations that are typical for this kind of problem. A formal specification of this problem is

$\lVert$ **con** N : int $\{N \geq 0\}$; X : **array** $[0..N)$ **of** int;
  var r : int;
  all zeros
  $\{r = (\mathbf{max}\, p, q : 0 \leq p \leq q \leq N \wedge (\forall i : p \leq i < q : X.i = 0) : q{-}p)\}$
$\rVert$.

Our first step is the introduction of a name for $(\forall i : p \leq i < q : X.i = 0)$. This does not only abbreviate the post-condition, but, more importantly, it enables us to find out which parts of the derivation are independent of the specific form of the predicate. For $0 \leq p \leq q \leq N$ we define $\mathcal{A}.p.q$ by

$\mathcal{A}.p.q \equiv (\forall i : p \leq i < q : X.i = 0)$

Post-condition R may then be written as

$R: \ r = (\mathbf{max}\, p, q : 0 \leq p \leq q \leq N \wedge \mathcal{A}.p.q : q{-}p)$

What can be said about predicate $\mathcal{A}$? Its term, $X.i = 0$, does not depend on p or q. It holds for empty segments, i.e.,

(0) $\mathcal{A}.n.n$ for $0 \leq n \leq N$ \hfill ($\mathcal{A}$ holds for empty segments)

Furthermore, $\mathcal{A}$ is *prefix-closed*, i.e., if a segment satisfies $\mathcal{A}$ then all prefixes of that segment satisfy $\mathcal{A}$ as well. More formally,

(1) $\mathcal{A}.p.q \Rightarrow (\forall i : p \leq i \leq q : \mathcal{A}.p.i)$ for $0 \leq p \leq q \leq N$ \hfill ($\mathcal{A}$ is prefix-closed)

and $\mathcal{A}$ is *postfix-closed*:

(2) $\mathcal{A}.p.q \Rightarrow (\forall i : p \leq i \leq q : \mathcal{A}.i.q)$ for $0 \leq p \leq q \leq N$ \hfill ($\mathcal{A}$ is postfix-closed)

Since the term, $X.i = 0$, in $\mathcal{A}$ neither depends on p nor on q, it does not matter whether we replace in R the constant 0 or the constant N by a variable. We propose as invariants P_0 and P_1 defined by

$P_0: \quad r = (\mathbf{max}\, p, q : 0 \leq p \leq q \leq n \wedge \mathcal{A}.p.q : q-p)$

and

$P_1: \quad 0 \leq n \leq N$

For the initialization, we derive

$\quad\quad (\mathbf{max}\, p, q : 0 \leq p \leq q \leq 0 \wedge \mathcal{A}.p.q : q-p)$
$= \quad \{\text{calculus}\}$
$\quad\quad (\mathbf{max}\, p, q : p = 0 \wedge q = 0 \wedge \mathcal{A}.p.q : q-p)$
$= \quad \{\mathcal{A}.0.0,\ \text{cf. (0)}\}$
$\quad\quad 0$

from which we infer that $P_0 \wedge P_1$ is initialized by $n, r := 0, 0$. Note that we used (0). For an increase of n by 1 we derive, assuming $P_0 \wedge P_1 \wedge n \neq N$,

$\quad\quad (\mathbf{max}\, p, q : 0 \leq p \leq q \leq n{+}1 \wedge \mathcal{A}.p.q : q-p)$
$= \quad \{\text{split off } q = n{+}1\}$
$\quad\quad (\mathbf{max}\, p, q : 0 \leq p \leq q \leq n \wedge \mathcal{A}.p.q : q-p)$
$\quad\quad \mathbf{max}\, (\mathbf{max}\, p : 0 \leq p \leq n{+}1 \wedge \mathcal{A}.p.(n{+}1) : n{+}1-p)$
$= \quad \{P_0\}$
$\quad\quad r\ \mathbf{max}\, (\mathbf{max}\, p : 0 \leq p \leq n{+}1 \wedge \mathcal{A}.p.(n{+}1) : n{+}1-p)$
$= \quad \{+ \text{ distributes over } \mathbf{max} \text{ for a non-empty range, } \mathcal{A}.(n{+}1).(n{+}1),\ \text{cf. (0)}\}$
$\quad\quad r\ \mathbf{max}\, (n+1 + (\mathbf{max}\, p : 0 \leq p \leq n{+}1 \wedge \mathcal{A}.p.(n{+}1) : -p)$
$= \quad \{\text{property of } \mathbf{max} \text{ and } \mathbf{min}\}$
$\quad\quad r\ \mathbf{max}\, (n+1 - (\mathbf{min}\, p : 0 \leq p \leq n{+}1 \wedge \mathcal{A}.p.(n{+}1) : p))$

leading to the introduction of integer variable s and accompanying invariant

$Q: \quad s = (\mathbf{min}\, p : 0 \leq p \leq n \wedge \mathcal{A}.p.n : p)$

(Why is s not defined as $s = (\mathbf{min}\, p : 0 \leq p \leq n{+}1 \wedge \mathcal{A}.p.(n{+}1) : p)$?) From

$\quad\quad (\mathbf{min}\, p : 0 \leq p \leq 0 \wedge \mathcal{A}.p.0 : p) = 0$

we infer that s should be initialized at zero and we obtain a program of the following form.

$$
\begin{aligned}
&\{N \geq 0 \land (\forall n : 0 \leq n \leq N : \mathcal{A}.n.n)\} \\
&n, r, s := 0, 0, 0 \\
&\{\text{invariant: } P_0 \land P_1 \land Q, \text{ bound: } N - n\} \\
&; \textbf{do } n \neq N \\
&\quad \rightarrow \text{ 'establish } Q(n := n{+}1)\text{'} \\
&\quad\quad ; r := r \max(n{+}1{-}s) \\
&\quad\quad ; n := n{+}1 \\
&\textbf{od} \\
&\{r = (\max p, q : 0 \leq p \leq q \leq N \land \mathcal{A}.p.q : q{-}p)\}
\end{aligned}
$$

This scheme leaves 'establish $Q(n := n{+}1)$' as a subproblem. Since $\mathcal{A}$ holds for empty segments, the range of the quantification in Q is non-empty and Q can be written as the conjunction of Q_0, Q_1, and Q_2, defined as

$Q_0: \ 0 \leq s \leq n$

$Q_1: \ \mathcal{A}.s.n$

$Q_2: \ (\forall p : 0 \leq p < s : \neg \mathcal{A}.p.n)$

Since $\mathcal{A}$ is prefix-closed, we have $\neg \mathcal{A}.p.n \Rightarrow \neg \mathcal{A}.p.(n{+}1)$ for $0 \leq p < n$, and, hence,

$\quad Q_2 \Rightarrow Q_2(n := n{+}1)$

We have $Q_0 \Rightarrow Q_0(n := n{+}1)$ as well and we conclude

$\quad Q_0 \land Q_2 \land \mathcal{A}.s.(n{+}1) \Rightarrow Q(n := n{+}1)$

The fact that $Q_2(n := n{+}1)$ is implied by Q_2 has another consequence. From

$\quad Q_2(n := n{+}1) \equiv (\forall p : 0 \leq p < s : \neg \mathcal{A}.p.(n{+}1))$

we infer

$\quad Q_2 \Rightarrow (\min p : 0 \leq p \leq n{+}1 \land \mathcal{A}.p.(n{+}1) : p) \geq s$

i.e., only values p for which $s \leq p \leq n+1$ have to be investigated. For $p = n+1$ we know that $\mathcal{A}.p.(n+1)$ holds, so we usually start our investigations with the calculation of $\mathcal{A}.p.(n+1)$ for $s \leq p \leq n$.

We return to *all zeros*, for which $\mathcal{A}.p.q \equiv (\forall i : p \leq i < q : X.i = 0)$, and we compute $\mathcal{A}.p.(n+1)$ for $s \leq p \leq n$:

$\quad \mathcal{A}.p.(n+1)$
$\equiv \quad \{\text{definition of } \mathcal{A}\}$
$\quad (\forall i : p \leq i < n+1 : X.i = 0)$
$\equiv \quad \{\text{split off } i = n,\, p \leq n\}$
$\quad (\forall i : p \leq i < n : X.i = 0) \wedge X.n = 0$
$\equiv \quad \{\text{definition of } \mathcal{A}\}$
$\quad \mathcal{A}.p.n \wedge X.n = 0$

Hence,

$$Q \wedge X.n = 0 \Rightarrow Q(n := n+1)$$

and

$$X.n \neq 0 \Rightarrow (\forall p : s \leq p \leq n : \neg \mathcal{A}.p.(n+1))$$

from which we infer, since $\mathcal{A}.(n+1).(n+1)$ holds

$$X.n \neq 0 \Rightarrow Q(n := n+1)(s := n+1)$$

This leads to the following solution to *all zeros*:

$\|[\,\textbf{var } n, s : \text{int};$
$\quad n, r, s := 0, 0, 0$
$\quad ; \textbf{do } n \neq N$
$\quad\quad \rightarrow \textbf{if } X.n = 0 \rightarrow \textbf{skip}$
$\quad\quad\quad [\!]\ X.n \neq 0 \rightarrow s := n+1$
$\quad\quad \textbf{fi}$
$\quad\quad ; r := r \max (n+1-s)$
$\quad\quad ; n := n+1$
$\quad \textbf{od}$
$]\!|.$

Note that we did not use the postfix-closedness of $\mathcal{A}$.

7.1.1 Left-minimal segments

As another example of the approach outlined in the previous section, we consider the problem of the computation of the length of a longest segment that is left-minimal. Its formal specification is

$$\begin{array}{l} \|[\, \mathbf{con}\ N : \mathbf{int}\ \{N \geq 0\};\ X : \mathbf{array}\ [0..N)\ \mathbf{of\ int}; \\ \quad \mathbf{var}\ r : \mathbf{int}; \\ \quad S \\ \quad \{r = (\mathbf{max}\, p, q : 0 \leq p \leq q \leq N \land (\forall i : p \leq i < q : X.p \leq X.i) : q{-}p)\} \\ \,]\!|. \end{array}$$

As before, we start with the introduction of $\mathcal{A}$ and define for $0 \leq p \leq q \leq N$

$$\mathcal{A}.p.q \equiv (\forall i : p \leq i < q : X.p \leq X.i)$$

Evidently, the term in $\mathcal{A}.p.q$ depends on p and does not depend on q. However, the following properties of $\mathcal{A}.p.q$ do hold:

(0) $\quad \mathcal{A}.n.n \quad$ for $0 \leq n \leq N \qquad\qquad$ ($\mathcal{A}$ holds for empty segments)

and

(1) $\quad \mathcal{A}.p.q \Rightarrow (\forall i : p \leq i \leq q : \mathcal{A}.p.i) \quad$ for $0 \leq p \leq N \quad$ ($\mathcal{A}$ is prefix-closed)

But $\mathcal{A}$ is not postfix-closed and the derivation of a program based on a replacement of the constant 0 by a variable is quite difficult, as the reader may verify. As in the previous section we define P_0, P_1, and Q (the conjunction of Q_0, Q_1, and Q_2) as

$P_0:\quad r = (\mathbf{max}\, p, q : 0 \leq p \leq q \leq n \land \mathcal{A}.p.q : q{-}p)$
$P_1:\quad 0 \leq n \leq N$
$Q_0:\quad 0 \leq s \leq n$
$Q_1:\quad \mathcal{A}.s.n$
$Q_2:\quad (\forall p : 0 \leq p < s : \neg \mathcal{A}.p.n)$

Since $\mathcal{A}$ is prefix-closed, we have, as before,

$$Q_0 \land Q_2 \land \mathcal{A}.s.(n{+}1) \Rightarrow Q(n := n{+}1)$$

We derive, assuming $Q \land 0 \leq n < N$, for $s \leq p \leq n$

Segment Problems

$$\mathcal{A}.p.(n+1)$$
$\equiv$ { definition of $\mathcal{A}$ }
$$(\forall i : p \leq i < n+1 : X.p \leq X.i)$$
$\equiv$ { split off $i = n$, $p \leq n < n+1$ }
$$(\forall i : p \leq i < n : X.p \leq X.i) \land X.p \leq X.n$$
$\equiv$ { definition of $\mathcal{A}$ }
$$\mathcal{A}.p.n \land X.p \leq X.n$$

hence,

$$Q \land X.s \leq X.n \Rightarrow Q(n := n+1)$$

When $X.n < X.s$, we have, starting with the last line of the derivation above,

$$\mathcal{A}.p.n \land X.p \leq X.n$$
$\Rightarrow$ { $X.n < X.s$ }
$$X.p < X.s$$
$\equiv$ { Q_1, definition of $\mathcal{A}.s.n$ }
$$X.p < X.s \land (\forall i : s \leq i < n : X.s \leq X.i)$$
$\equiv$ { $s \leq p \leq n$, $X.n < X.s$ }
$$p = n$$

from which we infer

$$Q \land X.s > X.n \Rightarrow Q(n := n+1)(s := n)$$

It is now easy to code the program:

```
‖[ var n, s : int;
    n, r, s := 0, 0, 0
  ; do n ≠ N
      → if X.s ≤ X.n  → skip
        ▯ X.s > X.n  → s := n
        fi
      ; r := r max (n+1−s)
      ; n := n+1
    od
 ]‖.
```

7.1.2 At most ten zeros

In this section we discuss a variation on the previous approach. Reconsider the program scheme of Section 7.1.0 in which 'establish $Q(n := n+1)$' has to be refined. We assume that $\mathcal{A}$ is prefix-closed and holds for empty segments.

The pre-condition of 'establish $Q(n := n+1)$' is Q, the conjunction of

$Q_0: \ 0 \leq s \leq n$
$Q_1: \ \mathcal{A}.s.n$
$Q_2: \ (\forall p: 0 \leq p < s: \neg \mathcal{A}.p.n)$

As stated before, we have $Q_0 \Rightarrow Q_0(n := n+1)$ and, since $\mathcal{A}$ is prefix-closed, we have $Q_2 \Rightarrow Q_2(n := n+1)$ as well. Thus, Q implies

$$0 \leq s \leq n+1 \land (\forall p: 0 \leq p < s: \neg \mathcal{A}.p.(n+1))$$

which may be used as invariant for a repetition with guard $\neg \mathcal{A}.s.(n+1)$ and bound function $n+1-s$ (the invariance of $s \leq n+1$ follows from $\mathcal{A}.(n+1).(n+1)$). Substitution of this linear search in the program scheme results in the program below.

$n, r, s := 0, 0, 0$
$; \mathbf{do}\ n \neq N$
$\quad \to\ \mathbf{do}\ \neg \mathcal{A}.s.(n+1) \to s := s+1\ \mathbf{od}$
$\quad\ ; r := r \max (n+1-s)$
$\quad\ ; n := n+1$
$\mathbf{od}$
$\{r = (\max p, q : 0 \leq p \leq q \leq N \land \mathcal{A}.p.q : q-p)\}$

To determine the time complexity of this 'program', we add ghost variable t:

$n, r, s := 0, 0, 0\ ; t := 0$
$; \mathbf{do}\ n \neq N$
$\quad \to\ \mathbf{do}\ \neg \mathcal{A}.s.(n+1) \to s := s+1\ ; t := t+1\ \mathbf{od}$
$\quad\ ; r := r \max (n+1-s)$
$\quad\ ; n := n+1\ ; t := t+1$
$\mathbf{od}$

Variable t is initialized at 0 and is incremented in each step of the outer repetition and in each step of the inner repetition. Hence, the final value of t is a good measure for the time complexity of the program. When s is incremented by 1 then t is incremented by 1 and the same holds for n and t. Thus, the value of $t - s - n$ is not changed during execution of the program. Initially this value is zero. Thus,

$$t = s + n$$

is an invariant of the program and holds initially. Since $s \leq n \leq N$ is also an invariant of the repetitions, we have

$$t \leq 2N$$

from which we conclude that the time complexity is $\mathcal{O}(N)$. In this discussion we have assumed that $\neg \mathcal{A}.s.(n+1)$ can be evaluated in constant time. If this is not the case, refinement of this expression may lead to a final program that is not linear at all.

We use this scheme for the derivation of a program for the computation of the length of a longest segment that contains at most 10 zeros. Its formal specification is

$\|[\,\textbf{con}\ N : \text{int}\ \{N \geq 0\};\ X : \textbf{array}\ [0..N)\ \textbf{of}\ \text{int};$
$\quad \textbf{var}\ r : \text{int};$
$\quad S$
$\quad \{r = (\max p, q : 0 \leq p \leq q \leq N \wedge (\#i : p \leq i < q : X.i = 0) \leq 10 : q - p)\}$
$\,]\|.$

With $\mathcal{A}.p.q$ defined as $(\#i : p \leq i < q : X.i = 0) \leq 10$, we have for $0 \leq s \leq n < N$

$\quad \neg \mathcal{A}.s.(n+1)$
$\equiv \quad \{\text{definition of } \mathcal{A}\}$
$\quad (\#i : s \leq i < n+1 : X.i = 0) > 10$

We introduce variable c and accompanying invariant Q' defined by

$Q' :\ c = (\#i : s \leq i < n : X.i = 0)$

Provided that $Q'(n := n+1)$, we may replace $\neg \mathcal{A}.s.(n+1)$ by $c > 10$.
From $(\#i : 0 \leq i < 0 : X.i = 0) = 0$ we conclude that c should be initialized at 0. We obtain the following $\mathcal{O}(N)$ solution.

Longest segments

```
‖[ var n, s, c : int;
    n, r, s, c := 0, 0, 0, 0
  ; do n ≠ N
       →  if X.n = 0 → c := c+1
          ▯ X.n ≠ 0 → skip
          fi
        {c = (#i : s ≤ i < n+1 : X.i = 0)}
        ; do c > 10
            →  if X.s = 0 → c := c−1
               ▯ X.s ≠ 0 → skip
               fi
             ; s := s+1
          od
        ; r := r max (n+1−s)
        ; n := n+1
     od
]‖.
```

The derivations of the selection statements in this program are straightforward and have been left to the reader.

7.1.3 All elements different

Our final example is a problem for which we derive a quadratic solution, despite the fact that the defining predicate holds for empty segments, is prefix-closed and is postfix-closed. The problem is to determine for a sequence X, the length of a longest segment in which all values are different. (Using more sophisticated data structures an $\mathcal{O}(N \log N)$ solution to this problem can be derived. However, the treatment of such data structures is beyond the scope of this book.) A formal specification of the problem is

```
‖[ con N : int {N ≥ 0}; X : array [0..N) of int;
   var r : int;
     S
   {r = (max p, q : 0 ≤ p ≤ q ≤ N ∧ A.p.q : q−p)}
]‖,
```

where for $0 \leq p \leq q \leq N$

$$\mathcal{A}.p.q \equiv (\forall i, j : p \leq i < j < q : X.i \neq X.j)$$

120 Segment Problems

Verify that $\mathcal{A}$ is prefix-closed, postfix-closed and holds for empty segments. We define P_0, P_1 and Q as before and we consider 'establish $Q(n := n{+}1)$'. Its pre-condition is

Q_0 : $0 \leq s \leq n$
Q_1 : $\mathcal{A}.s.n$
Q_2 : $(\forall p : 0 \leq p < s : \neg \mathcal{A}.p.n)$

Since $\mathcal{A}$ is prefix-closed, Q_2 implies $(\forall p : 0 \leq p < s : \neg \mathcal{A}.p.(n{+}1))$. Furthermore,

$\quad \mathcal{A}.s.(n{+}1)$
$\equiv \quad \{\text{definition of } \mathcal{A}\}$
$\quad (\forall i, j : s \leq i < j < n{+}1 : X.i \neq X, j)$
$\equiv \quad \{\text{split off } j = n\}$
$\quad (\forall i, j : s \leq i < j < n : X.i \neq X, j) \wedge (\forall i : s \leq i < n : X.i \neq X.n)$
$\equiv \quad \{\text{definition of } \mathcal{A}\}$
$\quad \mathcal{A}.s.n \wedge (\forall i : s \leq i < n : X.i \neq X.n)$

Hence, $Q(n := n{+}1)$ is the conjunction of the following four predicates:

$0 \leq s \leq n{+}1$
$\mathcal{A}.s.n$
$(\forall i : s \leq i < n : X.i \neq X.n)$
$(\forall p : 0 \leq p < s : \neg \mathcal{A}.p.(n{+}1))$

The first, second, and last conjunct are implied by Q and the third conjunct holds for $s = n$. As we did for the Bounded Linear Search, we introduce a fresh variable (h) and we define invariant U as the conjunction of U_0, U_1, U_2, and U_3:

U_0 : $s \leq h \leq n{+}1$
U_1 : $\mathcal{A}.s.n$
U_2 : $(\forall i : h \leq i < n : X.i \neq X.n)$
U_3 : $(\forall p : 0 \leq p < s : \neg \mathcal{A}.p.(n{+}1))$

These are initialized by $h := n$. As guard we choose, of course, $h \neq s$. Since $\mathcal{A}$ is postfix-closed, $s := h$ maintains U_1. A straightforward calculation yields

$\quad U \wedge h \neq s \wedge X.(h{-}1) \neq X.n \Rightarrow U(h := h{-}1)$
$\quad U \wedge h \neq s \wedge X.(h{-}1) = X.n \Rightarrow U(s := h)$

and we obtain as solution:

$$\begin{array}{l}
\|[\ \mathbf{var}\ n,s:\mathrm{int}; \\
\quad n,r,s := 0,0,0 \\
\quad ;\mathbf{do}\ n \neq N \\
\qquad \rightarrow\ \|[\ \mathbf{var}\ h:\mathrm{int}; \\
\qquad\qquad h := n \\
\qquad\qquad ;\mathbf{do}\ h \neq s \\
\qquad\qquad\qquad \rightarrow \mathbf{if}\ X.(h{-}1) \neq X.n\ \rightarrow h := h{-}1 \\
\qquad\qquad\qquad \ [\!]\ X.(h{-}1) = X.n\ \rightarrow s := h \\
\qquad\qquad\qquad \mathbf{fi} \\
\qquad\qquad \mathbf{od} \\
\qquad \ ]\!| \\
\qquad ;r := r\ \mathbf{max}\ (n{+}1{-}s) \\
\qquad ;n := n{+}1 \\
\quad \mathbf{od} \\
]\!|.
\end{array}$$

This program has time complexity $\mathcal{O}(N^2)$.

Exercises

Derive an $\mathcal{O}(N)$ solution to

$$\begin{array}{l}
\|[\ \mathbf{con}\ N:\mathrm{int}\ \{N \geq 1\};\ X:\mathbf{array}\ [0..N)\ \mathbf{of}\ \mathrm{int}; \\
\quad \mathbf{var}\ r:\mathrm{int}; \\
\qquad S \\
\quad \{r = (\mathbf{max}\,p,q:0 \leq p \leq q \leq N\ \wedge\ \mathcal{A}.p.q: q{-}p)\} \\
]\!|.
\end{array}$$

where $\mathcal{A}.p.q$ is defined as

0. $(\forall i,j : p \leq i \leq j < q : X.i = X.j)$

1. $X[p..q)$ is increasing.

2. $(\forall i : p \leq i < q : X.i \leq X.(q{-}1))$

3. $(\#i : p \leq i < q : X.i = 0) = 2$

4. The product of any two elements of $X[p..q)$ is at least zero.

5. $X[p..q)$ is monotonic (i.e. ascending or descending).

6. $(\Sigma i : p \leq i < q : X.i) \bmod 3 = 0$

The following exercises are more complicated and may be skipped at first reading.

7. $X[p..q)$ contains at most two distinct values.

8. $(\forall i : p \leq i < q : |X.p| \geq X.i)$

9. $(\forall i, j : p \leq i \leq j < q : 0 \leq X.i - X.j \leq 1)$

10. $(\forall i, j : p \leq i \leq j < q : |X.i - X.j| \leq 1)$

11. $(\forall i, j : p \leq i \leq j < q : X.i - X.j \leq 1)$

7.2 Shortest segments

We present only one example of a shortest segment problem. In this section we show that the approach for longest segment problems may lead to rather complicated solutions when applied to a shortest segment problem. This section may be skipped at first reading: in Chapter 8 the same problem is solved in a much better way.

The problem is to compute the length of a shortest segment that contains at least two zeros. It is formally specified as

$$[\![\textbf{con } N : \text{int } \{N \geq 0\}; X : \textbf{array } [0..N) \textbf{ of } \text{int};$$
$$\textbf{var } r : \text{int};$$
$$S$$
$$\{r = (\textbf{min } p, q : 0 \leq p \leq q \leq N \wedge \mathcal{A}.p.q : q - p)\}$$
$$]\!].$$

where, for $0 \leq p \leq q \leq N$,

$$\mathcal{A}.p.q \equiv (\# i : p \leq i < q : X.i = 0) \geq 2$$

It is not known whether segments satisfying $\mathcal{A}$ exist. When, for instance, $X[0..N)$ does not contain a zero then the post-condition is $r = \infty$.

Predicate $\mathcal{A}$ does not hold for empty segments, is not prefix-closed and not postfix-closed. However, $\neg \mathcal{A}$, defined by $(\neg \mathcal{A}).p.q \equiv \neg(\mathcal{A}.p.q)$, does have these properties.

Shortest segments

The duality between longest and shortest segment problems is studied in more detail in Chapter 8.

We may try to derive a program along the same lines as we did for longest segments, by defining

P_0 : $r = (\min p, q : 0 \leq p \leq q \leq n \wedge \mathcal{A}.p.q : q{-}p)$

P_1 : $0 \leq n \leq N$

Q : $s = (\max p : 0 \leq p \leq n \wedge \mathcal{A}.p.n : p)$

Redoing all calculations of Section 7.1.0 with **max** replaced by **min** and vice versa does not work. The problem is that the ranges of the quantifications may be empty and, hence, no distribution of + over **min** can be applied. We conclude that if we want to stick to the approach of the previous sections, we should ensure that the ranges in the quantifications are non-empty. Then all results of the preceding sections may be used (with the replacements indicated above). Note that $\mathcal{A}.0.n$ guarantees that the ranges are non-empty. Thus, we arrive at the following program scheme:

> 'establish $P_0 \wedge P_1 \wedge Q \wedge \mathcal{A}.0.n$'
> {invariant: $P_0 \wedge P_1 \wedge Q \wedge \mathcal{A}.0.n$, bound: $N - n$}
> ; **do** $n \neq N$
> $\quad \to$ 'establish $Q(n := n{+}1)$'
> $\qquad ; r := r \min (n{+}1{-}s)$
> $\qquad ; n := n{+}1$
> **od**
> $\{r = (\min p, q : 0 \leq p \leq q \leq N \wedge \mathcal{A}.p.q : q{-}p)\}$

We postpone the discussion of 'establish $P_0 \wedge P_1 \wedge Q \wedge \mathcal{A}.0.n$' and we consider 'establish $Q(n := n{+}1)$' first. We derive

$\quad Q$
$\equiv \quad \{ \text{definition of } Q \}$
$\quad s = (\max p : 0 \leq p \leq n \wedge \mathcal{A}.p.n : p)$
$\equiv \quad \{ \mathcal{A}.0.n, \text{ hence, the range is non-empty} \}$
$\quad 0 \leq s \leq n \wedge \mathcal{A}.s.n \wedge (\forall p : s < p \leq n : \neg \mathcal{A}.p.n)$
$\equiv \quad \{ \text{definition of } \mathcal{A} \}$

$$\equiv \quad 0 \leq s \leq n \wedge (\#i : s \leq i < n : X.i = 0) \geq 2 \wedge (\#i : s < i < n : X.i = 0) < 2$$
$$\{\text{calculus}\}$$
$$0 \leq s < n \wedge X.s = 0 \wedge (\#i : s < i < n : X.i = 0) = 1$$

and, hence,

$$Q(n := n+1) \equiv 0 \leq s < n+1 \wedge X.s = 0 \wedge (\#i : s < i < n+1 : X.i = 0) = 1$$

Evidently

$$Q \wedge X.n \neq 0 \Rightarrow Q(n := n+1)$$

whereas

$$Q \wedge X.n = 0 \Rightarrow (\#i : s < i < n+1 : X.i = 0) = 2$$

In the latter case s should be replaced by the unique t, $s < t < n$, for which $X.t = 0$. This leads to the introduction of variable t with accompanying invariant Q' defined by

$$Q' : \quad s < t < n \wedge X.t = 0$$

Then

$$Q \wedge Q' \wedge X.n \neq 0 \Rightarrow X.s = 0 \wedge X.t = 0 \wedge (\#i : s < i < n+1 : X.i = 0) = 1$$

and

$$Q \wedge Q' \wedge X.n = 0 \Rightarrow X.t = 0 \wedge X.n = 0 \wedge (\#i : t < i < n+1 : X.i = 0) = 1$$

which yields for 'establish $Q(n := n+1)$'

if $X.n \neq 0 \rightarrow$ **skip** $[\!]\ X.n = 0 \rightarrow s, t := t, n$ **fi**

The only thing that is left to be done is 'establish $P_0 \wedge P_1 \wedge Q \wedge Q'$'. Let us summarize these invariants.

P_0 : $r = (\min p, q : 0 \leq p \leq q \leq n \wedge \mathcal{A}.p.q : q - p)$
P_1 : $0 \leq n \leq N$
Q : $s = (\max p : 0 \leq p \leq n \wedge \mathcal{A}.p.n : p)$
Q' : $s < t < n \wedge X.t = 0$

When $X[0..N)$ contains less than two zeros, these invariants cannot be established. Thus, we perform case analysis and we introduce integer variable c for which

$$c = (\#i : 0 \leq i < n : X.i = 0) \wedge c \leq 2 \wedge (c = 2 \vee n = N)$$

is the post-condition of a repetition. Its derivation is straightforward. When $c < 2$ then ∞ is assigned to r, otherwise P_1, Q, and Q' are initialized such that

$$n-s = (\min p, q : 0 \leq p \leq q \leq n \wedge \mathcal{A}.p.q : q-p)$$

Since a more elegant solution is derived in Chapter 8, we do not show the calculations, but merely present the resulting program:

$\|[$ **var** $n, c :$ int;
  $\quad n, c := 0, 0$
  $\quad ;$ **do** $n \neq N \wedge c \neq 2$
  $\qquad \rightarrow \quad$ **if** $X.n = 0 \rightarrow c := c+1 \;[\!]\; X.n \neq 0 \rightarrow$ skip **fi**
  $\qquad \quad ; n := n+1$
  $\quad$ **od**
  $\quad ;$ **if** $c < 2 \rightarrow r := \infty$
  $\quad \;[\!]\; c = 2$
  $\qquad \rightarrow \|[$ **var** $s, t :$ int;
  $\qquad\qquad s := 0 \,;$ **do** $X.s \neq 0 \rightarrow s := s+1$ **od**
  $\qquad\qquad ; t := s+1 \,;$ **do** $X.t \neq 0 \rightarrow t := t+1$ **od**
  $\qquad\qquad ; n := t+1$
  $\qquad\qquad ; r := n-s$
  $\qquad\qquad ;$ **do** $n \neq N$
  $\qquad\qquad\quad \rightarrow$ **if** $X.n \neq 0 \rightarrow$ skip $[\!]\; X.n = 0 \rightarrow s, t := t, n$ **fi**
  $\qquad\qquad\qquad ; r := r \min (n+1-s)$
  $\qquad\qquad\qquad ; n := n+1$
  $\qquad\qquad$ **od**
  $\qquad]\!|$
  $\quad$ **fi**
$]\!|.$

Exercises

0. Solve

$\lVert$ **con** N : int $\{N \geq 0\}$; X : **array** $[0..N)$ **of** int;
$\{(\forall i : 0 \leq i < N : 0 \leq X.i \leq 2)\}$
var r : int;
  S
$\{r = (\min p, q : 0 \leq p \leq q \leq N \land \mathcal{A}.p.q : q-p)\}$
$\rVert$.

where $\mathcal{A}.p.q$ is defined as

Values 0,1, and 2 occur in $X[p..q]$.

Chapter 8

Slope Search

8.0 Introduction

Slope Search, also known as *Saddleback Search*, is a technique which is applicable to a large class of problems that involve quantifications over two bound variables, i.e., over an area contained in $\mathcal{Z} \times \mathcal{Z}$. In most applications the term of such a quantification is a monotonic function of the bound variables, for instance, ascending in both variables or increasing in one variable and decreasing in the other variable. Examples are the longest and shortest segment problems discussed in Chapter 7. For these problems the term is $q - p$, which is an increasing function of q and a decreasing function of p.

In Section 8.1 we discuss the basic principle of the slope search and we provide various examples of its use. In Section 8.2 slope search is applied to segment problems.

8.1 The basic principle

Let M and N be natural numbers and let array $f : [0..M] \times [0..N] \to \mathcal{Z}$ be ascending in both arguments, i.e.,

$$(\forall i : 0 \leq i \leq M : (\forall j : 0 \leq j < N : f.i.j \leq f.i.(j+1)))$$
$$\land (\forall j : 0 \leq j \leq N : (\forall i : 0 \leq i < M : f.i.j \leq f.(i+1).j))$$

Assume that a value X occurs in f, i.e.,

$$(\exists i, j : 0 \leq i \leq M \land 0 \leq j \leq N : f.i.j = X)$$

We are asked to derive a program that establishes for integer variables a and b

$$0 \leq a \leq M \land 0 \leq b \leq N \land f.a.b = X$$

128   Slope Search

Array f is ascending in both arguments. Hence, f has its minimum in $(0,0)$ and its maximum in (M, N). Since X occurs in f, we have

$$f.0.0 \leq X \leq f.M.N$$

Having this information, it does not help much to inspect $f.0.0$ or $f.M.N$. Two other points of $[0..M] \times [0..N]$ are possible candidates for inspection: $(0, N)$ and $(M, 0)$. We consider $(0, N)$. Since f is ascending in its first argument, we have

$$f.0.N = (\min i : 0 \leq i \leq M : f.i.N)$$

hence,

$$f.0.N > X \;\Rightarrow\; (\forall i : 0 \leq i \leq M : f.i.N > X)$$

i.e., when $f.0.N > X$ then the search area may be reduced to $[0..M] \times [0..N-1]$. Since f is ascending in its second argument, we have

$$f.0.N = (\max j : 0 \leq j \leq N : f.0.j)$$

hence,

$$f.0.N < X \;\Rightarrow\; (\forall j : 0 \leq j \leq N : f.0.j < X)$$

i.e., when $f.0.N < X$ then the search area may be reduced to $[1..M] \times [0..N]$.

We formalize this discussion as follows. Let I and J be such that

$$0 \leq I \leq M \;\land\; 0 \leq J \leq N \;\land\; f.I.J = X$$

The 'search area' is characterized by $(I, J) \in [a..M] \times [0..b]$ or, equivalently, we choose as invariant for a repetition

$$P:\; 0 \leq a \leq I \;\land\; J \leq b \leq N$$

which is established by $a, b := 0, N$. The reduction of the search area in terms of P is given by the following derivations.

$$\quad f.a.b < X$$
$$\Rightarrow \quad \{\, f \text{ is ascending in its second argument, } J \leq b \,\}$$
$$\quad f.a.J < X$$
$$\Rightarrow \quad \{\, f.I.J = X \,\}$$
$$\quad a \neq I$$
$$\equiv \quad \{\, P, \text{ in particular, } a \leq I \,\}$$
$$\quad a+1 \leq I$$

and

$\quad\quad f.a.b > X$
$\Rightarrow\quad \{\,f\text{ is ascending in its first argument, } a \leq I\,\}$
$\quad\quad f.I.b > X$
$\Rightarrow\quad \{\,f.I.J = X\,\}$
$\quad\quad b \neq J$
$\equiv\quad \{\,P,\text{ in particular, } J \leq b\,\}$
$\quad\quad J \leq b-1$

We conclude

$$P \wedge f.a.b < X \Rightarrow P(a := a+1) \quad \text{and} \quad P \wedge f.a.b > X \Rightarrow P(b := b-1)$$

This yields the following solution:

$\quad a, b := 0, N\ \{\text{invariant: } P,\text{ bound: } N - a + b\}$
$\quad ;\mathbf{do}\ f.a.b < X \rightarrow a := a+1$
$\quad\ \ [\!]\ \ f.a.b > X \rightarrow b := b-1$
$\quad \mathbf{od}$
$\quad \{f.a.b = X\}$

This program has time complexity $\mathcal{O}(M+N)$. A similar program is obtained when we choose $(M, 0)$ as starting point.

An operational interpretation of this technique is the following. The three-dimensional surface $z = f.x.y$ has as lowest point $(0, 0, f.0.0)$ and as highest point $(M, N, f.M.N)$. Somewhere in between position X occurs. To find that position one should not start at a minimum or at a maximum, but somewhere in between, for instance, at $(0, N, f.0.N)$ or at $(M, 0, f.M.0)$, and move along the slope of the surface in such a way that position X is approximated as well as possible, i.e., by going down when the value is too high and by going up when the value is too low. Because of this interpretation, which will not be pursued any further, this technique is called Slope Search.

Note that the points where f attains its minimum or its maximum are not important. The other two points, that are either the maximum of a row and the minimum of a column, or the minimum of a row and the maximum of a column, are useful. When, for instance, f is ascending in its first argument and descending in its second argument, suitable invariants are $0 \leq a \leq I \wedge 0 \leq b \leq J$ or $I \leq a \leq M \wedge J \leq b \leq N$.

The reduction of the search area, i.e., the reduction of the problem to a smaller problem of the same form, usually leads to the introduction of a tail invariant. For the above program, we have

Slope Search

$$(\exists i, j : 0 \leq i \leq M \land 0 \leq j \leq N : f.i.j = X)$$
$$\equiv$$
$$(\exists i, j : a \leq i \leq M \land 0 \leq j \leq b : f.i.j = X)$$

as tail invariant. In the following sections we use tail invariants of this form.

8.1.0 Searching

In the previous section we solved the problem of searching for a value in a two-dimensional array, given that the value occurs in the array. In this section we consider the following problem: we are given integers M and N, $M \geq 0 \land N \geq 0$, and integer array $f[0..M] \times [0..N]$ such that f is ascending in both arguments. We are asked to determine whether value X occurs in f. A formal specification is

$\|[$ **con** M, N, X : int $\{M \geq 0 \land N \geq 0\}$; f : **array** $[0..M] \times [0..N]$ **of** int;
$\{f$ is ascending in both arguments$\}$
var r : bool;
$\quad S$
$\{r \equiv (\exists i, j : 0 \leq i < M \land 0 \leq j < N : f.i.j = X)\}$
$]\|.$

Following the strategy explained in the previous section, we define 'tail' $G.a.b$ for $0 \leq a \leq M \land 0 \leq b \leq N$ by

$$G.a.b \equiv (\exists i, j : a \leq i < M \land 0 \leq j < b : f.i.j = X)$$

In terms of G, the post-condition of the specification may be written as

$R : \quad r \equiv G.0.N$

We introduce integers a and b and define tail invariant P_0 by

$P_0 : \quad r \lor G.a.b \equiv G.0.N$

The bounds for a and b are specified by invariant P_1 :

$P_1 : \quad 0 \leq a \leq M \land 0 \leq b \leq N$

A proper initialization of $P_0 \land P_1$ is $a, b, r := 0, N,$ false. For $a = M \lor b = 0$ the range of the quantification in G is empty, hence,

$P_0 \wedge (a = M \vee b = 0)$
$\Rightarrow$ { definitions of P_0 and G }
$r \vee \text{false} \equiv G.0.N$
$\equiv$ { predicate calculus }
$r \equiv G.0.N$
$\equiv$ { definition of R }
R

Furthermore, when r is true, then $r \vee G.a.b \equiv r$, hence,

$r \vee G.a.b \equiv G.0.N$
$\equiv$ { $r \vee G.a.b \equiv r$ }
$r \equiv G.0.N$

and we conclude $P \wedge (a = M \vee b = 0 \vee r) \Rightarrow R$. Thus, we choose

$a \neq M \wedge b \neq 0 \wedge \neg r$

as guard of a repetition.

We investigate an increase of a by 1. Assuming $0 \leq a < M \wedge 0 < b \leq N$, then

$G.a.b$
$\equiv$ { definition of G }
$(\exists i, j : a \leq i < M \wedge 0 \leq j < b : f.i.j = X)$
$\equiv$ { split off $i = a$ }
$G.(a+1).b \vee (\exists j : 0 \leq j < b : f.a.j = X)$
$\equiv$ { f is ascending in its second argument, $0 \leq b-1$, assuming $f.a.(b-1) < X$ }
$G.(a+1).b \vee \text{false}$
$\equiv$ { predicate calculus }
$G.(a+1).b$

Hence,

$f.a.(b-1) < X \Rightarrow (G.a.b \equiv G.(a+1).b)$

Similarly, we have for a decrease of b by 1:

$\quad\quad G.a.b$
$\equiv\quad\quad\{\text{definition of } G\}$
$\quad\quad (\exists i,j : a \leq i < M \land 0 \leq j < b : f.i.j = X)$
$\equiv\quad\quad \{\text{split off } j = b{-}1\}$
$\quad\quad G.a.(b{-}1) \lor (\exists i : a \leq i < M : f.i.(b{-}1) = X)$
$\equiv\quad\quad \{f \text{ is ascending in its first argument, } a < M, \text{ assuming } f.a.(b{-}1) > X\}$
$\quad\quad G.a.(b{-}1) \lor \text{false}$
$\equiv\quad\quad \{\text{predicate calculus}\}$
$\quad\quad G.a.(b{-}1)$

Hence,

$$f.a.(b{-}1) > X \Rightarrow (G.a.b \equiv G.a.(b{-}1))$$

For the remaining case $f.a.(b{-}1) = X$, we derive for $0 \leq a < M \land 0 < b \leq N$

$\quad\quad P_0 \land f.a.(b{-}1) = X$
$\equiv\quad\quad \{\text{definition of } P_0\}$
$\quad\quad (r \lor G.a.b \equiv G.0.N) \land f.a.(b{-}1) = X$
$\Rightarrow\quad\quad \{\text{definition of } G\}$
$\quad\quad r \lor \text{true} \equiv G.0.N$
$\equiv\quad\quad \{\text{predicate calculus}\}$
$\quad\quad \text{true} \lor G.a.b \equiv G.0.N$
$\equiv\quad\quad \{\text{definition of } P_0\}$
$\quad\quad P_0(r := \text{true})$

These derivations lead to the following solution

$\|[\textbf{var } a, b : \text{int};$
$\quad\quad a, b, r := 0, N, \text{false } \{\text{invariant: } P_0 \land P_1, \text{bound: } M - a + b + \#.(\neg r)\}$
$\quad\quad ; \textbf{do } a \neq M \land b \neq 0 \land \neg r$
$\quad\quad\quad \rightarrow \textbf{if } f.a.(b{-}1) < X \rightarrow a := a+1$
$\quad\quad\quad\quad [\!] \ f.a.(b{-}1) > X \rightarrow b := b-1$
$\quad\quad\quad\quad [\!] \ f.a.(b{-}1) = X \rightarrow r := \text{true}$
$\quad\quad\quad \textbf{fi}$
$\quad\quad \textbf{od}$
$\,]\!|.$

This program has *optimal* time complexity $\mathcal{O}(M+N)$, which is proved as follows. Let $h[0..N]$ be an integer array, then a program for the computation of

$$(\exists i : 0 \leq i \leq N : h.i = X)$$

has at least time complexity $\mathcal{O}(N)$, since any correct program will inspect all $h.i$ in the case that X does not occur in h. Define array $f[0..N] \times [0..N]$ by

$$\begin{array}{ll} f.i.j = -\infty & \text{if } i+j < N \\ f.i.j = \infty & \text{if } i+j > N \\ f.i.j = h.i & \text{if } i+j = N \end{array}$$

Then f is ascending in both arguments and a correct program for the computation of

$$(\exists i, j : 0 \leq i \leq N \wedge 0 \leq j \leq N : f.i.j = X)$$

will inspect all $f.i.(N-i)$ in the case that X does not occur in f.

8.1.1 Decomposition in a sum of two squares

As our second example, we derive a program for the computation of the number of ways in which a natural number N can be written as the sum of two squares. We supply an annotated program together with its numbered derivations.

The first thing to do is to supply a formal specification:

$\|[\textbf{con } N : \text{int } \{N \geq 0\};$
$\quad \textbf{var } r : \text{int};$
$\quad S$
$\quad \{r = (\# x, y : 0 \leq x \leq y : x^2 + y^2 = N)\}$
$\,]\|.$

Since $x^2 + y^2$ is increasing in both arguments on the domain $0 \leq x \leq y$, we define $G.a.b$ as

$$G.a.b = (\# x, y : a \leq x \leq y \leq b : x^2 + y^2 = N)$$

and we choose as invariants

$P_0: \quad r + G.a.b = (\# x, y : 0 \leq x \leq y : x^2 + y^2 = N)$
$P_1: \quad 0 \leq a$

Slope Search

In the following proofs we present the calculations for a solution.

Proof 0

$\quad G.a.b$
$= \quad \{ \text{definition of } G \}$
$\quad (\# x, y : a \leq x \leq y \leq b : x^2 + y^2 = N)$
$= \quad \{ \text{provided } a > b \}$
$\quad 0$

Hence, $P_0 \wedge a > b$ implies the post-condition.

Proof 1

For the initialization, we derive for $0 \leq b$

$\quad G.0.b$
$= \quad \{ \text{definition of } G \}$
$\quad (\# x, y : 0 \leq x \leq y \leq b : x^2 + y^2 = N)$
$= \quad \{ \text{range split} \}$
$\quad (\# x, y : 0 \leq x \leq y : x^2 + y^2 = N) - (\# x, y : 0 \leq x \leq y \wedge y > b : x^2 + y^2 = N)$
$= \quad \{ \text{provided } b^2 \geq N,\ 0 \leq b \}$
$\quad (\# x, y : 0 \leq x \leq y : x^2 + y^2 = N)$

Hence,

$\quad r = 0 \wedge a = 0 \wedge 0 \leq b \wedge b^2 \geq N$
$\Rightarrow \quad \{ \text{see above} \}$
$\quad r + G.a.b = (\# x, y : 0 \leq x \leq y : x^2 + y^2 = N) \wedge 0 \leq a$
$\equiv \quad \{ \text{definitions of } P_0 \text{ and } P_1 \}$
$\quad P_0 \wedge P_1$

Proof 2

We investigate an increase of a by 1. For $0 \leq a \leq b$, we derive

$\quad G.a.b$
$= \quad \{ \text{definition of } G \}$
$\quad (\# x, y : a \leq x \leq y \leq b : x^2 + y^2 = N)$
$= \quad \{ \text{split off } x = a \}$

$$G.(a+1).b + (\# y : a \leq y \leq b : a^2 + y^2 = N)$$
$= \quad \{ a^2 + y^2 \text{ is increasing in } y, \, a \leq b \}$
$$\begin{cases} G.(a+1).b + 0 & \text{if } a^2 + b^2 < N \\ G.(a+1).b + 1 & \text{if } a^2 + b^2 = N \end{cases}$$

Proof 3

We investigate a decrease of b by 1. For $0 \leq a \leq b$, we derive

$G.a.b$
$= \quad \{ \text{definition of } G \}$
$(\# x, y : a \leq x \leq y \leq b : x^2 + y^2 = N)$
$= \quad \{ \text{split off } y = b \}$
$G.a.(b-1) + (\# x : a \leq x \leq b : x^2 + b^2 = N)$
$= \quad \{ x^2 + b^2 \text{ is increasing in } x, \, a \leq b \}$
$$\begin{cases} G.a.(b-1) + 0 & \text{if } a^2 + b^2 > N \\ G.a.(b-1) + 1 & \text{if } a^2 + b^2 = N \end{cases}$$

Solution:

$\|[\ \mathbf{var}\ a, b : \text{int};$
$\quad r, a := 0, 0$
$\quad \{\text{Linear Search:}\}$
$\quad ; b := 0\ ;\mathbf{do}\ b * b < N \rightarrow b := b+1\ \mathbf{od}$
$\quad \{\text{invariant: } P_0 \wedge P_1, \text{ Proof 1, bound: } b - a\}$
$\quad ; \mathbf{do}\ a \leq b$
$\qquad \rightarrow \mathbf{if}\ a*a + b*b < N \rightarrow a := a+1\ \{\text{Proof 2}\}$
$\qquad \quad [\!]\ a*a + b*b > N \rightarrow b := b-1\ \{\text{Proof 3}\}$
$\qquad \quad [\!]\ a*a + b*b = N \rightarrow r, a := r+1, a+1\ \{\text{Proof 2}\}$
$\qquad \quad [\!]\ a*a + b*b = N \rightarrow r, b := r+1, b-1\ \{\text{Proof 3}\}$
$\qquad \mathbf{fi}$
$\quad \mathbf{od}$
$\quad \{r = (\# x, y : 0 \leq x \leq y : x^2 + y^2 = N), \text{ Proof 0}\}$
$]\!|.$

This concludes the presentation of the solution. This program has time complexity $\mathcal{O}(\sqrt{N})$. Initializing b by $b := N$ leads to a program that has time complexity $\mathcal{O}(N)$ which is as bad as a brute force search in the area $[0..\sqrt{N}] \times [0..\sqrt{N}]$.

One may wonder whether the two guarded commands

$a*a + b*b = N \to r, a := r+1, a+1$
$a*a + b*b = N \to r, b := r+1, b-1$

may be replaced by

$a*a + b*b = N \to r, a, b := r+1, a+1, b-1$

The only way to find out is by calculation: assume $0 \le a \le b \wedge a^2 + b^2 = N$, then

$\quad G.a.b$
$=\quad \{\text{definition of } G\}$
$\quad (\# x, y : a \le x \le y \le b : x^2 + y^2 = N)$
$=\quad \{\text{split off } y = b\}$
$\quad G.a.(b-1) + (\# x : a \le x \le b : x^2 + b^2 = N)$
$=\quad \{\text{split off } x = a \text{ in } G.a.(b-1)\}$
$\quad G.(a+1).(b-1) + (\# y : a \le y \le b-1 : a^2 + y^2 = N)$
$\quad\quad\quad\quad\quad\quad + (\# x : a \le x \le b : x^2 + b^2 = N)$
$=\quad \{a^2 + b^2 = N\}$
$\quad G.(a+1).(b-1) + 1$

Hence, this replacement is allowed, leading to

$\|[$ **var** a, b : int;
$\quad r, a := 0, 0$
$\quad ; b := 0\ ;$ **do** $b*b < N \to b := b+1$ **od**
$\quad ;$ **do** $a \le b$
$\quad\quad\quad \to$ **if** $a*a + b*b < N \to a := a+1$
$\quad\quad\quad\quad [\!]\ a*a + b*b > N \to b := b-1$
$\quad\quad\quad\quad [\!]\ a*a + b*b = N \to r, a, b := r+1, a+1, b-1$
$\quad\quad\quad$ **fi**
$\quad$ **od**
$]\!|.$

8.1.2 Minimal distance

Our next example is the derivation of a program for the computation of the minimal distance of two ascending sequences. It is specified by

$\|[\textbf{con}\ M, N : \textbf{int}\ \{M \geq 0 \wedge N \geq 0\};$
$\qquad f : \textbf{array}\ [0..M)\ \textbf{of}\ \textbf{int}\ \{f \text{ is ascending}\};$
$\qquad g : \textbf{array}\ [0..N)\ \textbf{of}\ \textbf{int}\ \{g \text{ is ascending}\};$
$\textbf{var}\ r : \textbf{int};$
$\quad S$
$\{r = (\min x, y : 0 \leq x < M \wedge 0 \leq y < N : |f.x - g.y|)\}$
$]|.$

Note that $f.x - g.y$ is ascending in x and descending in y and $g.y - f.x$ is descending in x and ascending in y. The expression $|f.x - g.y|$, being equal to $(f.x - g.y)\max(g.y - f.x)$, does not have these properties. However, as will emerge from the derivations, a slope search still is possible. Since $f.x - g.y$ and $g.y - f.x$ have both ascending and descending properties, we define $G.a.b$ for $0 \leq a \leq M \wedge 0 \leq b \leq N$ as:

$$G.a.b = (\min x, y : a \leq x < M \wedge b \leq y < N : |f.x - g.y|)$$

The post-condition may be written as

$R: \quad r = G.0.0$

and we propose as invariants

$P_0: \quad r \min G.a.b = G.0.0$
$P_1: \quad 0 \leq a \leq M \wedge 0 \leq b \leq N$

These are initialized by $a, b, r := 0, 0, \infty$. Furthermore,

$\quad P_0 \wedge (a = M \vee b = N)$
$\Rightarrow \quad \{\text{minimum over an empty range is } \infty\}$
$\quad r \min \infty = G.0.0$
$\equiv \quad \{\text{calculus}\}$
$\quad r = G.0.0$

This yields as guard $a \neq M \wedge b \neq N$. For $0 \leq a < M \wedge 0 \leq b < N$ we have

$\quad G.a.b$
$= \quad \{\text{definition of } G\}$
$\quad (\min x, y : a \leq x < M \wedge b \leq y < N : |f.x - g.y|)$
$= \quad \{\text{split off } x = a\}$

$$G.(a+1).b \text{ min } (\text{min } y : b \le y < N : |f.a - g.y|)$$
$$= \quad \{ g \text{ is ascending, assume } g.b \ge f.a \}$$
$$G.(a+1).b \text{ min } (\text{min } y : b \le y < N : g.y - f.a)$$
$$= \quad \{ g \text{ is ascending} \}$$
$$G.(a+1).b \text{ min } (g.b - f.a)$$

Hence,

$$g.b \ge f.a \;\Rightarrow\; G.a.b = G.(a+1).b \text{ min } (g.b - f.a)$$

On account of the symmetry of the specification in f and g, we have

$$f.a \ge g.b \;\Rightarrow\; G.a.b = G.a.(b+1) \text{ min } (f.a - g.b)$$

as well. We now have all ingredients for the solution:

```
|[ var a, b : int;
     r, a, b := ∞, 0, 0
   ; do a ≠ M ∧ b ≠ N
        → if g.b ≥ f.a  →  a, r := a+1, r min (g.b - f.a)
          [] f.a ≥ g.b  →  b, r := b+1, r min (f.a - g.b)
          fi
     od
]|.
```

When we know how to approach these problems, the derivations are rather simple and a program is easily constructed.

Exercises

Derive programs for the following problems.

0. $|[$ **con** M, N : int $\{M \ge 0 \land N \ge 0\}$;
    $\quad f$: **array** $[0..M)$ **of** int $\{f$ is increasing$\}$;
    $\quad g$: **array** $[0..N)$ **of** int $\{g$ is increasing$\}$;
    var r : int;
    coincidence count
    $\{r = (\# x, y : 0 \le x < M \land 0 \le y < N : f.x = g.y)\}$
    $]|.$

1. [[**con** N : int $\{N \geq 0\}$;
   var r : int;
   S
   $\{r = (\# x, y : 0 \leq x \land 0 \leq y : x^3 + y^2 = N)\}$
   ]].

2. [[**con** M, N : int $\{M \geq 0 \land N \geq 0\}$; f : **array** $[0..M) \times [0..N)$ **of** int;
   $\{f$ is ascending in both arguments$\}$
   var r : int;
   S
   $\{r = (\# i, j : 0 \leq i < M \land 0 \leq j < N : f.i.j = 0)\}$
   ]].
   (Hint: $(\# i : R : h.i = 0) = (\# i : R : h.i \geq 0) - (\# i : R : h.i > 0)$).

3. The *Welfare Crook*: The sets U, V, and W are represented by increasing integer arrays $f[0..K)$, $g[0..L)$, and $h[0..M)$. Derive a program for the computation of an element of $U \cap V \cap W$, given that such an element exists.

4. [[**con** N : int $\{N \geq 0\}$;
   var r : bool;
   S
   $\{r \equiv (\exists x, y : 0 \leq x \land 0 \leq y : N = 2^x + 3^y)\}$
   ]].

5. [[**con** M : int $\{M \geq 0\}$; f : **array** $[0..M)$ **of** int;
   $\{(\forall i : 0 \leq i < M : f.i \geq 0)\}$
   var r : int;
   S
   $\{r = (\# p, q : 0 \leq p \leq q \leq M : (\Sigma i : p \leq i < q : f.i) < 7)\}$
   ]].

6. N points, numbered from 0 onwards, are located on a circle (in the rest of this exercise all point numbers should be taken **mod** N). Point $i+1$ is the clockwise neighbor of point i. An integer array, dist$[0..N)$, is given such that dist.i is the distance (along the circle) between points i and $i+1$.

   (i) Derive a program to determine whether there exist two points at opposite ends of a diameter of the circle.

   (ii) Derive a program for the computation of two points that have maximal Euclidian distance.

8.2 Longest and shortest segments

In Chapter 7 we discussed longest and shortest segment problems. Longest segment problems are of the form

$$[\![\, \mathbf{con}\ N : \text{int}\ \{N \geq 0\};$$
$$\mathbf{var}\ r : \text{int};$$
$$\quad maxseg$$
$$\{\, r = (\,\mathbf{max}\, p, q : 0 \leq p \leq q \leq N \land \mathcal{A}.p.q : q{-}p)\,\}$$
$$]\!].$$

where $\mathcal{A}$ is a predicate, typically related to some integer array $X[0..N]$. Examples of such predicates are

$$\mathcal{A}.p.q \equiv (\forall i, j : p \leq i < q \land p \leq j < q : X.i = X.j) \quad (X[p..q]\ \text{is constant})$$
$$\mathcal{A}.p.q \equiv (\forall i, j : p \leq i \leq j < q : X.i \leq X.j) \quad (X[p..q]\ \text{is ascending})$$
$$\mathcal{A}.p.q \equiv (\#i : p \leq i < q : X.i = 0) \leq 60 \quad (X[p..q]\ \text{contains at most 60 zeros})$$

For these examples, $\mathcal{A}$ satisfies $(0 \leq p \leq q \leq N)$:

(0) $\mathcal{A}.p.p$ the empty segment is an $\mathcal{A}$-segment
(1) $\mathcal{A}.p.q \Rightarrow (\forall s : p \leq s \leq q : \mathcal{A}.p.s)$ $\mathcal{A}$ is prefix-closed
(2) $\mathcal{A}.p.q \Rightarrow (\forall s : p \leq s \leq q : \mathcal{A}.s.q)$ $\mathcal{A}$ is postfix-closed

Shortest segment problems are of the form

$$[\![\, \mathbf{con}\ N : \text{int}\ \{N \geq 0\};$$
$$\mathbf{var}\ r : \text{int};$$
$$\quad minseg$$
$$\{\, r = (\,\mathbf{min}\, p, q : 0 \leq p \leq q \leq N \land \mathcal{A}.p.q : q{-}p)\,\}$$
$$]\!].$$

Examples of predicates for these problems are

$$\mathcal{A}.p.q \equiv (\exists i, j, k : p \leq i, j, k < q : X.i = 0 \land X.j = 1 \land X.k = 2)$$
(values 0, 1, and 2 occur in $X[p..q]$)

$$\mathcal{A}.p.q \equiv (\#i : p \leq i < q : X.i = 0) \geq 60 \quad (X[p..q]\ \text{contains at least 60 zeros})$$

For these examples, $\mathcal{A}$ satisfies $(0 \leq p \leq q \leq N)$:

(0') $\neg \mathcal{A}.p.p$ the empty segment is a $\neg \mathcal{A}$-segment
(1') $\neg \mathcal{A}.p.q \Rightarrow (\forall s : p \leq s \leq q : \neg \mathcal{A}.p.s)$ $\neg \mathcal{A}$ is prefix-closed
(2') $\neg \mathcal{A}.p.q \Rightarrow (\forall s : p \leq s \leq q : \neg \mathcal{A}.s.q)$ $\neg \mathcal{A}$ is postfix-closed

Note that

$$\mathcal{A} \text{ satisfies } (0), (1), \text{ and } (2) \equiv \neg\mathcal{A} \text{ satisfies } (0'), (1'), \text{ and } (2')$$

When we have a solution to *maxseg* for predicates that satisfy (0) and (1), then we have, by applying this solution to the reverse of X, a solution for predicates that satisfy (0) and (2). A similar remark pertains to *minseg*.

In Section 8.2.0 we derive a program scheme for *maxseg* for the case that (0) and (1) hold. In Section 8.2.1 a program scheme is derived for *minseg*, for which (0') and (2') are assumed. These schemes are derived by means of the Slope Search technique. In Section 8.2.2 we apply such a scheme to obtain a program for the computation of the length of a shortest segment $X[p..q]$ that contains at least two zeros, i.e.,

$$\mathcal{A}.p.q \equiv (\# i : p \leq i < q : X.i = 0) \geq 2$$

The same problem was solved in Section 7.2, but that solution is not very satisfactory.

8.2.0 Longest segments

Let $N \geq 0$ and let predicate $\mathcal{A}$ in the range $0 \leq p \leq q \leq N$ satisfy

(0) $\mathcal{A}.p.p$ the empty segment is an $\mathcal{A}$-segment
(1) $\mathcal{A}.p.q \Rightarrow (\forall s : p \leq s \leq q : \mathcal{A}.p.s)$ $\mathcal{A}$ is prefix-closed

We derive a program that has post-condition

R: $r = (\max p, q : 0 \leq p \leq q \leq N \wedge \mathcal{A}.p.q : q-p)$

Since $q-p$ is ascending in q and descending in p, we define $G.a.b$ for $0 \leq a \leq b \leq N$ by

$$G.a.b = (\max p, q : a \leq p \leq q \leq N \wedge b \leq q \leq N \wedge \mathcal{A}.p.q : q-p)$$

Then R may be formulated as

R: $r = G.0.0$

As invariants for a repetition we choose

Slope Search

$P_0:$ $\quad r \max G.a.b = G.0.0$
$P_1:$ $\quad 0 \leq a \leq b \leq N$

These may be initialized by $a, b, r := 0, 0, -\infty$. However, since $\mathcal{A}.0.0$ holds, $a, b, r := 0, 0, 0$ is also correct. We derive

$\quad G.a.N$
$=\quad$ { definition of G }
$\quad (\max p : a \leq p \leq N \wedge \mathcal{A}.p.N : N{-}p)$
$=\quad$ { assume $\mathcal{A}.a.N$, $N{-}p$ is descending in p, $a \leq N$ }
$\quad N{-}a$

Hence,

$$P_0 \wedge b = N \wedge \mathcal{A}.a.b \;\Rightarrow\; R(r := r \max (N{-}a))$$

which yields $b \neq N \vee \neg\mathcal{A}.a.b$ as guard of the repetition. To determine a condition under which b may be increased, we derive for $0 \leq a \leq b < N$:

$\quad G.a.b$
$=\quad$ { definition of G, split off $q = b$ }
$\quad G.a.(b{+}1) \max (\max p : a \leq p \leq b \wedge \mathcal{A}.p.b : b{-}p)$
$=\quad$ { assume $\mathcal{A}.a.b$, $b{-}p$ is descending in p, $a \leq b$ }
$\quad G.a.(b{+}1) \max (b{-}a)$

Hence,

$$\mathcal{A}.a.b \;\Rightarrow\; G.a.b = G.a.(b{+}1) \max (b{-}a)$$

Note that

$$P_1 \wedge (b \neq N \vee \neg\mathcal{A}.a.b) \wedge \mathcal{A}.a.b \;\Rightarrow\; b < N$$

For the case $\neg\mathcal{A}.a.b$ we investigate an increase in a.
Due to (0), we have $\neg\mathcal{A}.a.b \Rightarrow a \neq b$, hence $a \leq b$ is not violated by $a := a{+}1$ in this case. We derive for $0 \leq a \leq b \leq N \wedge \neg\mathcal{A}.a.b$

$G.a.b$
=   { definition of G, split off $p = a$ }
$G.(a+1).b$ **max** (**max** $q : a \leq q \leq N \wedge b \leq q \leq N \wedge \mathcal{A}.a.q : q-a$)
=   { $a \leq b$ }
$G.(a+1).b$ **max** (**max** $q : b \leq q \leq N \wedge \mathcal{A}.a.q : q-a$)
=   { (1), $\neg \mathcal{A}.a.b$, hence, ($\forall q : b \leq q \leq N : \neg \mathcal{A}.a.q$) }
$G.(a+1).b$

Hence,

$$\neg \mathcal{A}.a.b \Rightarrow G.a.b = G.(a+1).b$$

This concludes our derivation. The program scheme for *maxseg* is shown below. As bound function, $2N - a - b$ will do.

---

    maxseg: $[\![$ **var** a, b : int;
                 $a, b, r := 0, 0, 0$
                ; **do** $b \neq N \vee \neg \mathcal{A}.a.b$
                    $\rightarrow$ **if** $\mathcal{A}.a.b \rightarrow r := r$ **max** $(b-a)$; $b := b+1$
                         $[\!]$ $\neg \mathcal{A}.a.b \rightarrow a := a+1$
                       fi
                od
                ; $r := r$ **max** $(N-a)$
                { $r = ($ **max** $p, q : 0 \leq p \leq q \leq N \wedge \mathcal{A}.p.q : q-p)$ }
           $]\!]$.

Note that we did not use the fact that $q - p$ is ascending in q, only that it is descending in p. A closer look at the range of the quantification in the post-condition (using the fact that $\mathcal{A}$ is prefix-closed) reveals that on the one hand the descendingness plays a role and on the other hand the specific form of the range is important.

To obtain a final program, one has to replace $\mathcal{A}.a.b$ by a boolean expression. For instance, we may try to add invariant $c \equiv \mathcal{A}.a.b$, which is initialized by $c :=$ true. Since $0 \leq a \leq b \leq N$, this invariant is well defined.

8.2.1 Shortest segments

We now consider *minseg* and we assume that $\mathcal{A}$ satisfies

(0') $\neg\mathcal{A}.p.p$ the empty segment is a $\neg\mathcal{A}$-segment
(2') $\neg\mathcal{A}.p.q \Rightarrow (\forall s : p \leq s \leq q : \neg\mathcal{A}.s.q)$ $\neg\mathcal{A}$ is postfix-closed

The following derivation is almost a copy of the derivation presented in the previous subsection and the reader is advised to compare both texts carefully. We define $G.a.b$ for $0 \leq a \leq b \leq N$ by

$$G.a.b = (\min p, q : a \leq p \leq q \leq N \land b \leq q \leq N \land \mathcal{A}.p.q : q-p)$$

Then post-condition R may be formulated as

$R: \quad r = G.0.0$

As invariants we propose

$P_0: \quad r \min G.a.b = G.0.0$
$P_1: \quad 0 \leq a \leq b \leq N$

which are established by $a, b, r := 0, 0, \infty$. We derive

$\quad G.a.N$
$=\quad \{\text{definition of } G\}$
$\quad (\min p : a \leq p \leq N \land \mathcal{A}.p.N : N-p)$
$=\quad \{\text{assume } \neg\mathcal{A}.a.N,\ \neg\mathcal{A} \text{ is postfix-closed}\}$
$\quad \infty$

Hence,

$\quad P_0 \land P_1 \land b = N \land \neg\mathcal{A}.a.b \Rightarrow R$

which yields $b \neq N \lor \mathcal{A}.a.b$ as guard of the repetition. To determine a condition under which b may be increased, we derive for $0 \leq a \leq b < N$:

$\quad G.a.b$
$=\quad \{\text{definition of } G, \text{split off } q = b\}$
$\quad G.a.(b+1) \min (\min p : a \leq p \leq b \land \mathcal{A}.p.b : b-p)$
$=\quad \{\text{assume } \neg\mathcal{A}.a.b,\ \neg\mathcal{A} \text{ is postfix-closed}\}$
$\quad G.a.(b+1)$

Hence,

$$\neg \mathcal{A}.a.b \;\Rightarrow\; G.a.b = G.a.(b+1)$$

Note that

$$P \wedge (b \neq N \vee \mathcal{A}.a.b) \wedge \neg \mathcal{A}.a.b \;\Rightarrow\; b < N$$

For the case $\mathcal{A}.a.b$ we investigate an increase in a.
Due to $(0')$, we have $\mathcal{A}.a.b \Rightarrow a \neq b$, hence $a \leq b$ is not violated by $a := a+1$ in this case. We derive for $0 \leq a \leq b \leq N \wedge \mathcal{A}.a.b$

$\quad G.a.b$
$= \quad$ { definition of G, split off $p = a$ }
$\quad G.(a+1).b \;\textbf{min}\; (\textbf{min}\, q : a \leq q \leq N \wedge b \leq q \leq N \wedge \mathcal{A}.a.q : q-a)$
$= \quad \{a \leq b\}$
$\quad G.(a+1).b \;\textbf{min}\; (\textbf{min}\, q : b \leq q \leq N \wedge \mathcal{A}.a.q : q-a)$
$= \quad \{\mathcal{A}.a.b,\; q - a \text{ is ascending in } q\}$
$\quad G.(a+1).b \;\textbf{min}\; (b - a)$

Hence,

$$\mathcal{A}.a.b \;\Rightarrow\; G.a.b = G.(a+1).b \;\textbf{min}\; (b-a)$$

This concludes our derivation. The program scheme for *minseg* is shown below. As bound function, $2N - a - b$ will do.

```
minseg:   |[ var a, b : int;
             a, b, r := 0, 0, ∞
           ; do b ≠ N ∨ 𝒜.a.b
               → if ¬𝒜.a.b → b := b+1
                  [] 𝒜.a.b → r := r min (b−a) ; a := a+1
                  fi
             od
             {r = (min p, q : 0 ≤ p ≤ q ≤ N ∧ 𝒜.p.q : q−p)}
           ]|.
```

8.2.2 At least two zeros revisited

In this subsection we apply the scheme for *minseg* to obtain an algorithm for the computation of the length of a shortest segment of integer array $X[0..N)$ that contains at least two zeros. For this problem

$$\mathcal{A}.a.b \equiv (\# i : a \leq i < b : X.i = 0) \geq 2$$

Then $\neg\mathcal{A}$ holds for empty segments and $\neg\mathcal{A}$ is postfix-closed. To express $\mathcal{A}.a.b$ as boolean expression, we introduce integer variable c and accompanying invariant

$$Q : \ c = (\# i : a \leq i < b : X.i = 0)$$

Then $\mathcal{A}.a.b \equiv c \geq 2$ and $\neg\mathcal{A}.a.b \equiv c < 2$. This leads to the following solution.

$$\begin{aligned}
&\|[\ \textbf{var}\ a,b,c : \text{int}; \\
&\quad r,a,b,c := \infty, 0, 0, 0 \\
&\ ;\textbf{do}\ b \neq N \vee c \geq 2 \\
&\quad\quad \rightarrow \textbf{if}\ c < 2 \rightarrow \quad \textbf{if}\ X.b = 0 \rightarrow c := c+1 \ [\!]\ X.b \neq 0 \rightarrow \textbf{skip}\ \textbf{fi} \\
&\quad\quad\quad\quad\quad\quad\quad\quad\quad ;b := b+1 \\
&\quad\quad\quad\quad [\!]\ c \geq 2 \rightarrow \quad r := r\ \textbf{min}\ (b-a) \\
&\quad\quad\quad\quad\quad\quad\quad\quad\quad ;\textbf{if}\ X.a = 0 \rightarrow c := c-1\ [\!]\ X.a \neq 0 \rightarrow \textbf{skip}\ \textbf{fi} \\
&\quad\quad\quad\quad\quad\quad\quad\quad\quad ;a := a+1 \\
&\quad\quad\quad\quad \textbf{fi} \\
&\quad \textbf{od} \\
&\ ]\!|.
\end{aligned}$$

Compare this program with the one derived in Chapter 7.

Exercises

0. $\|[\ \textbf{con}\ N : \text{int}\ \{N \geq 0\};\ X : \textbf{array}\ [0..N)\ \textbf{of}\ \text{int};$
   $\quad \{(\forall i : 0 \leq i < N : X.i \geq 1)\}$
   $\ \textbf{var}\ r : \text{int};$
   $\quad S$
   $\quad \{r = (\textbf{min}\ p, q : 0 \leq p \leq q \leq N \wedge (\Sigma i : p \leq i < q : X.i) \geq N : q - p)\}$
   $\ ]\!|.$

1. $[\![\,\mathbf{con}\ N : \mathbf{int}\ \{N \geq 1\};\ X : \mathbf{array}\ [0..N)\ \mathbf{of}\ \mathrm{int};$
   $\mathbf{var}\ r : \mathrm{int};$
   S
   $\{r = (\mathbf{max}\,p, q : 0 \leq p < q \leq N \wedge \mathcal{A}.p.q : q - p)\}$
   $]\!]$.
   where

   $\mathcal{A}.p.q \equiv (\#\,i : p < i < q : X.i = X.(i{-}1)) = 37$

2. $[\![\,\mathbf{con}\ N : \mathbf{int}\ \{N \geq 0\};\ X : \mathbf{array}\ [0..N)\ \mathbf{of}\ \mathrm{int};$
   $\{(\forall i : 0 \leq i < N : X.i \geq 0)\}$
   $\mathbf{var}\ r : \mathrm{int};$
   S
   $\{r = (\mathbf{max}\,p, q : 0 \leq p \leq q \leq N \wedge (\Sigma\,i : p \leq i < q : X.i) \leq 3 : q - p)\}$
   $]\!]$.

   How would you solve this problem if each element of X may be inspected only once ?

3. Let $N \geq 0$ and let $X[0..N)$ be an integer array. Derive a program for the computation of the length of a shortest segment that contains values 0,1, and 2.

Chapter 9

Mixed Problems

In the preceding chapters we showed how to reason about programs and how to derive them from specifications. Arrays were only used as constants. In the final chapters of this book we discuss array manipulations and we solve problems by introducing auxiliary arrays.

A number of programming techniques have been described in these chapters. These techniques can only be mastered by applying them to problems. To encourage the reader, we have chosen problems that can be solved with the theory of the preceding section. For instance, all the problems in Section 6.2 can be solved by a binary search and all the problems in Chapter 8 can be solved by a slope search. In this chapter we present a mix of problems. It is up to the reader to find out what strategies are most appropriate for the problem in hand. Each problem should be studied carefully: often more than one approach is applicable. All exercises admit a linear solution; however, for some of them an $\mathcal{O}(\log N)$ solution exists.

The derivation is as important as the resulting program. Both should not be complicated: exploit symmetry, avoid unnecessary case analysis, introduce suitable notation etc.

It is not necessary to complete these exercises before going on to the next chapters. This collection is presented here because all prerequisites needed to solve these exercises have been presented.

Some of the exercises are given by a formal specification. Others are formulated in English. For the latter, one has to supply a formal specification first.

Exercises

0. $\|[\,\mathbf{con}\ N : \text{int}\ \{N \geq 0\};\ A : \mathbf{array}\ [0..N)\ \mathbf{of}\ \text{bool};$
   $\mathbf{var}\ r : \text{int};$
   S
   $\{r = (\#p : 0 \leq p \leq N : (\forall i : 0 \leq i < p : A.i) \equiv (\exists i : 0 \leq i < p : A.i))\}$
   $\,]\|.$

1. $\|[\,\mathbf{con}\ N : \text{int}\ \{N \geq 0\};\ A : \mathbf{array}\ [0..N)\ \mathbf{of}\ \text{int};$
   $\mathbf{var}\ r : \text{int};$
   S
   $\{r = (\Sigma p, q : 0 \leq p < q < N : A.p + A.q)\}$
   $\,]\|.$

2. $\|[\,\mathbf{con}\ N : \text{int}\ \{N \geq 0\};\ f : \mathbf{array}\ [0..N)\ \mathbf{of}\ \text{int};$
   $\{f\ \text{is ascending}\}$
   $\mathbf{var}\ r : \text{int};$
   S
   $\{r = (\#p, q : 0 \leq p \leq p+q < N : f.(p+q) - f.p = 37)\}$
   $\,]\|.$

3. For integer arrays $f[0..N)$ and $g[0..N)$ relation $f \prec g$ is defined by

   $$f \prec g \equiv (\exists n : 0 \leq n < N : f.n < g.n \land (\forall i : 0 \leq i < n : f.i = g.i))$$

   The relation $\prec$ is called the *lexicographical order*. Derive for given f and g a program that assigns to boolean variables a, b, and c such values that

   $$(a \equiv f \prec g) \land (b \equiv f = g) \land (c \equiv f \succ g)$$

4. Integer array $f[0..N]$, $N \geq 0$, is *convex*, i.e.,

   $$(\forall i : 0 < i < N : f.i \leq \tfrac{1}{2}(f.(i-1) + f.(i+1)))$$

   Derive a program for the computation of $(\exists i : 0 \leq i < N : f.i = f.(i+1))$.

5. |[**con** N, A, B : int $\{N \geq 1\}$; f : **array** $[0..N)$ **of** int;
   var x : int;
   S
   $\{b \equiv (\forall p, q : 0 \leq p \leq q \leq N : A \leq (\Sigma i : p \leq i < q : f.i) \leq B)\}$
   ]|.

6. In the (x, y)-plane a collection G of M circles is represented by integer array $R[0..M)$. Circle i has centre $(0, 0)$ and radius $R.i$ ($R.i > 0$). Furthermore, a collection L of N lines is given by integer array $X[0..N)$. Line i has equation $x = X.i$. Both R and X are increasing. Derive a program for the computation of

   (i) There exists a line in L that is tangent to a circle of G.

   (ii) The number of intersection points of L and G.

7. |[**con** N : int $\{N \geq 0\}$; f : **array** $[0..N)$ **of** int;
   $\{f$ is increasing$\}$
   var r : int;
   S
   $\{r = (\# x, y : 0 \leq x \leq y < N : f.y - f.x > y - x)\}$
   ]|.

8. N points, numbered from 0 onwards, are located on a circle (in the rest of this exercise all point numbers should be taken **mod** N). Point $i+1$ is the clockwise neighbor of point i. An integer array, dist$[0..N)$, is given such that dist.i is the distance (along the circle) between points i and $i+1$. Derive a program to determine whether four of these points form a rectangle.

9. Array $f[0..N]$, $N \geq 0$, is increasing. Derive a program for the computation of

   $(\exists i : 0 \leq i \leq N : f.i = i)$

10. |[**con** N : int $\{N \geq 0\}$; f : **array** $[0..N)$ **of** int;
    var r : int;
    S
    $\{r = (\# p, q : 0 \leq p \leq N \wedge 0 \leq q \leq N :$
          $(\# i : 0 \leq i < p : f.i = 0) < (\# i : 0 \leq i < q : f.i = 1))\}$
    ]|.

11. For integers K and N, $0 < K \leq N$, and integer array $f[0..N)$, one is asked to compute the number of segments of length K on which f is ascending.

12. Sets V and W are represented by increasing integer arrays $f[0..M)$ and $g[0..N)$, $M \geq 0 \wedge N \geq 0$. Derive a program with post-condition

$$b \equiv V \subseteq W$$

13. For integer array $f[0..N]$, we have $f.0 = 0 \wedge f.N \neq 0$. Derive a program that establishes for integer x

$$f.x = 0 \wedge f.(x{+}1) \neq 0$$

14. For integer array $X[0..N)$, $N \geq 0$, determine the length of a longest segment on which X attains its maximum at most twice, i.e., a segment $[p..q)$ for which

$$(\#\,i : p \leq i < q : X.i = (\max j : p \leq j < q : X.j)) \leq 2$$

15. For integer array $X[0..N)$, $N \geq 0$, determine the length of a longest prefix of X that contains zeros only.

16. $[\![$ **con** $A, B, N : \text{int}\,\{A \geq 1 \wedge B \geq 1 \wedge N \geq 1\};$
    var $r : \text{int};$
    S
    $\{r = (\min p, q : 1 \leq p \leq N \wedge 1 \leq q \leq N : |A^p - B^q|)\}$
    $]\!]$.

Chapter 10

Array Manipulations

10.0 Introduction

In the preceding chapters arrays are used as constants. We now introduce statements that may change the value of an array. As we shall see in the following, these statements have quite complicated definitions. Thus, precision in invariant calculations is vital.

In Section 10.1 the array assignment is introduced. It is of the form $h.E := F$, where h is an array and E and F are expressions. It differs from the ordinary assignment in that its execution affects the value of an entire function. In the definition this is reflected by a substitution of functions for functions.

In Section 10.2 we discuss the swap operation which interchanges two function values. Many programming problems can be solved by means of swap operations on the arrays involved only. Sorting is one example of such a problem.

10.1 Array assignments

Throughout this section N is a natural number, $h[0..N]$ is an integer array and E and F are integer expressions. The array assignment is of the form $h.E := F$. Its operational interpretation is 'replace the value of $h.E$ by F'. Before we present a formal definition we show by a small example how much this assignment differs from an ordinary assignment and how easily one may draw incorrect conclusions.

Suppose $h.0 = 1$ and $h.1 = 1$. Then $h.(h.1) = h.1 = 1$ and statement $h.(h.1) := 0$ is equivalent to $h.1 := 0$ and will result in $h.(h.1) = h.0 = 1$. We conclude that

$$\{h.0 = 1 \land h.1 = 1\} \ h.(h.1) := 0 \ \{h.(h.1) = 1\}$$

is correct. This simple example shows a difference between an array assignment and an ordinary assignment for which we have, for example,

$$\{\text{true}\}\ x := 0\ \{x = 0\}$$

Apparently, $h.E := F$ changes the value of h but not necessarily the value of the expression $h.E$. To express the change in a function, we introduce the following notation. For $0 \leq x < N$ and integer A, the function $h(x{:}A) : [0..N) \to \mathcal{Z}$ is defined by

$$h(x{:}A).i = \begin{cases} h.i & \text{if } i \neq x \\ A & \text{if } i = x \end{cases}$$

We pronounce $h(x{:}A)$ as 'h except in x where its value is A'. As an example, let $h[0..3)$ be defined by $h.0 = 2$, $h.1 = 4$, $h.2 = 6$, then $h(1{:}5)$ is the function

$h(1{:}5).0 = 2$
$h(1{:}5).1 = 5$
$h(1{:}5).2 = 6$

With this notational convention, $h.E := F$ may now be defined by

$$\{P\}\ h.E := F\ \{Q\}\ \text{ is equivalent to }\ [P \Rightarrow Q(h := h(E{:}F))]$$

where, as usual, $Q(h := h(E{:}F))$ denotes Q in which h is replaced by $h(E{:}F)$. As an example of the use of the rule of the array assignment, we prove

$$\{h.0 = 1 \land h.1 = 1\}\ h.(h.1) := 0\ \{h.(h.1) = 1\}$$

Proof:

Assume $h.0 = 1 \land h.1 = 1$. We derive

$\quad (h.(h.1))(h := h(h.1{:}0))$
$= \quad \{\text{substitution}\}$
$\quad h(h.1{:}0).(h(h.1{:}0).1)$
$= \quad \{h.1 = 1\}$
$\quad h(1{:}0).(h(1{:}0).1)$
$= \quad \{\text{definition of } h(x{:}A),\ 1 = 1\}$
$\quad h(1{:}0).0$
$= \quad \{\text{definition of } h(x{:}A),\ 1 \neq 0\}$
$\quad h.0$
$= \quad \{h.0 = 1\}$
$\quad 1$

It can be seen that for many array assignments, it is difficult to predict the outcome without calculations. Fortunately, there are many cases in which the effect of $h.E := F$ can be easily computed.

In the definition of $x := E$ conjunct def.E occurs. For array assignment $h.E := F$ we require that E and F are well defined, and that the value of E is in the range of h. More formally, def.$(h.E)$ is defined by

$$[\text{def.}(h.E) \equiv \text{def.}E \wedge 0 \leq E < N]$$

and the formal definition of $h.E := F$ is

$$\boxed{\{P\}\, h.E := F \,\{Q\} \text{ is equivalent to } [P \Rightarrow \text{def.}F \wedge \text{def.}(h.E) \wedge Q(h := h(E{:}F))]}$$

In terms of weakest pre-conditions we have

$$[wp.(h.E := F).Q \equiv \text{def.}F \wedge \text{def.}(h.E) \wedge Q(h := h(E{:}F))]$$

In calculations conjunct $Q(h := h(E{:}F))$ is the starting point. One should, however, be aware of the other two conjuncts too.

Multiple array assignments are not allowed. If they were the program fragment

$$x, y := 0, 0 \;;\; h.x, h.y := 0, 1$$

would establish $h.0 = 0$ or $h.0 = 1$. This problem may be solved by the definition of an order (for instance, from left to right) in which substitutions are performed. We prefer to avoid it by not allowing multiple assignments in which an array assignment occurs.

We present two examples in which we use the formal definition of the array assignment. Then, at the end of this section, we present the 'simple array assignment rule' which simplifies calculations in certain cases.

As a first example of the derivation of a program in which array assignments are used, we solve *all zeros* specified by

$$\begin{array}{l} |[\, \textbf{con}\; N : \text{int}\; \{N \geq 0\}; \\ \quad \textbf{var}\; h : \textbf{array}\; [0..N)\, \textbf{of}\; \text{int}; \\ \quad \textit{all zeros} \\ \quad \{(\forall i : 0 \leq i < N : h.i = 0)\} \\ ]|. \end{array}$$

Replacement of the constant N by the integer variable n leads to invariants P_0 and P_1 :

P_0 : $(\forall i : 0 \leq i < n : h.i = 0)$
P_1 : $0 \leq n \leq N$

which are established by $n := 0$. We investigate an increase of n by 1 and we derive, assuming $P_0 \wedge P_1 \wedge n \neq N$,

$\quad (\forall i : 0 \leq i < n{+}1 : h.i = 0)$
$\equiv \quad \{\text{split off } i = n, 0 \leq n\}$
$\quad (\forall i : 0 \leq i < n : h.i = 0) \wedge h.n = 0$
$\equiv \quad \{P_0\}$
$\quad (\forall i : 0 \leq i < n : h.i = h.i) \wedge h.n = 0$
$\equiv \quad \{\text{definition of } h(x{:}A)\}$
$\quad (\forall i : 0 \leq i < n : h.i = h(n{:}0).i) \wedge h.n = h(n{:}0).n$
$\equiv \quad \{\text{import } i = n\}$
$\quad (\forall i : 0 \leq i < n{+}1 : h.i = h(n : 0).i)$

The last line says that replacing h by $h(n{:}0)$, i.e., $h.n := 0$, establishes $P_0(n := n{+}1)$. This yields as solution to *all zeros*

$\|[\textbf{var } n : \text{int};$
$\quad n := 0$
$\quad ; \textbf{do } n \neq N$
$\quad \quad \to \quad h.n := 0$
$\quad \quad \quad ; n := n{+}1$
$\quad \textbf{od}$
$]\|.$

As a second example we consider the problem of computing a frequency table for a series of outcomes of an experiment of throwing a die. A formal specification is

$\|[\textbf{con } N : \text{int } \{N \geq 0\}; X : \textbf{array }[0..N) \textbf{ of } \text{int};$
$\quad \{(\forall i : 0 \leq i < N : 1 \leq X.i \leq 6)\}$
$\quad \textbf{var } h : \textbf{array }[1..6] \textbf{ of } \text{int};$
$\quad \quad \textit{frequency table}$
$\quad \{(\forall i : 1 \leq i \leq 6 : h.i = (\# k : 0 \leq k < N : X.k = i))\}$
$]\|.$

Array Manipulations

Replacement of the constant N by variable n yields invariants

$P_0:$ $(\forall i : 1 \leq i \leq 6 : h.i = (\# k : 0 \leq k < n : X.k = i))$
$P_1:$ $0 \leq n \leq N$

Substitution of $n = 0$ into P_0 yields

$(\forall i : 1 \leq i \leq 6 : h.i = 0)$

for which we have seen a solution (viz. *all zeros*). For the increase of n by 1, we present the following derivation. Assume $P_0 \wedge P_1 \wedge n \neq N$. For any i, $1 \leq i \leq 6$, we have

$\quad (\# k : 0 \leq k < n{+}1 : X.k = i)$
$= \quad \{\text{split off } k = n,\ 0 \leq n\}$
$\quad (\# k : 0 \leq k < n : X.k = i) + \#.(X.n = i)$
$= \quad \{\text{case analysis}\}$
$\quad \begin{cases} (\# k : 0 \leq k < n : X.k = i) & \text{if } i \neq X.n \\ (\# k : 0 \leq k < n : X.k = i) + 1 & \text{if } i = X.n \end{cases}$
$= \quad \{P_0\}$
$\quad \begin{cases} h.i & \text{if } i \neq X.n \\ h.(X.n) + 1 & \text{if } i = X.n \end{cases}$
$= \quad \{\text{definition of } h(x{:}A)\}$
$\quad h(X.n: h.(X.n){+}1).i$

Hence, h has to be replaced by $h(X.n: h.(X.n){+}1)$. We arrive at the following solution to *frequency table*.

$\quad |[\ \mathbf{var}\ n : \text{int};$
$\qquad n := 0$
$\qquad ; |[\ \mathbf{var}\ m : \text{int}\ ; m := 1\ ; \mathbf{do}\ m \neq 7 \rightarrow h.m := 0\ ; m := m + 1\ \mathbf{od}\ ]|$
$\qquad ; \mathbf{do}\ n \neq N$
$\qquad\qquad \rightarrow h.(X.n) := h.(X.n) + 1$
$\qquad\qquad\ ; n := n{+}1$
$\qquad \mathbf{od}$
$\quad]|.$

We now introduce a simpler rule for the array assignment. As in *all zeros*, we often encounter a situation in which

$(\forall i : 0 \leq i < N : h.i = H.i)$

has to be established, where expression H is such that h does not occur in H. This may be solved by introducing integer variable n and invariant

$P: \quad 0 \leq n \leq N \wedge (\forall i : 0 \leq i < n : h.i = H.i)$

and the problem amounts to finding integer expression E such that

$$\{P \wedge n \neq N\} \; h.n := E \; \{(\forall i : 0 \leq i < n{+}1 : h.i = H.i)\}$$

We derive, for $0 \leq n < N$,

$\quad (\forall i : 0 \leq i < n{+}1 : h.i = H.i)(h := h(n{:}E))$
$\equiv \quad \{\text{substitution}, h \text{ does not occur in } H\}$
$\quad (\forall i : 0 \leq i < n{+}1 : h(n{:}E).i = H.i)$
$\equiv \quad \{\text{split off } i = n, \text{definition of } h(x{:}A)\}$
$\quad (\forall i : 0 \leq i < n : h.i = H.i) \wedge E = H.n$

Hence, we have the following rule.

Simple Array Assignment

> If h does not occur in H, then
>
> $\{P \wedge n \neq N \wedge E = H.n\}$
> $h.n := E$
> $\{P(n := n + 1)\}$
>
> where $P : 0 \leq n \leq N \wedge (\forall i : 0 \leq i < n : h.i = H.i)$

Substitution of $E = 0$ yields the solution to *all zeros*. It may be presented as follows.

$\|[\textbf{var } n : \text{int};$
$\quad n := 0$
$\quad \{\text{invariant}: 0 \leq n \leq N \wedge (\forall i : 0 \leq i < n : h.i = 0): \text{simple array assignment}\}$
$\quad ; \textbf{do } n \neq N$
$\quad\quad \rightarrow \; h.n := 0$
$\quad\quad\quad ; n := n + 1$
$\quad \textbf{od}$
$\quad \{(\forall i : 0 \leq i < N : h.i = 0)\}$
$\,]\!|.$

158   *Array Manipulations*

Exercises

Derive solutions for the following programming problems.

0. $[\![$ **con** $N : $ int $\{N \geq 1\}$; $f : $ **array** $[0..N)$ **of** int;
   var $h : $ **array** $[0..N)$ **of** int;
   summation
   $\{(\forall k : 0 \leq k < N : h.k = (\Sigma i : 0 \leq i \leq k : f.i))\}$
   $]\!]$.

1. $[\![$ **con** $N : $ int $\{N \geq 1\}$; $f : $ **array** $[0..N)$ **of** int;
   var $h : $ **array** $[0..N)$ **of** int;
   decomposition
   $\{(\forall k : 0 \leq k < N : f.k = (\Sigma i : 0 \leq i \leq k : h.i))\}$
   $]\!]$.

2. $[\![$ **con** $N : $ int $\{N \geq 1\}$;
   var $h : $ **array** $[0..N)$ **of** int;
   $\{(\forall i : 0 \leq i < N : h.i = F.i)\}$
   decomposition in situ
   $\{(\forall k : 0 \leq k < N : F.k = (\Sigma i : 0 \leq i \leq k : h.i))\}$
   $]\!]$.

   Note that F is a specification variable (cf. Section 2.0) and not a program variable.

3. $[\![$ **con** $N : $ int $\{N \geq 0\}$; $X : $ **array** $[0..N)$ **of** int;
   $\{(\forall i : 0 \leq i < N : 0 \leq X.i < 100)\}$
   var $h : $ **array** $[0..100)$ **of** int;
   S
   $\{(\forall i : 0 \leq i < 100 : h.i = (\min p : 0 \leq p < N \wedge X.p = i : p))\}$
   $]\!]$.

4. $[\![$ **con** $N : $ int $\{N \geq 1\}$; $X : $ **array** $[0..N)$ **of** int;
   $\{(\forall i : 0 \leq i < N : 0 \leq X.i < 100)\}$
   var $r : $ int;
   S
   $\{r = (\max p, q : 0 \leq p < q < N \wedge X.p = X.(q{-}1) : q - p)\}$
   $]\!]$.

   (Hint: introduce array $h[0..100)$ and use the previous exercise.)

5. Derive a program to determine for natural N the frequency of the decimal digits in the decimal representation of N.

6. $[\![\,\mathbf{con}\ N : \mathrm{int}\ \{N \geq 0\};\ X :\mathbf{array}\ [0..N)\,\mathbf{of}\ \mathrm{int};$
   $\mathbf{var}\ h : \mathbf{array}\ [0..N)\,\mathbf{of}\ \mathrm{int};$
   S
   $\{(\forall i : 0 \leq i < N : h.i = (\max j : 0 \leq j \leq i : X.j))\}$
   $]\!]$.

7. Prove:

   If h does not occur in H or E, then
   $\{(\forall i : i \neq E : h.i = H.i) \land F = G(h := h(E{:}F))\}$
   $h.E := F$
   $\{(\forall i : i \neq E : h.i = H.i) \land h.E = G\}$.

   and

   If h does not occur in H, E, or F, then
   $\{(\forall i : i \neq E : h.i = H.i)\}$
   $h.E := F$
   $\{(\forall i : i \neq E : h.i = H.i) \land h.E = F\}$.

10.2 Swaps

Many programming problems involving array manipulations can be solved by interchanging array values. Given integer array $h[0..N)$, and integer expressions E and F, we abbreviate the program fragment

$[\![\,\mathbf{var}\ r : \mathrm{int};\ r := h.E\,;h.E := h.F\,;h.F := r\,]\!]$

to

swap.E.F

Its informal interpretation is 'interchange the values of $h.E$ and $h.F$'. However, as in the case of an array assignment, this operational interpretation does not help very much. To express its meaning formally, we extend the notation $h(x{:}A)$ to two arguments and we define $h(x,y : A, B)$ by

160   Array Manipulations

$$h(x, y : A, B).i = \begin{cases} h.i & \text{if } i \neq x \land i \neq y \\ A & \text{if } i = x \\ B & \text{if } i = y \end{cases}$$

Then swap.$E.F$ may be characterized by

> $\{P\}$ swap.$E.F$ $\{Q\}$ is equivalent to
> $[P \Rightarrow \text{def.}(h.E) \land \text{def.}(h.F) \land Q(h := h(E, F : h.F, h.E))]$

As long as E and F do not depend on h (i.e., h does not occur in E or F) things are relatively easy. Otherwise, it is very difficult to predict the effect of a swap without performing the necessary calculations. This is illustrated by the following example. Let $h.0 = 0$ and $h.1 = 1$. Then swap.$(h.0).(h.1)$ is equivalent to swap.0.1 which establishes $h.0 = 1$ and $h.1 = 0$. In particular, we then have $h.(h.1) = h.0 = 1$. Hence,

$$\{h.(h.0) = 0\} \text{ swap.}(h.0).(h.1) \{h.(h.1) = 0\}$$

does *not* hold. So a naive operational interpretation is liable to be faulty. We leave it as an exercise to the reader to provide a formal proof of

$\{h.0 = 0 \land h.1 = 1 \text{ (hence, } h.(h.0) = 0)\}$
swap.$(h.0).(h.1)$
$\{h.(h.1) = 1\}$

Fortunately, the situation is not so bad if we restrict ourselves to swaps of the form swap.$E.F$ in which h does not occur in E or F. For this case it is easy to derive the following rule.

Simple swap statement:

> If h does not occur in E or F, then
>
> $\{(\forall i : i \neq E \land i \neq F : h.i = H.i) \land h.E = A \land h.F = B\}$
> swap.$E.F$
> $\{(\forall i : i \neq E \land i \neq F : h.i = H.i) \land h.E = B \land h.F = A\}$

We will use this rule frequently, without explicit reference. In the following subsections we present examples of its use.

10.2.0 The Dutch National Flag

As a first example, we derive a program that swaps the values of an array with elements red, white and blue, in such a way that its final value is in accordance with the Dutch National Flag. Its specification is

$\lVert$ **con** N : int $\{N \geq 0\}$;
  var h : **array** $[0..N)$ **of** $[$red, white, blue$]$;
   Dutch National Flag
   $\{(\exists p, q : 0 \leq p \leq q \leq N : (\forall i : 0 \leq i < p\ : h.i = \text{red})$
         $\land (\forall i : p \leq i < q\ : h.i = \text{white})$
         $\land (\forall i : q \leq i < N : h.i = \text{blue})$
   $)\}$
$\rrbracket$,

in which only swap operations are allowed as operations on h.

It seems hard to establish this post-condition without being able to indicate where the final boundaries of the colours are. Therefore, we introduce variables r and w and we derive a program with post-condition

$R:\quad (\forall i : 0 \leq i < r\ : h.i = \text{red})$
$\land (\forall i : r \leq i < w : h.i = \text{white})$
$\land (\forall i : w \leq i < N\!: h.i = \text{blue})$

There are several ways in which R may be weakened. A possible invariant is (introducing integer variable b):

$(\forall i : 0 \leq i < r\ : h.i = \text{red})$
$\land (\forall i : r \leq i < w\!: h.i = \text{white})$
$\land (\forall i : w \leq i < b\!: h.i = \text{blue})$

which is established by $r, w, b := 0, 0, 0$. This choice, however, leads to a rather complicated program. We have lost too much symmetry. Since three parts have to be determined, complete symmetry cannot be obtained. Therefore, we choose as invariants P_0 and P_1 defined by

$P_0:\quad P_r \land P_w \land P_b$
$P_1:\quad 0 \leq r \leq w \leq b \leq N$

with

Array Manipulations

P_r : $(\forall i : 0 \leq i < r : h.i = \text{red})$
P_w : $(\forall i : r \leq i < w : h.i = \text{white})$
P_b : $(\forall i : b \leq i < N : h.i = \text{blue})$

P_0 and P_1 are initialized by $r, w, b := 0, 0, N$. Furthermore,

$$P_0 \land w = b \Rightarrow R$$

This yields $w \neq b$ as guard of a repetition. For $w < b$, the elements of $[w..b)$ are candidates for inspection. Two choices are obvious: w and $b-1$. We choose w and we discuss the other possibility later. This leads to a first approximation of the solution:

```
|[ var r, w, b : int;
    r, w, b := 0, 0, N {invariant P_0 ∧ P_1, bound b−w}
   ;do w ≠ b
       → if  h.w = red    → S_r
          [] h.w = white  → S_w
          [] h.w = blue   → S_b
          fi
    od
]|.
```

Note that

$r =$ 'the number of red elements that have been detected'
$w - r =$ 'the number of white elements that have been detected'
$N - b =$ 'the number of blue elements that have been detected'

Hence, S_r will contain the statement $r := r+1$ and also $w := w+1$, keeping $w - r$ invariant. Similarly, we expect that S_w will contain the statement $w := w+1$ and S_b will contain $b := b-1$.

Statement S_w is the easiest one, since

$$P_0 \land P_1 \land h.w = \text{white} \Rightarrow (P_0 \land P_1)(w := w+1)$$

Hence, for S_w we choose $w := w+1$. Next we consider S_b, which has $h.w = \text{blue}$ as a pre-condition and for which $\text{swap}.w.(b-1)$ is appropriate. From $r \leq w < b$ we infer that $\text{swap}.w.(b-1)$ does not affect P_r, P_w, or P_b, and we have

$\{P_r \wedge P_w \wedge P_b \wedge w < b \wedge h.w = \text{blue}\}$
swap.w.($b{-}1$)
$\{P_r \wedge P_w \wedge P_b \wedge w < b \wedge h.(b{-}1) = \text{blue}\}$
;$b := b - 1$
$\{P_r \wedge P_w \wedge P_b \wedge w \leq b\}$

Hence, for S_b we choose swap.w.($b{-}1$) ;$b := b{-}1$. We are left with S_r, with precondition

$$P_r \wedge P_w \wedge P_b \wedge w < b \wedge h.w = \text{red}$$

Statement swap.w.r seems appropriate for establishing $P(w := w{+}1)$, but what can be said about $h.r$? From P_w we infer $r < w \Rightarrow h.r = \text{white}$, or, equivalently, $r = w \vee h.r = \text{white}$. This yields two cases.

Case (i): $r = w$

$\{P_r \wedge P_w \wedge P_b \wedge r = w < b \wedge h.w = \text{red}\}$
swap.w.r
$\{P_r \wedge P_b \wedge r = w < b \wedge h.r = \text{red}\}$
;$r, w := r{+}1, w{+}1$
$\{P_r \wedge P_b \wedge r = w \leq b$, hence, $P_r \wedge P_b \wedge P_w\}$

Case (ii): $h.r = \text{white}$

$\{P_r \wedge P_w \wedge P_b \wedge w < b \wedge h.w = \text{red} \wedge h.r = \text{white}\}$
swap.w.r
$\{P_r \wedge h.r = \text{red} \wedge (\forall i : r{+}1 \leq i < w : h.i = \text{white}) \wedge h.w = \text{white} \wedge P_b \wedge w < b\}$
;$r, w := r{+}1, w{+}1$
$\{P_r \wedge P_w \wedge P_b \wedge w \leq b\}$

We conclude that swap.w.r ;$r, w := r{+}1, w{+}1$ is a good choice for S_r. Taking all pieces together, we obtain the following program.

164   Array Manipulations

$\lVert$ **var** $r, w, b :$ int;
  $r, w, b := 0, 0, N$ {invariant $P_0 \wedge P_1$, bound $b-w$}
  ;**do** $w \neq b$
    $\rightarrow$ **if** $h.w =$ red $\rightarrow$ swap.$w.r$;$r, w := r+1, w+1$
       $[\!]$ $h.w =$ white $\rightarrow w := w+1$
       $[\!]$ $h.w =$ blue $\rightarrow$ swap.$w.(b-1)$;$b := b-1$
       fi
  od
$\rVert$.

This program has time complexity $\mathcal{O}(N)$. When the colours are uniformly distributed then $\frac{2}{3}N$ swaps are performed on the average. If one chooses to use $h.(b-1)$ instead of $h.w$ then a program is obtained whose execution takes N swaps on the average.

10.2.1   Rotation

In many problems that involve array manipulations the individual array elements do not play a specific role, and these problems may often be expressed, for instance, in terms of segments or sequences. In this subsection we solve such a problem by first deriving an abstract program. That program is then refined into a program in terms of array operations.

Assume that an integer array $h[0..N)$ and integer constant K, $0 \leq K < N$, have been defined. The problem is to rotate h over K places, using swap operations only. A formal specification is

$\lVert$ **con** $K, N :$ int $\{0 \leq K < N\}$;
  var $h :$ **array** $[0..N)$ **of** int;
  $\{(\forall i : 0 \leq i < N : h.i = H.i)\}$
    rotation
  $\{(\forall i : 0 \leq i < N : h.((i+K) \bmod N) = H.i)\}$
$\rVert$,

in which only swap operations are allowed on h.

Note that H is a specification variable (cf. Section 2.0) and not a program variable, i.e., H may not occur in statements. To eliminate **mod** N, we rewrite post-condition R as

$(\forall i : 0 \leq i < N-K : h.(i+K) = H.i) \wedge (\forall i : N-K \leq i < N : h.(i+K-N) = H.i)$

or, equivalently,

$$h[K..N) = H[0..N-K) \land h[0..K) = H[N-K..N)$$

Apparently, this problem can be stated in terms of sequences. Let us denote $H[0..N-K)$ by X and $H[N-K..N)$ by Y. Furthermore, catenation of sequences is denoted by juxtaposition, for instance, $H[0..N)$ corresponds to XY. The empty sequence is denoted by $[\,]$, and the length of sequence U is denoted as $l.U$. In terms of sequences the problem may be specified by

$\{h = XY\}$
rotation
$\{h = YX\}$

where X and Y are as defined above. When X and Y have the same length then the post-condition can be established easily. Indeed, swapping the corresponding elements of X and Y in h yields $h = YX$.

When $l.X < l.Y$ then h may be written as $h = XUV$, where $l.U = l.X$ and $UV = Y$, and we have to solve

$\{h = XUV \land l.U = l.X\}$
rotation
$\{h = UVX\}$

Let us denote the exchange in h, $h = ABCD$, of sequences B and C that have the same length by $SWAP.B.C$. Then this problem may be reduced to solving S in

$\{h = XUV \land YX = UVX \land l.X = l.U\}$
SWAP.X.U
$\{h = UXV\}$
S
$\{h = UVX\}$

i.e., XV has to be transformed into VX, a problem that is of the same form as the original one. From this point one may start the discussion again and consider the cases $l.X \leq l.V$ and $l.V \leq l.X$. Such an investigation leads to the following invariant:

$P: \quad h = AUVB \land YX = AVUB$

i.e., to establish the desired post-condition, U and V have to be interchanged. Since initially $h = XY$, P is established by

Array Manipulations

$$A, U, V, B := [\,], X, Y, [\,]$$

Furthermore, we have

$$P \land (U = [\,] \lor V = [\,]) \Rightarrow h = YX$$

This yields the following solution:

$A, U, V, B := [\,], X, Y, [\,]$
{invariant P, bound: $l.U + l.V$}
; **do** $U \neq [\,] \land V \neq [\,]$
    $\rightarrow$ **if** $l.U \geq l.V$
        $\rightarrow$ 'split $U : U = U_0 U_1 \land l.U_1 = l.V$'
          $\{h = AU_0 U_1 VB \land YX = AVU_0 U_1 B\}$
        ; SWAP.$U_1.V$
          $\{h = AU_0 V U_1 B \land YX = AVU_0 U_1 B\}$
        ; $U, B := U_0, U_1 B$
          $\{h = AUVB \land YX = AVUB\}$
    [] $l.V \geq l.U$
        $\rightarrow$ 'split $V : V = V_0 V_1 \land l.V_0 = l.U$'
          $\{h = AUV_0 V_1 B \land YX = AV_0 V_1 UB\}$
        ; SWAP.$U.V_0$
          $\{h = AV_0 U V_1 B \land YX = AV_0 V_1 UB\}$
        ; $A, V := AV_0, V_1$
          $\{h = AUVB \land YX = AVUB\}$
    fi
od
$\{h = YX\}$.

To encode this algorithm in terms of array h, we represent sequences A, U, V, and B by integer values a, b, k, and l, such that

$A = h[0..a)$
$B = h[b..N)$
$U = h[a..a+k)$, hence, $l.U = k$
$V = h[b-l..b)$, hence, $l.V = l$

These relations are called *coupling invariants*. Note that $a+k = b-l$ should be a coupling invariant as well. In terms of a, b, k, and l, the algorithm is

$\|[\, \textbf{var}\ a,b,k,l : \text{int};$
  $a,b,k,l := 0, N, N{-}K, K$
  $;\textbf{do}\ k \neq 0 \wedge l \neq 0$
    $\rightarrow \textbf{if}\ k \geq l$
      $\rightarrow \|[\, \textbf{var}\ n : \text{int}\ ; n := b{-}l\ ;\textbf{do}\ n \neq b \rightarrow \text{swap}.n.(n{-}l)\ ; n := n{+}1\ \textbf{od}\,]\|$
        $; k := k{-}l\ ; b := b{-}l$
      $[\!]\ l \geq k$
      $\rightarrow \|[\, \textbf{var}\ n : \text{int}\ ; n := a\ ;\textbf{do}\ n \neq a{+}k \rightarrow \text{swap}.n.(n{+}k)\ ; n := n{+}1\ \textbf{od}\,]\|$
        $; l := l{-}k\ ; a := a{+}k$
    $\textbf{fi}$
  $\textbf{od}$
$\,]\|.$

To determine the time complexity of this program, we add the auxiliary variable t to record the number of swaps performed during its execution. We leave out the variables that are not relevant to this discussion. This yields

$\|[\, \textbf{var}\ k,l,t : \text{int};$
  $k,l := N{-}K, K\ ; t := 0$
  $;\textbf{do}\ k \neq 0 \wedge l \neq 0$
    $\rightarrow \textbf{if}\ k \geq l \rightarrow t := t{+}l\ ; k := k{-}l$
      $[\!]\ l \geq k \rightarrow t := t{+}k\ ; l := l{-}k$
    $\textbf{fi}$
  $\textbf{od}$
$\,]\|.$

In this program, we recognize the algorithm for the computation of a greatest common divisor. Note that $t + k + l$ is constant during execution of the repetition. Initially, it has value $0 + K + N - K = N$, hence,

$$t + k + l = N$$

is an invariant of the repetition. What can be said about the final values of k and l? With respect to k and l, we have as invariant

$$k \gcd l = K \gcd (N{-}K)$$

and, since $0 \operatorname{\mathbf{gcd}} x = x \operatorname{\mathbf{gcd}} 0 = x = x+0$, we have as post-condition

$$k + l = K \operatorname{\mathbf{gcd}} (N-K) = K \operatorname{\mathbf{gcd}} N$$

and, since $t + k + l = N$, we conclude that $N - (K \operatorname{\mathbf{gcd}} N)$ swaps are performed.

Exercises

Derive solutions, with time complexity $\mathcal{O}(N)$, to the following problems. The only array manipulations allowed are swaps.

0. $[\![$ **con** N : int $\{N \geq 0\}$;
   var h : **array** $[0..N)$ **of** int;
   S
   $\{(\exists p : 0 \leq p \leq N : (\forall i : 0 \leq i < p : h.i \leq 0) \land (\forall i : p \leq i < N : h.i \geq 0))\}$
   $]\!]$.

1. $[\![$ **con** N : int $\{N \geq 0\}$;
   var h : **array** $[0..N)$ **of** int;
   S
   $\{(\forall i : 0 \leq i < N \land i \bmod 2 = 0 : h.i \bmod 2 = 0)$
   $\lor (\forall i : 0 \leq i < N \land i \bmod 2 = 1 : h.i \bmod 2 = 1)$
   $\}$
   $]\!]$.

2. $[\![$ **con** k, N : int $\{0 \leq k < N\}$;
   var h : **array** $[0..N)$ **of** int;
   S
   $\{h.k = (\mathbf{max} i : 0 \leq i < N : h.i)\}$
   $]\!]$.

3. $[\![$ **con** k, N : int $\{0 \leq k < N\}$;
   var h : **array** $[0..N)$ **of** int;
   S
   $\{(\exists p, q : 0 \leq p \leq q \leq N : (\forall i : 0 \leq i < p : h.i < h.k)$
   $\phantom{\{(\exists p, q : 0 \leq p \leq q \leq N : } \land (\forall i : p \leq i < q : h.i = h.k)$
   $\phantom{\{(\exists p, q : 0 \leq p \leq q \leq N : } \land (\forall i : q \leq i < N : h.i > h.k)$
   $)\}$
   $]\!]$.

Derive solutions, with time complexity $\mathcal{O}(N^2)$, to the following problem. The only array manipulations allowed are swaps.

4. $[\![\,\mathbf{con}\ N : \text{int}\ \{N \geq 0\};$
   $\mathbf{var}\ h : \mathbf{array}\ [0..N)\ \mathbf{of}\ \text{int};$
   $sort$
   $\{(\forall i, j : 0 \leq i \leq j < N : h.i \leq h.j)\}$
   $]\!]$.

   Use a repetition within a repetition and choose as invariants for the outer repetition $P_0 \wedge P_1$ and as invariant for the inner repetition Q where

   $P_1: \ 0 \leq n \leq N$

   and

   (i) $P_0: \ (\forall i, j : 0 \leq i \leq j < n : h.i \leq h.j)$
   $\ Q: \ (\forall i : k \leq i \leq n : h.i \leq h.n)$

   (ii) $P_0: \ (\forall i : 0 \leq i < n : (\forall j : i \leq j < N : h.i \leq h.j))$
   $\ Q: \ (\forall j : k \leq j \leq N : h.n \leq h.j)$

   (iii) $P_0: \ (\forall i : 0 \leq i < n : (\forall j : i \leq j < N : h.i \leq h.j))$
   $\ Q: \ (\forall j : n \leq j \leq k : h.n \leq h.j)$

Chapter 11

Sorting

11.0 Introduction

Many programming problems involving arrays admit efficient solutions if these arrays are ascending. Examples are Binary Search and Slope Search. This is one reason that makes sorting algorithms interesting. Another reason is that solving the sorting problem is a nice illustration of our programming techniques. In this chapter we discuss some sorting algorithms, i.e., algorithms that establish ascendingness of an integer array without changing the bag (multiset) of values of the array (bags are a generalization of sets in the sense that a bag may contain multiple occurrences of an element). The latter requirement is met if we restrict the array operations to swaps.

Let $h[0..N)$ be the integer array to be sorted. Define, for $0 \leq p < N$ and $0 \leq q < N$, inversion.$p.q$ by

$$\text{inversion}.p.q \equiv p < q \land h.p > h.q$$

'Array h is ascending' is equivalent to $(\# p, q : 0 \leq p < q < N : \text{inversion}.p.q) = 0$. The number of inversions is at most
$(\# p, q : 0 \leq p < q < N : \text{true}) = (\Sigma i : 0 \leq i < N : i) = \frac{1}{2}N(N-1)$. Swapping two neighbours in h decreases the number of inversions by at most 1 and so we conclude:

> A sorting algorithm in which only neighbours are swapped has time complexity of at least $\mathcal{O}(N^2)$.

In Section 11.1 sorting algorithms that have time complexity $\mathcal{O}(N^2)$ are derived. What can be said about the time complexity if elements are swapped that are not neighbours? To answer this question, we use the following argument. Assume that all elements of h are different. Then there are $N!$ (N factorial) different arrangements of these elements and only one of these is ascending. Each comparison of two elements has two possible outcomes and, hence, after k comparisons we have 2^k possible outcomes. To ensure that all $N!$ arrangements can be distinguished, 2^k must be at least $N!$, i.e., $k \geq {}^2\log N!$, and from mathematics (Stirling's formula) it is known that $\log N!$ is at least $C * N \log N$ for some $C > 0$. We formulate this result as follows.

A comparison-based sorting algorithm has time complexity of at least $\mathcal{O}(N \log N)$.

In Section 11.2 we present $\mathcal{O}(N \log N)$ sorting algorithms. An example of a non-comparison-based algorithm is *bucket sort*. This algorithm is applicable when the values of h are within a small range, say $[0..K)$. Using a frequency table (cf. Section 10.1), the frequency of each value that occurs in h can be computed and these values are assigned to h in ascending order, leading to an algorithm that has time complexity $\mathcal{O}(N+K)$.

The sorting problem discussed in this chapter has the following specification:

$\|[$ **con** N : int $\{N \geq 1\}$;
　　var h : **array** $[0..N)$ **of** int;
　　　sort
　　$\{(\forall i, j : 0 \leq i \leq j < N : h.i \leq h.j)\}$
$]\|$

in which only swap operations are allowed on h.

In solutions to this problem, we often encounter the following statement $(0 \leq i < N$ and $0 \leq j < N)$:

if $h.i \leq h.j \to$ skip
$[\!]\ h.i > h.j \to$ swap.$i.j$
fi

for which we have

$\{P\}$
if $h.i \leq h.j \to$ skip
$[\!]\ h.i > h.j \to$ swap.$i.j$
fi
$\{Q\}$

is equivalent to

$[P \Rightarrow Q(h := h(i, j : h.i \min h.j, h.i \max h.j))]$

172 Sorting

11.1 Quadratic sorting algorithms

In this section we derive some $\mathcal{O}(N^2)$ sorting algorithms, not because of their usefulness, but to illustrate the ways in which they may be derived and to show what kinds of problems are related to sorting. One should not try to memorize them and we do not supply average-case time complexity derivations, nor do we supply figures that compare these sorting algorithms with respect to some test inputs.

The post-condition R of the specification of *sort* may be rewritten in several ways, for instance, as

$$(\forall i : 0 < i < N : h.(i{-}1) \le h.i)$$
$$(\forall i,j : 0 \le i < j < N : h.i \le h.j)$$
$$(\forall i : 0 \le i < N{-}1 : (\forall j : i \le j < N : h.i \le h.j))$$

Each of these expressions may be generalized in several ways to obtain an invariant. In the following subsections we choose one of these and derive a corresponding algorithm, leading to *insertion sort*, *selection sort*, and *bubble sort* respectively. These are just three of the better-known quadratic solutions. Other investigations of this kind are left to the reader.

11.1.0 Insertion Sort

We choose as post-condition

$R: \quad (\forall i,j : 0 \le i < j < N : h.i \le h.j)$

Replacing the constant N by integer variable n yields invariants P_0 and P_1 defined by

$P_0: \quad (\forall i,j : 0 \le i < j < n : h.i \le h.j)$
$P_1: \quad 1 \le n \le N$

which are established by $n := 1$. As guard of a repetition we choose $n \ne N$ and as bound function $N{-}n$ will do. For $1 \le n < N$, we have

$$P_0(n := n{+}1) \equiv (\forall i,j : 0 \le i < j < n{+}1 : h.i \le h.j)$$

which equals P_0 apart from $j = n$, i.e., P_0 can be written as

$$(\forall i,j : 0 \le i < j < n{+}1 \land j \ne n : h.i \le h.j)$$

We generalize this expression, introducing the integer variable k, to

$Q_0: \ (\forall i, j : 0 \leq i < j < n+1 \land j \neq k : h.i \leq h.j)$

which is initialized by $k := n$. Furthermore, $Q_0 \land k = 0 \Rightarrow P_0(n := n+1)$ and also, because of the transitivity of $\leq$, we have, for $1 \leq k \leq n$,

$Q_0 \land h.(k-1) \leq h.k \Rightarrow P_0(n := n+1)$

as well. Hence,

$Q_0 \land (k = 0 \lor h.(k-1) \leq h.k) \Rightarrow P_0(n := n+1)$

For the case $k \geq 1 \land h.(k-1) > h.k$ we investigate a decrease of k by 1 and we derive

$\quad Q_0$
$\equiv \quad$ { definition of Q_0 }
$\quad (\forall i, j : 0 \leq i < j < n+1 \land j \neq k : h.i \leq h.j)$
$\equiv \quad$ { definition of **max** }
$\quad (\forall j : 0 \leq j < n+1 \land j \neq k : h.j = (\mathbf{max}\, i : 0 \leq i \leq j : h.i))$
$\equiv \quad$ { range split }
$\quad (\forall j : 0 \leq j < k-1 : h.j = (\mathbf{max}\, i : 0 \leq i \leq j : h.i)) \land$
$\quad (\forall j : k+1 \leq j < n+1 : h.j = (\mathbf{max}\, i : 0 \leq i \leq j : h.i)) \land$
$\quad h.(k-1) = (\mathbf{max}\, i : 0 \leq i \leq k-1 : h.i)$

The first and the second conjunct of the last line of this derivation are not affected by swap.$(k-1).k$. For the third conjunct, we have

$\quad h.(k-1) = (\mathbf{max}\, i : 0 \leq i \leq k-1 : h.i)$
$\Rightarrow \quad$ { **max** calculus }
$\quad h.(k-1) \, \mathbf{max} \, h.k = (\mathbf{max}\, i : 0 \leq i \leq k : h.i)$

Hence, if $h.(k-1) > h.k$ then swap.$(k-1).k$ establishes

$h.k = (\mathbf{max}\, i : 0 \leq i \leq k : h.i)$

and it can only falsify $h.(k-1) = (\mathbf{max}\, i : 0 \leq i \leq k-1 : h.i)$, from which we infer

$\{Q_0 \land k \geq 1 \land h.(k-1) > h.k\} \ \text{swap}.(k-1).k \ \{Q_0(k := k-1)\}$

One may be tempted to translate this result into the following program fragment for 'establish $P_0(n := n+1)$':

174   Sorting

$$\begin{array}{l}\|[\,\mathbf{var}\ k:\mathrm{int};\\ \quad k:=n\\ \quad ;\mathbf{do}\ k\neq 0\ \wedge\ h.(k{-}1)>h.k\ \rightarrow\ \mathrm{swap}.(k{-}1).k\ ;k:=k{-}1\ \mathbf{od}\\ \,]\!|.\end{array}$$

However, the guard $k\neq 0\ \wedge\ h.(k{-}1)>h.k$ is not defined for $k=0$. We solve this problem by defining the bounds for k by

$Q_1:\ 1\leq k\leq n$

and taking case $k=1$ out of the repetition. This leads to

Insertion Sort

$$\begin{array}{l}\|[\,\mathbf{var}\ n:\mathrm{int};\\ \quad n:=1\\ \quad ;\mathbf{do}\ n\neq N\\ \qquad \rightarrow\ \|[\,\mathbf{var}\ k:\mathrm{int};\\ \qquad\qquad k:=n\\ \qquad\qquad ;\mathbf{do}\ k\neq 1\ \wedge\ h.(k{-}1)>h.k\ \rightarrow\ \mathrm{swap}.(k{-}1).k\ ;k:=k{-}1\ \mathbf{od}\\ \qquad\qquad ;\mathbf{if}\ h.0>h.1\ \rightarrow\ \mathrm{swap}.0.1\ []\ h.0\leq h.1\ \rightarrow\ \mathrm{skip}\ \mathbf{fi}\\ \qquad \,]\!|\\ \qquad\qquad ;n:=n{+}1\\ \quad \mathbf{od}\\ \,]\!|.\end{array}$$

When this program is executed and h is initially decreasing then $\frac{1}{2}N(N{-}1)$ steps are performed. When h is initially ascending then only N steps are performed.

11.1.1 Selection Sort

We write the post-condition of *sort* as

$R:\ (\forall i:0\leq i<N:(\forall j:i\leq j<N:h.i\leq h.j))$

We replace the first occurrence of N by integer variable n. Replacement of both occurrences of N gives rise to Insertion Sort, as the reader may verify. Thus, we propose invariants P_0 and P_1 defined by

$P_0:\ (\forall i:0\leq i<n:(\forall j:i\leq j<N:h.i\leq h.j))$
$P_1:\ 0\leq n\leq N$

We derive for $0 \leq n < N$:

$P_0(n := n+1)$
$\equiv$ { substitution }
$(\forall i : 0 \leq i < n+1 : (\forall j : i \leq j < N : h.i \leq h.j))$
$\equiv$ { split off $i = n$, $0 \leq n < n+1$ }
$P_0 \wedge (\forall j : n \leq j < N : h.n \leq h.j)$
$\equiv$ { **min** calculus }
$P_0 \wedge h.n = (\min j : n \leq j < N : h.j)$

Hence, a possible solution to 'establish $P_0(n := n+1)$' is

$[\![$ **var** a : int;
 'establish $n \leq a < N \wedge h.a = (\min j : n \leq j < N : h.j)$ without changing h'
 ; swap.$n.a$
$]\!]$.

Note that swap.$n.a$ does not affect P_0. A solution to the problem above is obtained by applying Searching by Elimination (cf. *maxlocation* in Section 6.3) with invariant

$n \leq a \leq b < N \wedge (\min j : n \leq j < N : h.j) = (\min j : a \leq j \leq b : h.j)$

Thus, we obtain the following solution, known as Selection Sort:

$[\![$ **var** n : int;
 $n := 0$
 ; **do** $n \neq N$
  $\rightarrow [\![$ **var** a, b : int;
   $a, b := n, N-1$
   ; **do** $a \neq b$
    $\rightarrow$ **if** $h.a \leq h.b \rightarrow b := b-1$
    $[\!]$ $h.b \leq h.a \rightarrow a := a+1$
    fi
   od
   ; swap.$n.a$
  $]\!]$
  ; $n := n+1$
 od
$]\!]$.

This program will also take $\frac{1}{2}N(N-1)$ steps. The number of swaps is N.

11.1.2 Bubble Sort

Our final example of an $\mathcal{O}(N^2)$ sorting algorithm is known as *bubble sort*. We choose the same invariants as we did for Selection Sort:

$P_0: \quad (\forall i: 0 \le i < n : (\forall j : i \le j < N : h.i \le h.j))$

$P_1: \quad 0 \le n \le N$

Then (cf. previous derivation) we have

$$P_0(n := n+1) \equiv P_0 \wedge h.n = (\min j : n \le j < N : h.j)$$

Instead of computing a location of the minimum of $h[n..N]$, we replace in the last expression both occurrences of n by integer variable k and we define Q_0 and Q_1 by

$Q_0: \quad h.k = (\min j : k \le j < N : h.j)$

$Q_1: \quad n \le k \le N-1$

which are established by $k := N-1$. We derive

$\quad\quad Q_0$
$\equiv \quad$ { definition of Q_0 }
$\quad\quad h.k = (\min j : k \le j < N : h.j)$
$\Rightarrow \quad$ { Leibniz }
$\quad\quad h.(k-1) \min h.k = h.(k-1) \min (\min j : k \le j < N : h.j)$
$\equiv \quad$ { calculus }
$\quad\quad h.(k-1) \min h.k = (\min j : k-1 \le j < N : h.j)$

Hence, sorting $h.(k-1)$ and $h.k$ establishes $Q_0(k := k-1)$. This yields as solution a program known as Bubble Sort, which is presented below. Execution of this program takes $\frac{1}{2}N(N-1)$ steps. When the selection amounts to skip in each step of the inner repetition, we may conclude that $h[n..N]$ is ascending, and, hence, R holds. More precisely, we introduce boolean variable b and add invariant P_2 :

$P_2: \quad b \Rightarrow h[n..N)$ is ascending

Then $P_0 \wedge b \Rightarrow R$. To invariants Q_0 and Q_1 we add

$Q_2: \quad b \Rightarrow h[k..N)$ is ascending

This results in a second version of bubble sort (Bubble Sort (1)). For ascending arrays execution of this version takes N steps.

Bubble Sort (0)

$\lVert$ **var** n : int;
$\quad n := 0$
$\quad$; **do** $n \neq N$
$\quad\quad \rightarrow \lVert$ **var** k : int;
$\quad\quad\quad k := N{-}1$
$\quad\quad\quad$; **do** $k \neq n$
$\quad\quad\quad\quad \rightarrow$ **if** $h.(k{-}1) \leq h.k \rightarrow$ skip
$\quad\quad\quad\quad\quad [\!]\ h.(k{-}1) > h.k \rightarrow$ swap$.(k{-}1).k$
$\quad\quad\quad\quad$ **fi**
$\quad\quad\quad$ **od**
$\quad\quad\quad$; $k := k{-}1$
$\quad\quad]\!]$
$\quad\quad$; $n := n{+}1$
$\quad$ **od**
$]\!]$.

Bubble Sort (1)

$\lVert$ **var** n : int; b : bool;
$\quad n, b := 0,$ false
$\quad$; **do** $n \neq N \wedge \neg b$
$\quad\quad \rightarrow \lVert$ **var** k : int;
$\quad\quad\quad k, b := N{-}1,$ true
$\quad\quad\quad$; **do** $k \neq n$
$\quad\quad\quad\quad \rightarrow$ **if** $h.(k{-}1) \leq h.k \rightarrow$ skip
$\quad\quad\quad\quad\quad [\!]\ h.(k{-}1) > h.k \rightarrow b :=$ false ; swap$.(k{-}1).k$
$\quad\quad\quad\quad$ **fi**
$\quad\quad\quad$ **od**
$\quad\quad\quad$; $k := k{-}1$
$\quad\quad]\!]$
$\quad\quad$; $n := n{+}1$
$\quad$ **od**
$]\!]$.

The solutions discussed in this section are only suited for sorting relatively small arrays (of length at most 100). In the following section we consider some more advanced sorting algorithms.

Exercises

0. Solve:

$$[\![\, \mathbf{con}\ N : \mathrm{int}\ \{N \geq 1\};\ X : \mathbf{array}\ [0..N)\ \mathbf{of}\ \mathrm{int};$$
$$\mathbf{var}\ h : \mathbf{array}\ [0..N)\ \mathbf{of}\ \mathrm{int};$$
$$\mathrm{sort}$$
$$\{(\forall i : 0 \leq i < N : (\exists j : 0 \leq j < N : h.j = i))$$
$$\land (\forall i, j : 0 \leq i \leq j < N : X.(h.i) \leq X.(h.j))\}$$
$$]\!].$$

1. A sorting algorithm is called *stable* if the order of any two equal values is not changed. In terms of the previous exercise this means that the post-condition is to be strengthened by

$$i \leq j \land X.i = X.j \Rightarrow h.i \leq h.j$$

   Which of the sorting algorithms of this section are stable?

2. Derive a program that sorts N pairs lexicographically. The N pairs are $\langle x.i, y.i \rangle$ ($0 \leq i < N$) and point $\langle a, b \rangle$ is lexicographically smaller than $\langle c, d \rangle$ if

$$a < c \lor (a = c \land b < d)$$

3. Derive a program that sorts integer matrix $x : \mathbf{array}\ [0..M) \times [0..N)$ such that x is ascending in both arguments.

4. Derive a program that sorts integer matrix $x : \mathbf{array}\ [0..M) \times [0..N)$ such that $(\forall i, j : 0 \leq i \leq j < M : x.i$ is lexicographically at most $x.j)$.

11.2 Advanced sorting algorithms

In this section we present the more practical sorting algorithms *Quicksort*, *Mergesort* and *Heapsort*. Quicksort, invented by C.A.R. Hoare, has worst-case time complexity $\mathcal{O}(N^2)$. Its average time complexity, however, is $\mathcal{O}(N \log N)$. It uses $\mathcal{O}(\log N)$ auxiliary storage. Mergesort has worst-case time complexity $\mathcal{O}(N \log N)$. It uses an auxiliary array of length N. Heapsort, invented by J. Williams, also has worst-case time complexity $\mathcal{O}(N \log N)$, but no auxiliary array is needed.

Both Quicksort and Mergesort are more elegantly presented as *recursive* programs. The bag of integers that has to be sorted is divided into two subbags and the results of sorting these subbags are combined to obtain the sorted sequence corresponding to the original bag. For Quicksort the division into subbags is the essential part and for Mergesort the combination of the sorted sequences is the essential part. In this book, however, we do not treat recursion and both programs are presented as ordinary iterative programs.

11.2.0 Quicksort

As before, let $h[0..N)$ be the array to be sorted. Let $z = h.j$ for some j, $0 \leq j < N$. Performing the Dutch National Flag (DNF) algorithm of Section 10.2.0 with

red	: $h.i < z$
white	: $h.i = z$
blue	: $h.i > z$

establishes post-condition

$$(\forall i : 0 \leq i < r : h.i < z)$$
$$\wedge\ (\forall i : r \leq i < w : h.i = z)$$
$$\wedge\ (\forall i : w \leq i < N: h.i > z)$$

Hence, $h[0..r)$ and $h[w..N)$ still have to be sorted, i.e., this post-condition implies

h is ascending $\equiv$ $h[0..r)$ is ascending $\wedge$ $h[w..N)$ is ascending

We may apply a similar splitting to $h[0..r)$ and $h[w..N)$, leading to four smaller parts that still have to be sorted. A generalization of this idea is expressed by the following invariant:

P: $\quad h[0..N)$ is ascending $\equiv$ $(\forall v : v \in V : h$ is ascending on $v)$

where V is a set of disjoint subsegments of $[0..N)$ and where for subsegment v:

h is ascending on v $\equiv$ $(\forall i, j : i \in v \wedge j \in v \wedge i \leq j : h.i \leq h.j)$

A program based on P is presented below.

$V := \{[0..N)\}$
; **do** $V \neq \emptyset$
   $\to$ 'choose $\alpha \in V$'
       ; **if** length.$\alpha \leq 1 \to V := V \setminus \{\alpha\}$
       [] length.$\alpha \geq 2$
           $\to$ 'choose $j \in \alpha$'
               ; $z := h.j$
               ; 'perform DNF with z on α'
               $\{\alpha = \beta\gamma\delta \land (\forall i : i \in \beta : h.i < z)$
                                $\land (\forall i : i \in \gamma : h.i = z)$
                                $\land (\forall i : i \in \delta : h.i > z)$
               $\}$
               ; $V := (V \setminus \{\alpha\}) \cup \{\beta\} \cup \{\delta\}$
       fi
od

(Why does it terminate?) To obtain a program in the guarded command language, we have to find a suitable representation for V, and we have to refine 'choose $\alpha \in V$' and 'choose $j \in \alpha$'. The set V can be represented by two integer arrays x and y, and an integer variable k, such that

$$V = \{[x.i .. y.i) \mid 0 \leq i < k\}$$

The DNF part splits sequence α into three parts: β, γ, and δ. At least one of the segments β and δ has a length which is at most half the length of α. When 'choose $\alpha \in V$' is refined to 'choose an element of V of minimal length', we may hope that the number of elements of V will not be too large. Indeed, let $G.n$ be the maximum number of elements that V will contain if we start with a segment of length n and if we choose in each step an element of V of minimal length. Then

$G.1 = 1$
$G.n \leq 1 + G.(n \text{ div } 2) \quad (n \geq 2)$

from which we infer

$G.n \leq 1 + {}^2\!\log n$

We conclude that for x and y only arrays of length $1 + {}^2\!\log N$ are needed. Since splitting a minimal element of V into two parts yields a minimal element again, we represent V by

$$V = \{[x.i..y.i) \mid 0 \leq i < k\} \cup \{[p..q)\}$$

such that

$$(\forall i : 0 < i < k : y.i - x.i \leq y.(i-1) - x.(i-1))$$

and

$$(\forall i : 0 \leq i < k : q - p \leq y.i - x.i)$$

Then

$$P \wedge k = 0 \wedge q-p \leq 1 \Rightarrow h \text{ is ascending}$$

The value of $^2\log N$ is easily computed. For 'choose $j \in [p..q)$' we choose (for the sake of symmetry) $j = (p+q) \operatorname{\mathbf{div}} 2$, i.e., $z := h.((p+q)\operatorname{\mathbf{div}} 2)$. The complete solution is presented below. The first part consists of the computation of the upper bound for arrays x and y.

When this program is applied to an increasing sequence, then $h[p..q)$ is divided into two parts that both have length at most $(q-p)\operatorname{\mathbf{div}} 2$. Let $T.n$ denote the time complexity of sorting an increasing sequence of length n in this way. We have the following recurrence relation for T:

$$T.1 = 0$$
$$T.n = 2T.(\tfrac{1}{2}n) + n \text{ for } n \geq 2$$

(For the Dutch National Flag n steps are needed.)
This recurrence relation has $T.n = n \log n$ as solution: for an already increasing sequence execution of this program takes $\mathcal{O}(N \log N)$ steps.

When this program is applied to an arbitrary sequence and in each step the *median* of sequence $h[p..q)$ is assigned to z, the same recurrence relation is obtained. A linear program for the computation of the median does exist, but its derivation is beyond the scope of this book.

When all elements of h are different and in each step of the repetition the minimum of $h[p..q)$ is assigned to z, execution takes $\tfrac{1}{2}N(N+1)$ steps, which is the worst-case behavior of Quicksort. It can be shown that the average execution time over all permutations of $[0..N)$ is $\mathcal{O}(N \log N)$.

The complete program is presented below.

Sorting

Quicksort

|[**var** n, m : int;
    $n, m := 0, 1 \ \{m = 2^n\}$
   ; **do** $m < N \to n, m := n+1, m * 2$ **od**
    $\{n \geq {}^2\log N\}$
   ; |[**var** k, p, q : int; x, y : **array** $[0..n)$ **of** int;
        $k, p, q := 0, 0, N$
       ; **do** $k \neq 0 \ \lor \ q-p \geq 2$
             $\to$ **if** $q-p \leq 1 \to k := k-1; \ p, q := x.k, y.k$
                 [] $q-p \geq 2 \to$ |[**var** r, w, b, z : int;
                                       $z := h.((p+q) \ \mathbf{div} \ 2)$
                                     ; $r, w, b := p, p, q$
                                     ; **do** $w \neq b \to$ **if** $h.w < z \to$ swap.$r.w$; $r, w := r+1, w+1$
                                                          [] $h.w = z \to w := w+1$
                                                          [] $h.w > z \to b := b-1;$ swap.$b.w$
                                                          fi
                                       od
                                     ; **if** $r-p \leq q-w \to x.k := w; \ y.k := q; \ q := r$
                                       [] $q-w \leq r-p \to x.k := p; \ y.k := r; \ p := w$
                                       fi
                                     ; $k := k+1$
                                     ]|
             fi
        od
     ]|
]|.

Exercises

0. Let $N \geq 1$ and let $h[0..N)$ be an array of integers. Derive a program for the computation of the unique element of h that occupies position k when h is sorted ($0 \leq k < N$), without sorting the entire array h. (Hint: use the DNF part of Quicksort).

11.2.1 Mergesort

Mergesort is based on the fact that two ascending sequences can be merged into one ascending sequence in linear time. To define the merge **m** of integer sequences x and y, we use the following notation: for integer a and sequence x, the sequence consisting of a followed by sequence x is denoted as ax. The merge of two sequences is defined by

$x \, \mathbf{m} \, y = x$ if y is the empty sequence

$x \, \mathbf{m} \, y = y$ if x is the empty sequence

$ax \, \mathbf{m} \, by = \begin{cases} a(x \, \mathbf{m} \, by) & \text{if } a \leq b \\ b(ax \, \mathbf{m} \, y) & \text{if } b \leq a \end{cases}$

Then **m** has the following properties:

x is ascending $\wedge$ y is ascending $\Rightarrow$ $x \, \mathbf{m} \, y$ is ascending

The bag of elements of $x \, \mathbf{m} \, y$ is the sum of the bags of elements of x and y

These properties enable us to use merge in a sorting algorithm. Let us first present an algorithm for the computation of the merge of two sequences. Program *merge* is specified by

$\| [\, \mathbf{con}\ M, N : \text{int}\ \{M \geq 0 \wedge N \geq 0\};\ x : \mathbf{array}\ [0..M)\ \mathbf{of}\ \text{int};\ y : \mathbf{array}\ [0..N)\ \mathbf{of}\ \text{int};$
$\quad \mathbf{var}\ z : \mathbf{array}\ [0..M{+}N)\ \mathbf{of}\ \text{int};$
$\quad\quad merge$
$\quad \{z = x \, \mathbf{m} \, y\}$
$\,]\!|.$

From the definition of **m** we infer that a tail invariant is appropriate (cf. Section 4.4). Denoting catenation of sequences x and y by $x \mathbin{+\mkern-8mu+} y$, we define P_0 by

$P_0 : \ z[0..c) \mathbin{+\mkern-8mu+} (x[a..M) \, \mathbf{m} \, y[b..N)) \ = \ x \, \mathbf{m} \, y$

and P_1 by

$P_1 : \ 0 \leq a \leq M \wedge 0 \leq b \leq N \wedge 0 \leq c \leq M{+}N$

Then

$P_0 \wedge (a = M \vee b = N) \Rightarrow z[0..c) \mathbin{+\mkern-8mu+} x[a..M) \mathbin{+\mkern-8mu+} y[b..N) \ = \ x \, \mathbf{m} \, y$

This leads to the following solution to *merge*.

‖ **var** a, b, c : int;
 $a, b, c := 0, 0, 0$ {invariant $P_0 \wedge P_1$, bound: $M - a + N - b$}
 ; **do** $a \neq M \wedge b \neq N$
   $\rightarrow$ **if** $x.a \leq y.b \rightarrow z.c := x.a$; $a, c := a+1, c+1$
   [] $y.b \leq x.a \rightarrow z.c := y.b$; $b, c := b+1, c+1$
   fi
 od
 ; **do** $a \neq M \rightarrow z.c := x.a$; $a, c := a+1, c+1$ **od**
 ; **do** $b \neq N \rightarrow z.c := y.b$; $b, c := b+1, c+1$ **od**
 $\{P_0 \wedge a = M \wedge b = N$, hence $z = x \mathbf{\,m\,} y\}$
‖.

We can use *merge* for sorting as follows. Let α be an integer sequence of length N. Split α into two sequences of length $\frac{1}{2}N$ (approximately). Sort these two sequences (by any sorting algorithm) and merge them into the sorted version of α. When we have a sorting algorithm that takes N^2 steps for a sequence of length N, this approach yields an algorithm whose execution takes $\frac{1}{4}N^2 + \frac{1}{4}N^2 + N$ steps, which is approximately twice as fast as the original algorithm!

Of course (compare this to the discussion in Section 5.1), we may apply this idea again and sort the two parts of α in the way described above, leading to an algorithm that is approximately four times as fast as the original one. In general, we start with sequences of length 1: for integer array $h[0..N)$, we have that each segment $h[i..i+1)$ is ascending. This is generalized to

P_0 : $(\forall\, i : 0 \leq i : h[i{*}k\mathinner{..}(i{+}1){*}k)$ is ascending)

in which we define $h.i = \infty$ for $i \geq N$. The bound for integer k is given by

P_1 : $1 \leq k$

These invariants are established by $k := 1$, and

$\qquad P_0 \wedge k \geq N \Rightarrow h$ is ascending

To obtain an $\mathcal{O}(N \log N)$ program, we investigate the effect of $k := k{*}2$:

$P_0(k := k*2)$
$\equiv$ { substitution }
    $(\forall i : 0 \leq i : h[i*k*2 .. (i+1)*k*2)$ is ascending)
$\equiv$ { calculus }
    $(\forall i : 0 \leq i : h[2i*k .. (2i+2)*k)$ is ascending)
$\equiv$ { calculus }
    $(\forall i : 0 \leq i \wedge i \bmod 2 = 0 : h[i*k .. (i+2)*k)$ is ascending)

Hence, $P_0(k := k*2)$ is established by merging, for all i, $0 \leq i \wedge i \bmod 2 = 0$, sequences $h[i*k .. (i+1)*k)$ and $h[(i+1)*k .. (i+2)*k)$, and assigning the result to $h[i*k .. (i+2)*k)$. For this purpose, we introduce integer variable n for a repetition that has invariant $P_0 \wedge Q_0 \wedge Q_1$, where

Q_0 : $(\forall i : 0 \leq i < n \wedge i \bmod 2 = 0 : h[i*k .. (i+2)*k)$ is ascending)
Q_1 : $0 \leq n$

which are established by $n := 0$. Furthermore,

$$Q_0 \wedge (n+1)*k \geq N \Rightarrow P_0(k := k*2)$$

For the sake of convenience, we introduce variables a, b, and c, such that

$$a = n*k \wedge b = (n+1)*k \wedge c = ((n+2)*k) \min N$$

and we arrive at the following solution to 'establish $P_0(k := k*2)$':

$\|[$ **var** n, a, b, c : int;
    $n, a, b, c := 0, 0, k, (2*k) \min N$
    ; **do** $b < N$
        $\rightarrow$ $h[a..c) := h[a..b)$ **m** $h[b..c)$
            ; $n, a, b, c := n+2, a+2*k, b+2*k, (c+2*k) \min N$
    od
$]\|$.

Each step of this repetition takes $2k$ steps; since b is incremented by $2k$, the total number of steps is at most N. Since k is doubled at each step of the outer repetition, the time complexity of Mergesort is $\mathcal{O}(N \log N)$. From the program fragment above, variable n may be removed.

Sorting

The computation of $h[a..b)$ **m** $h[b..c)$ is not performed *in situ*: we introduce auxiliary array $z[a..c)$ and $h[a..c) := h[a..b)$ **m** $h[b..c)$ is implemented by

$z[a..c) := h[a..b)$ **m** $h[b..c)$
$; h[a..c) := z[a..c)$

The complete program is presented below.

Mergesort

⦇ **var** k : int;
  $k := 1$
  ; **do** $k < N \rightarrow$
        ⦇ **var** a, b, c : int;
          $a, b, c := 0, k, (2*k)$ **min** N
          ; **do** $b < N \rightarrow$
                ⦇ **var** p, q, r : int; z : **array** $[a..c)$ **of** int;
                  $p, q, r := a, b, a$
                  ; **do** $p \neq b \wedge q \neq c$
                        $\rightarrow$ **if** $h.p \leq h.q \rightarrow z.r := h.p$; $r, p := r+1, p+1$
                        ◻ $h.q \leq h.p \rightarrow z.r := h.q$; $r, q := r+1, q+1$
                        fi
                  od
                  ; **do** $p \neq b \rightarrow z.r := h.p$; $r, p := r+1, p+1$ **od**
                  ; **do** $q \neq c \rightarrow z.r := h.q$; $r, q := r+1, q+1$ **od**
                  ; $r := a$
                  ; **do** $r \neq c \rightarrow h.r := z.r$; $r := r+1$ **od**
                ⦈
                ; $a, b, c := a + 2*k, b + 2*k, (c + 2*k)$ **min** N
        od
        ⦈
        ; $k := k*2$
  od
⦈.

11.2.2 Heapsort

Our final sorting algorithm is called *heapsort*. To make the formulas needed for its explanation more manageable, we describe the algorithm for an array $h[1..N]$ of integers. The final algorithm is easily adapted such that it satisfies the sort specification for an array defined on $[0..N)$.

One of the algorithms derived in Section 12.1 is Selection Sort. In each step of the outer repetition of Selection Sort, the minimum value of $h[n..N]$ is determined and interchanged with $h.n$.

The invariant of Selection Sort was obtained by replacing in the post-condition of *sort* the constant N by variable n. A replacement of the constant 0 by variable n results in a similar program, i.e., in

$\quad n := N$
$\quad ; \mathbf{do}\ n \neq 1$
$\quad\quad \rightarrow\ $ 'establish $\ 1 \leq a \leq n\ \wedge\ h.a = (\mathbf{max}\,i : 1 \leq i \leq n : h.i)$'
$\quad\quad ;\ \mathrm{swap}.a.n$
$\quad\quad ;\ n := n-1$
$\quad \mathbf{od}$

with invariants:

$\quad h[n+1..N]$ is ascending
$\quad (\forall i, j : 1 \leq i \leq n\ \wedge\ n < j \leq N : h.i \leq h.j)$
$\quad 1 \leq n \leq N$

A straightforward refinement of 'establish $\ 1 \leq a \leq n \wedge h.a = (\mathbf{max}\,i : 1 \leq i \leq n : h.i)$' yields an $\mathcal{O}(N^2)$ algorithm. To obtain a more efficient program, we can, for instance, strengthen the invariants with

$\quad h.1 = (\mathbf{max}\,i : 1 \leq i \leq n : h.i)$

This yields

$\quad n := N$
$\quad ;$ 'establish $h.1 = (\mathbf{max}\,i : 1 \leq i \leq n : h.i)$'
$\quad ; \mathbf{do}\ n \neq 1$
$\quad\quad \rightarrow\ \ \mathrm{swap}.1.n$
$\quad\quad ;\ n := n-1$
$\quad\quad ;$ 're-establish $h.1 = (\mathbf{max}\,i : 1 \leq i \leq n : h.i)$'
$\quad \mathbf{od}$

188   *Sorting*

Again, a straightforward refinement of 're-establish $h.1 = (\max i : 1 \leq i \leq n : h.i)$' gives rise to an $\mathcal{O}(N^2)$ algorithm.

The idea of Heapsort is to strengthen $h.1 = (\max i : 1 \leq i \leq n : h.i)$ to the so-called *heap-condition* heap.n, defined in such a way that

$$\text{heap}.n \Rightarrow h.1 = (\max i : 1 \leq i \leq n : h.i)$$

The resulting program Heapsort has the following structure:

$n := N$
; 'establish heap.n'
; **do** $n \neq 1$
$\quad \rightarrow \quad$ swap.1.n
$\qquad ; n := n-1$
$\qquad ;$ 're-establish heap.n'
od

and heap.n is defined in such a way that 'establish heap.N' takes $\mathcal{O}(N \log N)$ steps and 're-establish heap.n' takes $\mathcal{O}(\log N)$ steps. The result is an $\mathcal{O}(N \log N)$ sorting algorithm.

Thus, heap.n should satisfy

(i) heap.$n \Rightarrow h.1 = (\max i : 1 \leq i \leq n : h.i)$

(ii) 'establish heap.N' has time complexity at most $\mathcal{O}(N \log N)$

(iii) 're-establish heap.n' has time complexity at most $\mathcal{O}(\log N)$

A possible choice for heap.n that satisfies (i) is '$h[1..n]$ is descending', but, in view of (ii), this choice begs the question. We weaken '$h[1..n]$ is descending' by defining a partial order $\rightarrow$ of which $\leq$ is a refinement. This partial order is defined on the positive integers by

$$i \rightarrow j \equiv (\exists k : k \geq 0 : j \text{ div } 2^k = i)$$

Verify that $\rightarrow$ is a partial order, i.e., for all $i, j, k \geq 1$:

$\quad i \rightarrow i \qquad\qquad\qquad\qquad$ (reflexivity)
$\quad i \rightarrow j \wedge j \rightarrow k \Rightarrow i \rightarrow k \quad$ (transitivity)
$\quad i \rightarrow j \wedge j \rightarrow i \equiv i = j \quad$ (anti-symmetry)

and that $\leq$ is a refinement of $\rightarrow$, i.e.,

$$i \to j \Rightarrow i \leq j$$

Note that the (immediate) successors of i with respect to $\to$ are $2i$ and $2i+1$.

The heap condition is defined for n, $1 \leq n \leq N$, by

$$\text{heap}.n \equiv (\forall i, j : 1 \leq i \leq j \leq n \wedge i \to j : h.i \geq h.j)$$

Since $(\forall j : 1 \leq j : 1 \to j)$, requirement (i) is met:

$$\text{heap}.n \Rightarrow h.1 = (\max j : 1 \leq j \leq n : h.j)$$

and, since heap.n is weaker than '$h[1..n]$ is descending', we may hope that requirements (ii) and (iii) can be satisfied as well.

We first discuss 'establish heap.N', i.e., establish

$$(\forall i, j : 1 \leq i \leq j \leq N \wedge i \to j : h.i \geq h.j)$$

A possible invariant is obtained by replacing N by variable n. However, since

$$(\forall i, j : N \,\mathbf{div}\, 2 < i \leq j \leq N : \neg(i \to j))$$

we prefer invariants P_0 and P_1 defined by

$P_0:\ (\forall i, j : n < i \leq j \leq N \wedge i \to j : h.i \geq h.j)$
$P_1:\ 0 \leq n$

which are established by $n := N \,\mathbf{div}\, 2$ and for which we have

$$P_0 \wedge n = 0 \Rightarrow \text{heap}.N$$

Since

$$P_0(n := n-1) \equiv (\forall i, j : n \leq i \leq j \leq N \wedge i \to j : h.i \geq h.j)$$

we choose (in a similar way as we did for Insertion Sort) as invariants for a repetition that has post-condition $P_0(n := n-1)$:

$Q_0:\ (\forall i, j : n \leq i \leq j \leq N \wedge i \to j \wedge i \neq k : h.i \geq h.j)$
$Q_1:\ n \leq k$

which are initialized by $k := n$, and for which we have

$$\begin{aligned}
&\quad P_0(n := n-1) \\
&\equiv \quad \{\text{definition of } P_0\} \\
&\quad (\forall i, j : n \leq i \leq j \leq N \wedge i \to j : h.i \geq h.j) \\
&\equiv \quad \{\text{definition of } Q_0\} \\
&\quad Q_0 \wedge (\forall j : k \leq j \leq N \wedge k \to j : h.k \geq h.j) \\
&\equiv \quad \{\text{definition of } \mathbf{max}\} \\
&\quad Q_0 \wedge h.k = (\mathbf{max}\, j : k \leq j < N \wedge k \to j : h.j) \\
&\equiv \quad \{\text{definition of } \to, \text{ transitivity of } \geq\} \\
&\quad Q_0 \wedge h.k \geq h.(2k)\,\mathbf{max}\,h.(2k+1)
\end{aligned}$$

where we take $h.i = -\infty$ for $i > N$. From this derivation we conclude

$$Q_0 \wedge 2k > N \equiv P_0(n := n-1)$$

which yields $2k \leq N$ as guard for the inner repetition. Let p be such that

$$(p = 2k \vee p = 2k+1) \wedge h.p = h.(2k)\,\mathbf{max}\,h.(2k+1)$$

In view of the derivation above, we consider statement

if $h.k \geq h.p \to$ skip $[\!]$ $h.k < h.p \to$ swap.$k.p$ **fi**

which establishes $h.k \geq h.(2k)\,\mathbf{max}\,h.(2k+1)$.

For any i, $n \leq i < k \wedge i \to k$, we have, on account of Q_0, $h.i \geq h.k$, $h.i \geq h.(2k)$, and $h.i \geq h.(2k+1)$. Hence, swap.$k.p$ does not affect $h.i \geq h.k$ for $n \leq i < k \wedge i \to k$.

Since $h.p$ may be decreased, only

$$(\forall j : p \leq j \leq N \wedge p \to j : h.p \geq h.j)$$

may be falsified (cf. the derivation of Insertion Sort), and we conclude that

if $h.k \leq h.p \to$ skip $[\!]$ $h.k > h.p \to$ swap.$k.p$ **fi**

establishes $Q_0(k := p)$.

For the sake of convenience, we introduce variable q with

$$(2k < N \Rightarrow q = 2k+1) \wedge (2k = N \Rightarrow q = N)$$

This leads to the following program for 'establish heap.N'.

Advanced sorting algorithms 191

|[**var** n : int;
$\quad n := N$ **div** 2 {invariant: $P_0 \wedge P_1$}
$\quad$; **do** $n \neq 0$
$\quad\quad \rightarrow$ |[**var** k, p, q : int;
$\quad\quad\quad k, p, q := n, 2{*}n, (2{*}n + 1) \min N$
$\quad\quad\quad$ {invariant: $Q_0 \wedge Q_1 \wedge p = 2k \wedge q = (2k+1) \min N$}
$\quad\quad\quad$; **do** $p \leq N$
$\quad\quad\quad\quad \rightarrow$ **if** $h.p \geq h.q \rightarrow$ skip $[\!]$ $h.p < h.q \rightarrow p := q$ **fi**
$\quad\quad\quad\quad\quad$ {$(p = 2k \vee p = 2k+1) \wedge h.p = h.(2k) \max h.(2k+1)$}
$\quad\quad\quad\quad$; **if** $h.k \geq h.p \rightarrow$ skip $[\!]$ $h.k < h.p \rightarrow$ swap.$k.p$ **fi**
$\quad\quad\quad\quad$; $k, p, q := p, 2{*}p, (2{*}p + 1) \min N$
$\quad\quad\quad$ **od**
$\quad\quad$]|
$\quad\quad$; $n := n{-}1$
$\quad$ **od**
]|
{heap.N}

This algorithm has time complexity $\mathcal{O}(N)$, which is shown as follows. Variable k is initialized at n and in each step of the inner repetition k is replaced by at least $2k$ until $2k \geq N$. Hence, the inner repetition takes at most ${}^2\log \frac{N}{2n}$ steps. The total number of steps is at most:

$(\Sigma n : 1 \leq n \leq N$ **div** $2 : {}^2\log \frac{N}{2n})$
$\approx \quad$ { calculus }
$\int_1^{N/2} {}^2\log \frac{N}{2x} \, dx$
$= \quad$ { calculus }
$\frac{1}{2} \int_1^N {}^2\log \frac{N}{x} \, dx$
$\approx \quad$ { calculus }
$\frac{1}{1.4} \int_1^N \ln \frac{N}{x} \, dx$
$\approx \quad$ { calculus }
$\frac{1}{1.4} N$

So much for 'establish heap.N'. Annotation of the remaining part of the program yields

192   *Sorting*

$\quad\quad$ **do** $n \neq 1$
$\quad\quad\quad\quad \rightarrow \ \{\text{heap}.n, \text{ hence, heap}.(n-1)\}$
$\quad\quad\quad\quad\quad\quad \text{swap}.1.n$
$\quad\quad\quad\quad\quad\quad ; n := n - 1$
$\quad\quad\quad\quad\quad\quad \{(\forall i, j : 1 \leq i \leq j \leq n \wedge i \rightarrow j \wedge i \neq 1 : h.i \geq h.j)\}$
$\quad\quad\quad\quad\quad\quad ; \text{'re-establish heap}.n\text{'}$
$\quad\quad$ **od**

The pre-condition of 're-establish heap.n':

$$(\forall i, j : 1 \leq i \leq j \leq n \wedge i \rightarrow j \wedge i \neq 1 : h.i \geq h.j)$$

equals $Q_0(n, k, N := 1, 1, n)$, leading to a solution which is similar to the inner repetition of the previous program:

$\quad$ |[**var** k, p, q : int;
$\quad\quad\quad k, p, q := 1, 2, 3 \min n$
$\quad\quad\quad ; \mathbf{do}\ p \leq n$
$\quad\quad\quad\quad \rightarrow \mathbf{if}\ h.p \geq h.q \rightarrow \text{skip}\ [\!]\ h.p < h.q \rightarrow p := q\ \mathbf{fi}$
$\quad\quad\quad\quad\quad ; \mathbf{if}\ h.k \geq h.p \rightarrow \text{skip}\ [\!]\ h.k < h.p \rightarrow \text{swap}.k.p\ \mathbf{fi}$
$\quad\quad\quad\quad\quad ; k, p, q := p, 2{*}p, (2{*}p + 1) \min n$
$\quad\quad\quad$ **od**
$\quad$]|
$\quad$ {heap.n}

Execution of this program fragment takes at most $^2\!\log n$ steps and, hence, the total time complexity of Heapsort is $\mathcal{O}(N \log N)$. The complete algorithm is presented below.

$\quad\quad$ The heap structure is used in many algorithms. Often an algorithm is derived in terms of sets. When the operations on such a set V, say, are

$$V := V \cup \{x\}$$

and

$$V := V \setminus \{x\} \quad \text{where} \quad x = (\mathbf{max}\,i : i \in V : i)$$

then a heap (also called a 'max-heap') may be used to implement these operations efficiently.

Heapsort

|[**var** n : int;
   $n := N$ **div** 2
  ; **do** $n \neq 0$
      $\rightarrow$ |[**var** k, p, q : int;
          $k, p, q := n, 2{*}n, (2{*}n + 1) \min N$
        ; **do** $p \leq N$
            $\rightarrow$ **if** $h.p \geq h.q \rightarrow$ skip [] $h.p < h.q \rightarrow p := q$ **fi**
              ; **if** $h.k \geq h.p \rightarrow$ skip [] $h.k < h.p \rightarrow$ swap.$k.p$ **fi**
              ; $k, p, q := p, 2{*}p, (2{*}p + 1) \min N$
        od
      ]|
      ; $n := n{-}1$
  od
; $n := N$
; **do** $n \neq 1$
      $\rightarrow$ |[**var** k, p, q : int;
          swap.$1.n$
        ; $n := n{-}1$
        ; $k, p, q := 1, 2, 3 \min n$
        ; **do** $p \leq n$
            $\rightarrow$ **if** $h.p \geq h.q \rightarrow$ skip [] $h.p < h.q \rightarrow p := q$ **fi**
              ; **if** $h.k \geq h.p \rightarrow$ skip [] $h.k < h.p \rightarrow$ swap.$k.p$ **fi**
              ; $k, p, q := p, 2{*}p, (2{*}p + 1) \min n$
        od
      ]|
  od
]|.

Exercises

0. Derive an $\mathcal{O}(N \log N)$ program that establishes heap.N, using invariant

    heap.$n \land 1 \leq n \leq N$

1. (*Museum peak attendance*). Integer arrays $x[0..N)$ and $y[0..N)$ are given. A museum is visited by N people ($N \geq 1$). Person i, $0 \leq i < N$, arrives at moment

$x.i$, is present during interval $[x.i\mathinner{\ldotp\ldotp} y.i)$ and leaves at moment $y.i$. Array x is ascending. Derive a program for the computation of the maximum number of visitors that are simultaneously present in the museum.

Chapter 12

Auxiliary Arrays

Calculations with expressions that occur in an invariant often give rise to the introduction of (auxiliary) variables, together with an accompanying invariant (cf. Section 4.3). In this chapter we discuss some programming problems for which these calculations give rise to the introduction of arrays.

12.0 At most K zeros

Our first example is a segment problem (cf. Chapter 7). For integer array $X[0..N)$ and natural K, we are asked to derive a program for the computation of the length of a longest segment that has at most K zeros. As an additional restriction, it is not allowed to inspect an element of X more than once (X may, for example, be a sequential file that can be read only once). A formal specification of the problem is

$\lVert$ **con** N, K : int $\{N \geq 0 \land K \geq 0\}$; X : **array** $[0..N)$ **of** int;
 var r : int;
  S
 $\{r = (\max p, q : 0 \leq p \leq q \leq N \land \mathcal{N}.p.q \leq K : q-p)\}$
$\rVert$.

where

$\mathcal{N}.p.q = (\# i : p \leq i < q : X.i = 0)$

Note that $\mathcal{N}.p.q \leq K$ holds for empty segments, is prefix-closed and is postfix-closed. Following the strategy explained in Chapter 7, we introduce as invariants

Auxiliary Arrays

$P_0:\quad r = (\max p, q : 0 \leq p \leq q \leq n \land \mathcal{N}.p.q \leq K : q-p)$
$P_1:\quad 0 \leq n \leq N$
$Q:\quad s = (\min p : 0 \leq p \leq n \land \mathcal{N}.p.n \leq K : p)$

leading to a program of the following form.

$\quad n, r, s := 0, 0, 0$
$\quad ; \mathbf{do}\ n \neq N$
$\qquad \rightarrow\ $ 'establish $Q(n := n+1)$'
$\qquad\quad ; r := r \max (n+1-s)$
$\qquad\quad ; n := n+1$
$\quad \mathbf{od}$

For $Q(n := n+1)$, we derive $(0 \leq n < N)$

$\quad (\min p : 0 \leq p \leq n+1 \land \mathcal{N}.p.(n+1) \leq K : p)$
$=\quad \{\text{split off } p = n+1,\ \mathcal{N}.(n+1).(n+1) = 0,\ 0 \leq K\ \}$
$\quad (\min p : 0 \leq p \leq n \land \mathcal{N}.p.(n+1) \leq K : p)\ \min\ (n+1)$

and for $0 \leq p \leq n < N$:

$\quad \mathcal{N}.p.(n+1) \leq K$
$=\quad \{\text{definition of } \mathcal{N}\}$
$\quad (\#i : p \leq i < n+1 : X.i = 0) \leq K$
$=\quad \{\text{split off } i = n,\ p \leq n\ \}$
$\quad \mathcal{N}.p.n + \#.(X.n = 0) \leq K$
$=\quad \{\text{case analysis}\}$
$\quad \begin{cases} \mathcal{N}.p.n \leq K & \text{if } X.n \neq 0 \\ \mathcal{N}.p.n \leq K-1 & \text{if } X.n = 0 \end{cases}$

From this derivation we conclude that for the invariance of Q

$\quad (\min p : 0 \leq p \leq n \land \mathcal{N}.p.n \leq K-1 : p)$

is needed. Of course, for this expression

$\quad (\min p : 0 \leq p \leq n \land \mathcal{N}.p.n \leq K-2 : p)$

is needed too, and so on. Therefore, we replace integer s by integer array $s[0..K]$, with

At most K zeros   197

$Q:\quad (\forall k: 0 \leq k \leq K : s.k = (\min p : 0 \leq p \leq n \wedge \mathcal{N}.p.n \leq k : p))$

For $0 < k \leq K$, we have

$\quad (\min p : 0 \leq p \leq n{+}1 \wedge \mathcal{N}.p.(n{+}1) \leq k : p)$

$=\quad \{\, k > 0 \text{ implies } \mathcal{N}.n.(n{+}1) \leq k\,\}$

$\quad (\min p : 0 \leq p \leq n \wedge \mathcal{N}.p.(n{+}1) \leq k : p)$

$=\quad \{\text{ previous derivation with } K \text{ replaced by } k\,\}$

$\quad \begin{cases} (\min p : 0 \leq p \leq n \wedge \mathcal{N}.p.n \leq k : p) & \text{if } X.n \neq 0 \\ (\min p : 0 \leq p \leq n \wedge \mathcal{N}.p.n \leq k{-}1 : p) & \text{if } X.n = 0 \end{cases}$

$=\quad \{\,Q\,\}$

$\quad \begin{cases} s.k & \text{if } X.n \neq 0 \\ s.(k{-}1) & \text{if } X.n = 0 \end{cases}$

and (for $k = 0$)

$\quad (\min p : 0 \leq p \leq n{+}1 \wedge \mathcal{N}.p.(n{+}1) \leq 0 : p)$

$=\quad \{\text{ case analysis, } Q\,\}$

$\quad \begin{cases} s.0 & \text{if } X.n \neq 0 \\ n{+}1 & \text{if } X.n = 0 \end{cases}$

This yields the following solution.

$|[\,\mathbf{var}\ n : \text{int};\ s : \mathbf{array}\,[0..K]\,\mathbf{of}\ \text{int};$
$\quad n := 0$
$\quad ;|[\,\mathbf{var}\ a : \text{int};\ a := 0\ ;\ \mathbf{do}\ a \neq K{+}1 \to s.a := 0\ ;\ a := a{+}1\ \mathbf{od}\,]|$
$\quad \{\text{invariant: } P_0 \wedge P_1 \wedge Q\}$
$\quad ;\mathbf{do}\ n \neq N$
$\qquad \to \mathbf{if}\ X.n \neq 0 \to \text{skip}$
$\qquad\quad [\!]\ X.n = 0 \to |[\,\mathbf{var}\ a : \text{int};$
$\qquad\qquad\qquad\qquad a := K$
$\qquad\qquad\qquad\qquad ;\mathbf{do}\ a \neq 0 \to s.a := s.(a{-}1)\ ;\ a := a{-}1\ \mathbf{od}$
$\qquad\qquad\qquad\qquad ;s.0 := n{+}1$
$\qquad\qquad\qquad]|$
$\qquad\quad \mathbf{fi}$
$\qquad ;r := r\,\mathbf{max}\,(n{+}1{-}s.K)$
$\qquad ;n := n{+}1$
$\quad \mathbf{od}$
$]|.$

198 Auxiliary Arrays

When all elements of X are zero, execution of this program takes $K * N$ steps. In the inner repetition array s is rotated over one place. Using s as a so-called *circular array*, such a rotation corresponds to a shift of the origin over one position. More precisely, introduce integer variable h and replace Q by

$$Q': \quad (\forall k : 0 \leq k \leq K : s.(h \oplus k) = (\min p : 0 \leq p \leq n \wedge \mathcal{N}.p.n \leq k : p))$$

where $\oplus$ denotes addition modulo $K+1$. This results in

$$\begin{aligned}
&\|[\textbf{var } n : \text{int};\ s : \textbf{array } [0..K] \textbf{ of } \text{int};\\
&\quad n, h := 0, 0\\
&\quad ; \|[\textbf{var } a : \text{int};\ a := 0\ ;\ \textbf{do } a \neq K{+}1 \to s.a := 0\ ;\ a := a{+}1\ \textbf{od}\ ]\|\\
&\quad ; \textbf{do } n \neq N\\
&\qquad \to \textbf{if } X.n \neq 0 \to \text{skip}\\
&\qquad\quad [\!]\ X.n = 0 \to h := h \oplus K\ ;\ s.h := n{+}1\\
&\qquad \textbf{fi}\\
&\qquad ; r := r \max (n{+}1 - s.(h \oplus K))\\
&\qquad ; n := n{+}1\\
&\quad \textbf{od}\\
&]\!|.
\end{aligned}$$

This program has time complexity $\mathcal{O}(N + K)$.

12.1 Largest square under a histogram

For histogram $X[0..N)$, i.e., integer array X for which $(\forall i : 0 \leq i < N : X.i \geq 0)$ holds, we are asked to compute the largest square that fits under it. A formal specification is

$$\begin{aligned}
&\|[\textbf{con } N : \text{int } \{N \geq 0\};\ X : \textbf{array } [0..N) \textbf{ of } \text{int } \{(\forall i : 0 \leq i < N : X.i \geq 0)\};\\
&\quad \textbf{var } r : \text{int};\\
&\quad S\\
&\quad \{r = (\max p, q : 0 \leq p \leq q \leq N \wedge \mathcal{A}.p.q : q{-}p)\}\\
&]\!|.
\end{aligned}$$

where

$$\mathcal{A}.p.q \ \equiv\ (\forall i : p \leq i < q : X.i \geq q{-}p)$$

Note that $\mathcal{A}$ holds for empty segments, is prefix-closed, and is postfix-closed. Hence, we may apply the program scheme maxseg of Section 8.2:

$$\begin{aligned}
&\|[\textbf{ var } a, b : \text{int}; \\
&\quad a, b, r := 0, 0, 0 \\
&\quad ; \textbf{do } b \neq N \vee \neg \mathcal{A}.a.b \\
&\qquad \rightarrow \textbf{if } \quad \mathcal{A}.a.b \rightarrow r := r \max (b-a) \,; b := b+1 \\
&\qquad \qquad [\!] \; \neg \mathcal{A}.a.b \rightarrow a := a+1 \\
&\qquad \textbf{fi} \\
&\quad \textbf{od} \\
&\quad ; r := r \max (N-a) \\
&\quad \{\, r = (\max p, q : 0 \leq p \leq q \leq N \wedge \mathcal{A}.p.q : q-p)\,\} \\
&\,]\!|,
\end{aligned}$$

for which $0 \leq a \leq b \leq N$ is one of the invariants. We introduce boolean variable c and add

$$c \equiv \mathcal{A}.a.b$$

as an additional invariant. Since $\mathcal{A}.0.0$ holds, c is initialized at true. We consider $b := b+1$, which is guarded by $\mathcal{A}.a.b$:

$$\begin{aligned}
&\mathcal{A}.a.(b+1) \\
\equiv \quad & \{\,\text{definition of } \mathcal{A}\,\} \\
&(\forall i : a \leq i < b+1 : X.i \geq b+1-a) \\
\equiv \quad & \{\,\text{split off } i = b,\ a \leq b\,\} \\
&(\forall i : a \leq i < b : X.i \geq b+1-a) \wedge X.b \geq b+1-a \\
\equiv \quad & \{\,\text{heading for } \mathcal{A}.a.b\,\} \\
&(\forall i : a \leq i < b : X.i \geq b-a \wedge X.i \neq b-a) \wedge X.b \geq b+1-a \\
\equiv \quad & \{\,\mathcal{A}.a.b\,\} \\
&(\forall i : a \leq i < b : X.i \neq b-a) \wedge X.b \geq b+1-a \\
\equiv \quad & \{\,\text{express as 'number of'}\,\} \\
&(\# i : a \leq i < b : X.i = b-a) = 0 \wedge X.b \geq b+1-a
\end{aligned}$$

The value of $b-a$ is within the range $[0..N]$, hence, $\mathcal{A}.a.(b+1)$ equals

$$f.(b-a) = 0 \wedge X.b \geq b+1-a$$

provided that we add additional invariant

$Q_0 : \quad (\forall j : 0 \leq j \leq N : f.j = (\# i : a \leq i < b : X.i = j))$

The change from universal quantification to 'number of' quantification is a general technique. The first step of the derivation above is

$$\mathcal{A}.a.(b+1) \equiv (\forall i : a \leq i < b+1 : X.i \geq b+1-a)$$

and one might be tempted to add $d = (\min i : a \leq i < b : X.i)$ to the invariants. This yields no problems to $b := b+1$, but it does pose a problem to $a := a+1$, since **min** has no inverse. The introduction of the 'number of' quantification solves this problem. Such a transition is also applicable to existential and universal quantifications.

In the second alternative, guarded by $\neg\mathcal{A}.a.b$, we have an increase of a by 1. Note that $\neg\mathcal{A}.a.b$ implies $a < b$ and, hence, $X.(b-1)$ is well defined. For $a+1 < b$, we have

$\quad\mathcal{A}.(a+1).b$
$\equiv\quad$ { definition of $\mathcal{A}$ }
$\quad(\forall i : a+1 \leq i < b : X.i \geq b-a-1)$
$\equiv\quad$ { split off $i = b-1$, $a+1 \leq b-1$ }
$\quad(\forall i : a+1 \leq i < b-1 : X.i \geq b-a-1) \wedge X.(b-1) \geq b-a-1$
$\equiv\quad$ { see below }
$\quad X.(b-1) \geq b-a-1$

provided that $(\forall i : a+1 \leq i < b-1 : X.i \geq b-a-1)$. Since $\mathcal{A}$ is postfix-closed, this is implied by $\mathcal{A}.a.(b-1)$ and we add

$Q_1 : \quad \mathcal{A}.a.(b-1)$

to the invariants. Initially Q_1 holds, the increase of b by 1 has guard $\mathcal{A}.a.b$ and, since $\mathcal{A}$ is postfix-closed, it is not violated by $a := a+1$.

For the case $a+1 = b$, we have

$\quad\mathcal{A}.(a+1).b$
$\equiv\quad$ { $a+1 = b$, definition of $\mathcal{A}$ }
$\quad$ true
$\equiv\quad$ { $(\forall i : 0 \leq i < N : X.i \geq 0)$ }
$\quad X.(b-1) \geq 0$
$\equiv\quad$ { $a+1 = b$ }
$\quad X.(b-1) \geq b-a-1$

and we conclude that, in either case, $\mathcal{A}.(a+1).b \equiv X.(b-1) \geq b-a-1$.

The introduction of Q_1 may be surprising. It is, however, from the general program scheme of maxseg immediately clear that for postfix-closed $\mathcal{A}$, Q_1 is an invariant. In many applications of this program scheme, the invariance of $\mathcal{A}.a.(b-1)$ turns out to be crucial.

The statements needed for the invariance of Q_0 are easily derived, and we obtain the following program.

$\lVert$ **var** $a, b :$ int; $c :$ bool; $f :$ **array** $[0..N]$ **of** int;
$\quad a, b, r, c := 0, 0, 0,$ true
$\quad ; \lVert$ **var** $k :$ int; $k := 0$; **do** $k \neq N{+}1 \rightarrow f.k := 0$; $k := k{+}1$ **od** $\rVert$
$\quad ;$ **do** $b \neq N \lor \neg c$
$\qquad \rightarrow$ **if** $\ c \ \rightarrow \ r := r \max (b{-}a)$
$\qquad\qquad\qquad ; c := f.(b{-}a) = 0 \land X.b \geq b{+}1{-}a$
$\qquad\qquad\qquad ;$ **if** $X.b \leq N \rightarrow f.(X.b) := f.(X.b) + 1 \ [\!]\ X.b > N \rightarrow$ skip **fi**
$\qquad\qquad\qquad ; b := b{+}1$
$\qquad\quad [\!] \ \neg c \ \rightarrow \ c := X.(b{-}1) \geq b{-}a{-}1$
$\qquad\qquad\qquad ;$ **if** $X.a \leq N \rightarrow f.(X.a) := f.(X.a) - 1 \ [\!]\ X.a > N \rightarrow$ skip **fi**
$\qquad\qquad\qquad ; a := a{+}1$
$\qquad\quad$ **fi**
$\quad$ **od**
$\quad ; r := r \max (N{-}a)$
$\rVert$.

12.2 The length of a longest common subsequence

Our next example is a program for the computation of the length of a longest common subsequence of two sequences. A subsequence of sequence s is obtained by removing zero or more elements of s. A common subsequence of sequences s and t is a subsequence of both s and t. The length of a sequence is its number of elements. We consider two integer sequences, represented by integer arrays $X[0..M)$ and $Y[0..N)$ for which the length of a longest common subsequence has to be computed.

Let lcs.$m.n$ $(0 \leq m \leq M \land 0 \leq n \leq N)$ denote the length of a longest common subsequence of $X[0..m)$ and $Y[0..n)$. Then

$\quad$ lcs.$m.0 = 0$
$\quad$ lcs.$0.n = 0$

For $0 \leq m < M \wedge 0 \leq n < N$, we express lcs.$(m+1).(n+1)$ as follows.
When $X.m = Y.n$, each common subsequence of $X[0..m)$ and $Y[0..n)$ can be extended by $X.m$, hence,

$$X.m = Y.n \Rightarrow \text{lcs}.(m+1).(n+1) = 1 + \text{lcs}.m.n$$

When $X.m \neq Y.n$ then each common subsequence of $X[0..m+1)$ and $Y[0..n+1)$ is either a common subsequence of $X[0..m+1)$ and $Y[0..n)$ or a common subsequence of $X[0..m)$ and $Y[0..n+1)$, hence,

$$X.m \neq Y.n \Rightarrow \text{lcs}.(m+1).(n+1) = \text{lcs}.(m+1).n \textbf{ max } \text{lcs}.m.(n+1)$$

We conclude that lcs is formally defined by

lcs.$m.0 = 0$
lcs.$0.n = 0$
$$\text{lcs}.(m+1).(n+1) = \begin{cases} 1 + \text{lcs}.m.n & \text{if } X.m = Y.n \\ \text{lcs}.(m+1).n \textbf{ max } \text{lcs}.m.(n+1) & \text{if } X.m \neq Y.n \end{cases}$$

A formal specification of the problem is

$\lVert$ **con** M, N : int $\{M \geq 0 \wedge N \geq 0\}$;
  X : **array** $[0..M)$ **of** int;
  Y : **array** $[0..N)$ **of** int;
var r : int;
  S
  $\{r = \text{lcs}.M.N\}$
$\rVert$.

In the post-condition two constants (M and N) occur. We may replace both of them by variables and try as invariant

$r = \text{lcs}.m.n$

This invariant is established by, for instance, $r, m, n := 0, 0, 0$, $r, m, n := 0, M, 0$, or $r, m, n := 0, 0, N$. This indicates that this invariant is rather weak. Moreover, as guard of a repetition, we would have $m \neq M \vee n \neq N$ and, hence, inspection of $X.m$ or $Y.n$ has to be guarded. In view of these problems, we replace only one of the constants by a variable (thereby destroying the symmetry) and we consider invariant

$r = \text{lcs}.m.N$

The length of a longest common subsequence

which is established by $r, m := 0, 0$. An increase of m by 1 yields expression $\text{lcs}.(m+1).N$ and, according to the definition of lcs, $\text{lcs}.m.(N-1)$, $\text{lcs}.m.N$, and $\text{lcs}.(m+1).(N-1)$ are needed for its computation. The last expression gives rise to $\text{lcs}.m.(N-2)$, etc. Therefore, we introduce integer array $h[0..N]$ and accompanying invariant

$$P_0: \quad (\forall i : 0 \leq i \leq N : h.i = \text{lcs}.m.i)$$

where the bounds for m are given by

$$P_1: \quad 0 \leq m \leq M$$

Then

$$P_0(m := 0) \equiv (\forall i : 0 \leq i \leq N : h.i = 0)$$

and

$$P_0 \wedge m = M \Rightarrow h.N = \text{lcs}.M.N$$

Furthermore, we have

$$\begin{aligned}
& P_0(m := m+1) \\
\equiv \quad & \{\text{ definition of } P_0 \} \\
& (\forall i : 0 \leq i \leq N : h.i = \text{lcs}.(m+1).i)
\end{aligned}$$

which is established by another repetition, replacing constant N by variable n with invariants

$$Q_0: \quad (\forall i : 0 \leq i \leq n : h.i = \text{lcs}.(m+1).i) \wedge (\forall i : n < i \leq N : h.i = \text{lcs}.m.i)$$
$$Q_1: \quad 0 \leq n \leq N$$

for which we have $P_0 \Rightarrow Q_0(n := 0)$ and $Q_0 \wedge n = N \Rightarrow P_0(m := m+1)$. For $0 \leq n < N$, we derive

$$\begin{aligned}
& Q_0(n := n+1) \\
\equiv \quad & \{\text{ definition of } Q_0 \} \\
& (\forall i : 0 \leq i \leq n+1 : h.i = \text{lcs}.(m+1).i) \wedge (\forall i : n+1 < i \leq N : h.i = \text{lcs}.m.i) \\
\equiv \quad & \{\text{ split off } i = n+1 \} \\
& (\forall i : 0 \leq i \leq n : h.i = \text{lcs}.(m+1).i) \wedge (\forall i : n+1 < i \leq N : h.i = \text{lcs}.m.i) \\
& \wedge\ h.(n+1) = \text{lcs}.(m+1).(n+1)
\end{aligned}$$

204   Auxiliary Arrays

The first two conjuncts of the last predicate are implied by Q_0, hence,

$$h.(n+1) = \text{lcs}.(m+1).(n+1)$$

has to be established, for which we have

$\quad\quad\text{lcs}.(m+1).(n+1)$
$=\quad\quad\{\text{ definition of lcs }\}$
$\quad\quad\begin{cases} 1+\text{lcs}.m.n & \text{if } X.m = Y.n \\ \text{lcs}.(m+1).n \;\textbf{max}\; \text{lcs}.m.(n+1) & \text{if } X.m \neq Y.n \end{cases}$
$=\quad\quad\{Q_0\}$
$\quad\quad\begin{cases} 1+\text{lcs}.m.n & \text{if } X.m = Y.n \\ h.n \;\textbf{max}\; h.(n+1) & \text{if } X.m \neq Y.n \end{cases}$

Evidently, we need lcs.$m.n$ as well, and we add to the invariants

$Q_2: \quad a = \text{lcs}.m.n$

The invariance of Q_2 is no problem: Q_0 implies $h.(n+1) = \text{lcs}.m.(n+1)$. Thus, we have

$\{Q_0 \wedge Q_1 \wedge Q_2 \wedge n \neq N\}$
if $X.m = Y.n \rightarrow a, h.(n+1) := h(n+1), 1+a$
$[\!]\; X.m \neq Y.n \rightarrow a, h.(n+1) := h(n+1), h.n \;\textbf{max}\; h.(n+1)$
fi
$\{(Q_0 \wedge Q_1 \wedge Q_2)(n := n+1)\}$

Since multiple assignments are not allowed when arrays are involved, local variable b is introduced. The resulting program is presented below.

|[**var** m : int; h : **array** $[0..N]$ **of** int;
    $m := 0$
  ; |[k : int; $k := 0$; **do** $k \neq N{+}1 \rightarrow h.k := 0$; $k := k{+}1$ **od**]|
  $\{P_0 \wedge P_1\}$
  ; **do** $m \neq M$
      $\rightarrow$ |[**var** n, a : int;
            $n, a := 0, 0$
            $\{Q_0 \wedge Q_1 \wedge Q_2\}$
          ; **do** $n \neq N$
              $\rightarrow$ |[**var** b : int;
                    $b := h.(n{+}1)$
                  ; **if** $X.m = Y.n \rightarrow h.(n{+}1) := 1 + a$
                    [] $X.m \neq Y.n \rightarrow h.(n{+}1) := h.n \max h.(n{+}1)$
                    fi
                  ; $a := b$
                 ]|
               ; $n := n{+}1$
            od
         ]|
       ; $m := m{+}1$
    od
  ; $r := h.N$
]|.

12.3 A shortest segment problem

In our final example, we demonstrate how an efficient solution to a programming problem can be obtained in a number of steps. These steps are not specific for this particular problem but they occur in derivations of many other programming problems as well. To illustrate these steps, we use the following segment problem.

For integer array $X[0..N]$, $N \geq 1$, we wish to derive a program for the computation of the length of a shortest segment in which the maximum value on that segment occurs exactly twice. A formal specification is

$$\begin{aligned}
&\|[\,\mathbf{con}\ N : \text{int}\ \{N \geq 1\};\ X : \mathbf{array}\ [0..N]\ \mathbf{of}\ \text{int};\\
&\quad \mathbf{var}\ r : \text{int};\\
&\quad S\\
&\quad \{r = (\mathbf{min}\, p, q : 0 \leq p \leq q \leq N \wedge \mathcal{A}.p.q : q-p)\}\\
&\,]\|
\end{aligned}$$

where

$$\mathcal{A}.p.q \equiv (\# i : p \leq i < q : X.i = (\mathbf{max}\, j : p \leq j < q : X.j)) = 2$$

The 'shortest segment properties' of Section 8.2 do not hold for predicate $\mathcal{A}$. Even when we change $\mathcal{A}$ to

$$(\# i : p \leq i < q : X.i = (\mathbf{max}\, j : p \leq j < q : X.j)) \geq 2$$

(which does not affect the specification of S), we only have '$\neg \mathcal{A}$ holds for empty segments'. As a consequence, we need a different approach to solve this problem.

A shortest segment $[p..q]$ that satisfies $\mathcal{A}$ is characterized by

$$0 \leq p < q < N \wedge X.p = X.q \wedge (\forall i : p < i < q : X.i < X.q)$$

It has length $q+1-p$. Hence, we may rewrite the post-condition of the specification as

$$r = (\mathbf{min}\, p, q : 0 \leq p < q < N \wedge \mathcal{B}.p.q : q+1-p)$$

where

$$\mathcal{B}.p.q \equiv X.p = X.q \wedge (\forall i : p < i < q : X.i < X.q)$$

Replacing the constant N by integer variable n leads to

$P_0:\quad r = (\min p, q : 0 \leq p < q < n \land \mathcal{B}.p.q : q+1-p)$
$P_1:\quad 1 \leq n \leq N$

which are established by $n, r := 1, \infty$. For $P_0(n := n+1)$, a straightforward derivation yields the expression

$$(\min p : 0 \leq p < n \land X.p = X.n \land (\forall i : p < i < n : X.i < X.n) : n+1-p)$$

The equation

$$p : 0 \leq p < n \land X.p = X.n \land (\forall i : p < i < n : X.i < X.n) \qquad (*)$$

has at most one solution; if it exists, then it equals the solution of

$$p : 0 \leq p < n \land X.p \geq X.n \land (\forall i : p < i < n : X.i < X.n)$$

This equation also has at most one solution; if it exists, then it equals the solution of

$$p : 0 \leq p < n \land (p = 0 \lor X.p \geq X.n) \land (\forall i : p < i < n : X.i < X.n)$$

This equation has, since $n \geq 1$, precisely one solution, viz.

$$(\min p : 0 \leq p < n \land (\forall i : p < i < n : X.i < X.n) : p)$$

So, for s defined by

$$(s = 0 \lor X.s \geq X.n) \land 0 \leq s < n \land (\forall i : s < i < n : X.i < X.n)$$

we have

$X.s = X.n \Rightarrow s$ is the solution of $(*)$
$X.s \neq X.n \Rightarrow (*)$ has no solution

The relation

$$(s = 0 \lor X.s \geq X.n) \land 0 \leq s < n \land (\forall i : s < i < n : X.i < X.n)$$

is established by a repetition that is guarded by $s \neq 0 \land X.s < X.n$ and has invariant

$Q:\quad 0 \leq s < n \land (\forall i : s < i < n : X.i < X.n)$

This leads to the first solution:

208 Auxiliary Arrays

$$
\begin{aligned}
&\|[\,\textbf{var}\ n : \text{int};\\
&\quad n, r := 1, \infty\\
&\quad \{\text{invariant: } P_0 \wedge P_1,\ \text{bound: } N{-}n\}\\
&\quad ;\textbf{do}\ n \neq N\\
&\quad\quad \to \|[\,\textbf{var}\ s : \text{int};\\
&\quad\quad\quad s := n{-}1\\
&\quad\quad\quad \{\text{invariant: } Q,\ \text{bound: } s\}\\
&\quad\quad\quad ;\textbf{do}\ s \neq 0 \wedge X.s < X.n \to s := s{-}1\ \textbf{od}\\
&\quad\quad\quad ;\textbf{if}\ X.s = X.n \to r := r \min (n{+}1{-}s)\\
&\quad\quad\quad \quad [\!]\ X.s \neq X.n \to \text{skip}\\
&\quad\quad\quad \textbf{fi}\\
&\quad\quad \,]\!|\\
&\quad\quad ; n := n{+}1\\
&\quad \textbf{od}\\
&\,]\!|.
\end{aligned}
$$

For increasing X, execution of the inner repetition takes $n{-}1$ steps and, hence, this program has time complexity $\mathcal{O}(N^2)$. A more efficient program is obtained when s can be decreased by more than one. We reconsider the definition of s and we define for $1 \leq j \leq N$

$$f.j = (\min p : 0 \leq p < j \wedge (\forall i : p < i < j : X.i < X.j) : p)$$

The program fragment

$$
\begin{aligned}
&s := n{-}1\\
&\{Q : 0 \leq s < n \wedge (\forall i : s < i < n : X.i < X.n)\}\\
&;\textbf{do}\ s \neq 0 \wedge X.s < X.n \to s := s{-}1\ \textbf{od}
\end{aligned}
$$

establishes $s = f.n$. We derive

$$
\begin{aligned}
&\quad Q \wedge s \neq 0 \wedge X.s < X.n\\
&\equiv \quad \{\,\text{definition of } Q\,\}\\
&\quad (\forall i : s < i < n : X.i < X.n) \wedge 0 < s < n \wedge X.s < X.n\\
&\equiv \quad \{\,\text{definition of } f\,\}\\
&\quad (\forall i : s < i < n : X.i < X.n) \wedge 0 < s < n \wedge X.s < X.n\\
&\quad \wedge (\forall i : f.s < i < s : X.i < X.s) \wedge 0 \leq f.s < s\\
&\Rightarrow \quad \{\,\text{transitivity of } <\,\}
\end{aligned}
$$

$$\equiv \quad \begin{array}{l}(\forall i: f.s < i < n : X.i < X.n) \land 0 \leq f.s < n \\ \{\text{definition of } Q\}\end{array}$$
$$Q(s := f.s)$$

Hence, $s := s-1$ may be replaced by $s := f.s$. We introduce integer array $f[1..N]$ and accompanying invariant

$P_2: \quad (\forall j : 1 \leq j < n : f.j = (\min p : 0 \leq p < j \land (\forall i : p < i < j : X.i < X.j) : p))$

This leads to the second solution:

$\|[\mathbf{var}\ n : \text{int};\ f : \mathbf{array}\ [1..N]\ \mathbf{of}\ \text{int};$
$\quad n, r := 1, \infty$
$\quad \{\text{invariant: } P_0 \land P_1 \land P_2,\ \text{bound: } N-n\}$
$\quad ; \mathbf{do}\ n \neq N$
$\quad\quad \rightarrow \|[\mathbf{var}\ s : \text{int};$
$\quad\quad\quad\quad s := n-1$
$\quad\quad\quad\quad \{\text{invariant: } Q,\ \text{bound: } s\}$
$\quad\quad\quad\quad ; \mathbf{do}\ s \neq 0 \land X.s < X.n \rightarrow s := f.s\ \mathbf{od}$
$\quad\quad\quad\quad ; f.n := s$
$\quad\quad\quad\quad ; \mathbf{if}\ X.s = X.n \rightarrow r := r \min (n+1-s)$
$\quad\quad\quad\quad\quad [\!]\ X.s \neq X.n \rightarrow \text{skip}$
$\quad\quad\quad\quad \mathbf{fi}$
$\quad\quad\quad]\!|$
$\quad\quad\quad ; n := n+1$
$\quad \mathbf{od}$
$]\!|.$

To determine its time complexity, we add the ghost variable k to the inner repetition. We leave out the statements that are irrelevant for this discussion and obtain

$\quad n := 1$
$\quad ; \mathbf{do}\ n \neq N$
$\quad\quad \rightarrow s := n-1\ ; k := 0$
$\quad\quad\quad ; \mathbf{do}\ s \neq 0 \land X.s < X.n \rightarrow s := f.s\ ; k := k+1\ \mathbf{od}$
$\quad\quad\quad ; f.n := s$
$\quad\quad\quad ; n := n+1$
$\quad \mathbf{od}$

Auxiliary Arrays

An invariant of the inner repetition is

$$s = f^k.(n{-}1) \land (\forall i : 0 \leq i < k : f^i.(n{-}1) \neq 0)$$

where $f^i.x$ is defined by

$$f^0.x = x \text{ and } f^{i+1}.x = f.(f^i.x) \text{ for } i \geq 0.$$

Since $0 \leq f.x < x$ for $x > 0$, sequence $f^i.(n{-}1)$ is a decreasing sequence with final element 0. Let a denote the length of this sequence, i.e., add integer variable a and invariant

$$a = (\min i : i \geq 0 \land f^i.(n{-}1) = 0 : i)$$

where $f.0$ is defined as 0. The inner repetition has post-condition

$$s = f^k.(n{-}1) \land s = f.n \land (\forall i : 0 \leq i < k : f^i.(n{-}1) \neq 0)$$

For $i \geq 1$, we have

$$\quad f^i.n$$
$= \quad$ { definition of f^i, $i \geq 1$ }
$$\quad f^{i-1}.(f.n)$$
$= \quad$ { $s = f.n \land s = f^k.(n{-}1)$ }
$$\quad f^{i-1}.(f^k.(n{-}1))$$
$= \quad$ { definition of f^i }
$$\quad f^{i+k-1}.(n{-}1)$$

and, hence,

$$\quad (\min i : i \geq 0 \land f^i.n = 0 : i)$$
$= \quad$ { $f^0.n = n$ and $n \neq 0$ }
$$\quad (\min i : i \geq 1 \land f^i.n = 0 : i)$$
$= \quad$ { derivation above }
$$\quad (\min i : i \geq 1 \land f^{i+k-1}.(n{-}1) = 0 : i)$$
$= \quad$ { dummy change: $i := i{-}k{+}1$ }
$$\quad (\min i : i \geq k \land f^i.(n{-}1) = 0 : i{-}k{+}1)$$
$= \quad$ { $(\forall i : 0 \leq i < k : f^i.(n{-}1) \neq 0)$ }
$$\quad (\min i : i \geq 0 \land f^i.(n{-}1) = 0 : i{-}k{+}1)$$
$= \quad$ { definition of a }
$$\quad a{-}k{+}1$$

This leads to

$n, a := 1, 0$
$; \mathbf{do}\ n \neq N$
  $\rightarrow\ s := n{-}1\ ; k := 0$
  $; \mathbf{do}\ s \neq 0 \land X.s < X.n \rightarrow s := f.s\ ; k := k{+}1\ \mathbf{od}$
  $; a := a{-}k{+}1$
  $; f.n := s$
  $; n := n{+}1$
$\mathbf{od}$

In each step of the outer repetition a is incremented by 1 and decremented by the number of steps of the inner repetition. Since the outer repetition takes $N{-}1$ steps, the final value of a equals

$N - 1 -$ (the total number of steps of the inner repetition)

From the invariance of $a \geq 0$, we conclude that the total number of steps of the inner repetition is at most $N{-}1$. Hence, the program is linear.

Although the second program is quite satisfactory, there is another interesting transformation possible. From the invariance of

$$s = f^k.(n{-}1)$$

we infer that only the values of sequence $f^i.(n{-}1)$, $1 \leq i \leq a$ are needed for the computation of $f.n$. Moreover, sequence $f^i.n$ is obtained from sequence $f^i.(n{-}1)$ by removing the first k elements and adding the value of s in front of it. An easy way to record the sequence $f^i.(n{-}1)$ is by the introduction of an integer array $h[0..N)$ with accompanying invariant of the outer repetition:

$$(\forall i : 1 \leq i \leq a : h.(a{-}i) = f^i.(n{-}1))$$

This yields the third solution:

|[**var** n, a : int; h: **array** $[0..N)$ **of** int;
$\quad n, a, r := 1, 0, \infty$
$\quad$; **do** $n \neq N$
$\quad\quad \rightarrow$ |[**var** s : int;
$\quad\quad\quad s := n-1$
$\quad\quad\quad$; **do** $s \neq 0 \land X.s < X.n \rightarrow a := a-1\,; s := h.a$ **od**
$\quad\quad\quad$; $h.a := s\,; a := a+1$
$\quad\quad\quad$; **if** $X.s = X.n \rightarrow r := r \min (n+1-s)$
$\quad\quad\quad\quad [\!]\ X.s \neq X.n \rightarrow$ skip
$\quad\quad\quad$ **fi**
$\quad\quad$]|
$\quad\quad$; $n := n+1$
$\quad$ **od**
]|.

This program has the same complexity as the second solution. The main difference is that array h may be implemented as a so-called *stack*: elements are added and removed from its 'top' and only the storage that is needed (i.e., the maximal value that a may have) is used. Some people prefer the third solution. Since the second solution is obtained in a more calculational way, we prefer that.

Exercises

Solve the following programming problems.

0. |[**con** N : int $\{N \geq 0\}$; X : **array** $[0..N)$ **of** int;
$\quad$ **var** r : int;
$\quad\quad S$
$\quad \{r = (\min p, q : 0 \leq p \leq q \leq N \land \mathcal{A}.p.q : q-p)\}$
]|.
where $\mathcal{A}.p.q$ is defined by

$$\mathcal{A}.p.q \equiv (\forall i : 0 \leq i < 60 : (\exists j : p \leq j < q : X.j = i))$$

1. (*Balanced segments*)

   $\|[\mathbf{con}\ N : \text{int}\ \{N \geq 0\};\ X : \mathbf{array}\ [0..N)\ \mathbf{of}\ \text{int};$
   $\mathbf{var}\ r : \text{int};$
   S
   $\{r = (\mathbf{max}\,p,q : 0 \leq p \leq q \leq N \wedge \mathcal{A}.p.q : q-p)\}$
   $\,]\!|.$

   where $\mathcal{A}.p.q$ is defined by

   $\mathcal{A}.p.q \equiv (\#i : p \leq i < q : X.i = 0) = (\#i : p \leq i < q : X.i = 1)$

2. Let N be a natural number. A partition of N is a bag of positive integers that has sum N. For example, 4 has the following partitions:

   $[4],\ [1,3],\ [2,2],\ [1,1,2],$ and $[1,1,1,1]$.

   One is asked to derive an $\mathcal{O}(N^2)$ program for the computation of the number of partitions of natural number N.

   (Hint: define for natural p and q function $C.p.q$ by

   $C.p.q =$ 'the number of partitions of q in which each element is at most p'

   and derive a suitable recurrence relation for C.)

3. Derive an $\mathcal{O}(N)$ program for the computation of the number of subsequences of integer array $X[0..N)$ that equal the sequence $0..K$ ($0 \leq N \wedge 0 \leq K$).

4. (*Longest upsequence*) Derive an $\mathcal{O}(N \log N)$ program for the computation of the length of a longest increasing subsequence of the integer array $X[0..N)$, $N \geq 1$.

5. A partition of a set V is a collection of non-empty subsets of V whose union equals V. For example, the partitions of $\{a,b,c\}$ are

   $\{\{a,b,c\}\},\ \{\{a,b\},\{c\}\},\ \{\{a\},\{b,c\}\},\ \{\{a,c\},\{b\}\},$ and $\{\{a\},\{b\},\{c\}\}$.

   Derive a program for the computation of the number of partitions of a set of N, $N \geq 0$, elements.

6. (*Largest rectangle*) For integer N, $N \geq 1$, and histogram $X[0..N)$, i.e., $(\forall i : 0 \leq i < N : X.i \geq 0)$, one is asked to derive a program for the computation of the size of a rectangle that fits under X and that has maximal area.

Index

abort, 16
absorption, 6
all elements different, 119
all zeros, 111
annotation, 22
array, 40
array assignment, 152
    multiple, 154
ascending, 48
assignment, 17
    multiple, 18
associative, 44
associativity, 6
at least two zeros, 146
at most K zeros, 195
at most ten zeros, 117
auxiliary arrays, 195

balanced segments, 213
Binary Search, 100, 102
bool, 13
bound function, 30
bound variable, 9
Bounded Linear Search, 95, 96
bubble sort, 176
bucket sort, 171

catenation, 20
celebrity, 107
circular array, 198
coincidence count, 138
commutative, 44
commutativity, 6
complement rule, 7
con, 39

conjunction, 4
constant, 38
convex, 149
coupling invariant, 167
credit, 71

De Morgan, 6
decreasing, 48
def, 19
descending, 48
Dijkstra, Edsger W., 29
disjunction, 4
distributivity, 6
div, 18
divmod, 83
dummy, 9
Dutch National Flag, 161

efficiency, 51
equivalence, 4, 6
exponentiation, 57, 77

false-true rules, 6
Fibolucci, 82, 91
Fibonacci, 63, 88
frequency table, 155
function application, 40
fusc, 79

ghost variable, 86
greatest common divisor, 29
guard, 23
guarded command, 23
guarded command language, 13

h-sequence, 80

Index

heap condition, 189
Heapsort, 193

idempotence, 6
identity, 44
implication, 4, 6
increasing, 48
inference rule, 13
inner block, 38
insertion sort, 174
int, 13
Invariance Theorem, 31
invariant, 29
inversion, 170

largest rectangle, 213
largest square under a histogram, 198
lcm, 56
left-minimal segments, 115
Leibniz's Rule, 5
lexicographical order, 149
linear combinations, 88
Linear Search, 94
longest common subsequence, 201
longest segments, 110
longest upsequence, 213

max, 45
maximum occurs twice, 206
maxlocation, 106
maxseg, 143
maxsegsum, 67
merge, 183
Mergesort, 186
min, 45
minimal distance, 136
minseg, 145
mod, 18
monotonic, 122
museum peak attendance, 193

negation, 4, 6
non-determinism, 15

number of, 48

$\mathcal{O}$, 51

partition, 213
post-condition, 13
postfix-closed, 111
pre-condition, 13
    weakest, 15
predicate, 4
predicate transformer, 14
prefix-closed, 111

quantification, 44
    existential, 8
    universal, 8
Quicksort, 182

range, 9, 45
    empty, 9
    non-empty, 9
rotation, 164

Saddleback Search, 127
scope, 40
searching, 92
Searching by Elimination, 105, 106
segment, 40
segment problems, 110, 140
selection, 23
selection sort, 175
semi-colon, 21
shortest segments, 122
Simple Array Assignment, 157
simple swap statement, 160
skip, 16
Slope Search, 127
sorting, 170
specification variables, 13
square root, 55, 87, 102
square brackets, 5, 10
stable, 178
stack, 212

starting pit location, 109
state space, 4, 13
statement, 13
stronger, 7
strongest solution, 8
subsequence, 201
substitution, 8
sum of two squares, 133
swap, 159

tail invariant, 74
tail recursion, 73
Teacher's Manual, x
term, 9, 45
termination, 30
type, 13

var, 13

weaker, 7
weakest solution, 7
Welfare Crook, 139

zero, 46